# The Illustrated Guide to Btrieve

**for Btrieve version 5.x**

MIDI America

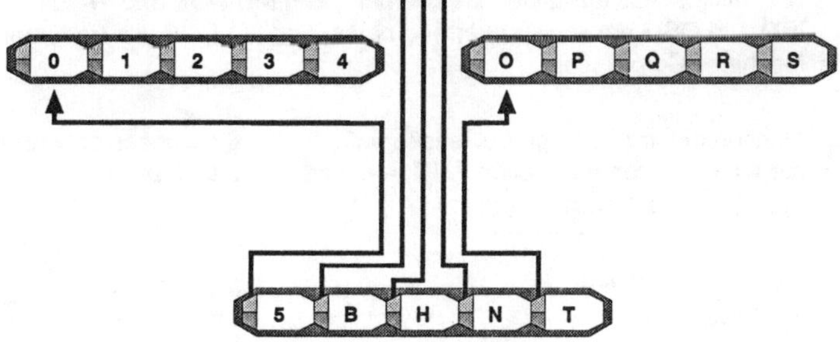

**Published by MIDI America, Inc., 2103 N. Decatur Rd., Suite 160, Decatur, Georgia 30033**

ISBN 0-9623397-7-6

Printed and bound in the United States of America.

**DISCLAIMER**

MIDI America, Inc. makes no representations or warranties with respect to the contents or use of this publication, and specifically disclaims any express or implied warranties of merchantability or fitness for any particular purpose. Further, MIDI America, Inc. reserves the right to revise this publication and to make changes to its content, at any time, without obligation to notify any person or entity of such revisions or changes.

Further, MIDI America, Inc. makes no representations or warranties with respect to any software, and specifically disclaims any express or implied warranties of merchantability or fitness for any particular purpose. Further, MIDI America, Inc. reserves the right to make changes to any and all parts of the software, at any time, without obligation to notify any person or entity of such changes.

**TRADEMARKS**

MIDI America, Inc. has made every effort to supply trademark information about company names, products, and services. All trademarks, registered trademarks, and servicemarks contained in this book are acknowledged to be the property of the companies or individuals that own those marks. Trademarks indicated below were derived from various sources.

Novell, NetWare, Btrieve, XQL are registered trademarks, NetWare Loadable Module (NLM), NetWare SQL, TTS, NetWare Btrieve, and Xtrieve PLUS are trademarks, and Professional Developers' (PDP), NetWire, and Direct Connect are servicemarks of Novell, Inc. Intel is a registered trademark of Intel Corporation. 1-2-3 and Lotus are registered trademarks of Lotus Development Corporation. dBASE III Plus and dBASE IV are trademarks of Ashton-Tate Corporation. Paradox, Turbo C, and Turbo Pascal are registered trademarks of Ansa-Borland. CompuServe is a registered trademark of CompuServe Corporation. Microsoft is a registered trademark, and MS-DOS and Windows are trademarks of Microsoft, Inc. IBM and OS/2 are registered trademarks, and PC-DOS is a trademark of International Business Machines Corporation.

Mention of third-party products is for informational purposes only and constitutes neither and endorsement nor a recommendation. MIDI America, Inc. assumes no responsibility with respect to the performance or use of these products.

March 1992 Edition
For Btrieve v5.x

# Table of Contents

**Preface** . . . . . . . . . . . . . . . . . . . . . . . . . . . **9**

**Chapter 1: Introduction to Btrieve** . . . . . . . . . . . **11**

What is Btrieve? . . . . . . . . . . . . . . . . . . . . . . . . . 11

Why Use Btrieve? . . . . . . . . . . . . . . . . . . . . . . . . 12

How does Btrieve work? . . . . . . . . . . . . . . . . . . . . 14

The NetWare Database Product Line . . . . . . . . . . . 15

NetWare Btrieve . . . . . . . . . . . . . . . . . . . . . . 15

Btrieve Developer's Kits . . . . . . . . . . . . . . . . 16

Xtrieve PLUS . . . . . . . . . . . . . . . . . . . . . . . 18

NetWare SQL and XQL . . . . . . . . . . . . . . . . . 19

Novell's Developer Support Services . . . . . . . . . . . 21

Bug Patches . . . . . . . . . . . . . . . . . . . . . . . . 21

Phone Support . . . . . . . . . . . . . . . . . . . . . . . 21

Fax Support . . . . . . . . . . . . . . . . . . . . . . . . 21

CompuServe Support . . . . . . . . . . . . . . . . . . 22

Professional Developers' Program . . . . . . . . . . 22

Novell Education . . . . . . . . . . . . . . . . . . . . . 23

**Chapter 2: Tools for Btrieve Programming** . . . . . . **25**

Choosing the Right Compiler . . . . . . . . . . . . . . . . 25

Choosing the Best Language . . . . . . . . . . . . . 26

C Language . . . . . . . . . . . . . . . . . . . . . . . . 26

BASIC . . . . . . . . . . . . . . . . . . . . . . . . . . . . 27

Pascal . . . . . . . . . . . . . . . . . . . . . . . . . . . . 27

COBOL . . . . . . . . . . . . . . . . . . . . . . . . . . . 28

FORTRAN . . . . . . . . . . . . . . . . . . . . . . . . . . 28

Other Languages . . . . . . . . . . . . . . . . . . . . . 28

The Btrieve Interface . . . . . . . . . . . . . . . . . . 29

Compiler Independence . . . . . . . . . . . . . . . . 29

Btrieve Utilities . . . . . . . . . . . . . . . . . . . . . . . . . 31

Btrieve Function Executors . . . . . . . . . . . . . 32

Btrieve Debuggers . . . . . . . . . . . . . . . . . . . . 32

File Utilities . . . . . . . . . . . . . . . . . . . . . . . . . 32

Monitoring Btrieve . . . . . . . . . . . . . . . . . . . . 34

Data Dictionary and Development Systems . . . . . 35

Utilities for Windows . . . . . . . . . . . . . . . . . . 37

The Tutorial Diskette . . . . . . . . . . . . . . . . . . . . 37

**Chapter 3: Calling Btrieve . . . . . . . . . . . . . . . . 39**

Flow of Control . . . . . . . . . . . . . . . . . . . . . . . . 39

Btrieve Operations . . . . . . . . . . . . . . . . . . . . . . 40

The Btrieve Function Call . . . . . . . . . . . . . . 43

Interfacing with Btrieve for DOS . . . . . . . . . . . 45

Interfacing with Btrieve for Windows . . . . . . . . . . . 47

Interfacing with Btrieve for OS/2 . . . . . . . . . . . . . 50

Multiple Thread Support . . . . . . . . . . . . . . . 51

**Chapter 4: Btrieve File Architecture . . . . . . . . . . . 53**

Btrieve Pages . . . . . . . . . . . . . . . . . . . . . . . . . 53

Packing Files and Re-indexing . . . . . . . . . . . . 55

File Control Record (FCR) . . . . . . . . . . . . . . . . 55

Data Pages . . . . . . . . . . . . . . . . . . . . . . . . . . . 56

Fixed-Length Record Pages . . . . . . . . . . . . . 56

Record Addressing . . . . . . . . . . . . . . . . . . . . 58

Variable-Length Record Pages . . . . . . . . . . . 59

Free Space Threshold . . . . . . . . . . . . . . . . . . 59

Blank Truncation . . . . . . . . . . . . . . . . . . . . . 59

Data Compression . . . . . . . . . . . . . . . . . . . . 60

Index Pages . . . . . . . . . . . . . . . . . . . . . . . . . . . 60

Data-Only Files . . . . . . . . . . . . . . . . . . . . . . . . 60

Choosing the Optimal Page Size . . . . . . . . . . . . . 61

Performance Considerations . . . . . . . . . . . . . . 61

Optimal Page Size for Disk Utilization . . . . . . . . . 61
Btrieve's Memory Scheme . . . . . . . . . . . . . . . . . 62
Pre-Imaging . . . . . . . . . . . . . . . . . . . . . . . 63
Fundamentals of Indexing . . . . . . . . . . . . . . . . 64
Btrieve Indexes . . . . . . . . . . . . . . . . . . . . 64
B-tree Indexes . . . . . . . . . . . . . . . . . . . . . 65
Key Segments . . . . . . . . . . . . . . . . . . . . . . 66
Key Segment Definition Elements . . . . . . . . . . . 67
Duplicate Key Indexes . . . . . . . . . . . . . . . . . 69
Duplicate Keys on Permanent Indexes . . . . . . . . 69
Duplicate Keys on Supplemental Indexes . . . . . . . 70

**Chapter 5: Basic File Access Techniques . . . . . . 73**
Creating Files . . . . . . . . . . . . . . . . . . . . . . 73
Opening and Closing Files . . . . . . . . . . . . . . . . 80
Inserting Records . . . . . . . . . . . . . . . . . . . . 81
Traversing . . . . . . . . . . . . . . . . . . . . . . . . 84
Positioning . . . . . . . . . . . . . . . . . . . . . . . 84
Index Traversal . . . . . . . . . . . . . . . . . . . . . 85
Physical Record Traversal . . . . . . . . . . . . . . . 87
Searching . . . . . . . . . . . . . . . . . . . . . . . . 89
Updating Records . . . . . . . . . . . . . . . . . . . . 91

**Chapter 6: Advanced File Access Techniques . . . . 93**
Advanced Indexing . . . . . . . . . . . . . . . . . . . . 93
Record Grouping . . . . . . . . . . . . . . . . . . . . . 93
Supplemental Indexes . . . . . . . . . . . . . . . . . . 95
Extended Operations . . . . . . . . . . . . . . . . . . . 97
Extended Inserts . . . . . . . . . . . . . . . . . . . . 100
Extended Retrieval Operations . . . . . . . . . . . . 102
Reject Count . . . . . . . . . . . . . . . . . . . . . . 103
Maximum Number of Records . . . . . . . . . . . . . 104
Multiuser programming . . . . . . . . . . . . . . . . . 109
Passive Concurrency . . . . . . . . . . . . . . . . . . 109

Record Locking . . . . . . . . . . . . . . . . . . . . 110
Network Simulation with Btrieve . . . . . . . . . . . 112
Transaction Processing . . . . . . . . . . . . . . . . . . . . 113
Initiating a Transaction . . . . . . . . . . . . . . . . . 114
Writing Btrieve NLMs . . . . . . . . . . . . . . . . . . . . 115

**Chapter 7: Loading Btrieve . . . . . . . . . . . . . . . 117**
Operating Modes . . . . . . . . . . . . . . . . . . . . . . 117
Mixed Mode . . . . . . . . . . . . . . . . . . . . . . . 118
Load Options . . . . . . . . . . . . . . . . . . . . . . . . 119
Loading Btrieve for DOS (workstation mode) . . . . . . . 120
Loading Btrieve for Windows 3.0 (workstation mode) . . 122
Loading Btrieve for OS/2 (workstation mode) . . . . . . . 123
Loading NetWare Btrieve (client-server mode) . . . . . . 124
Installing NetWare v3.x Btrieve . . . . . . . . . . . 124
Installing NetWare v2.x Btrieve . . . . . . . . . . . 126
Loading the Btrieve Requester for DOS . . . . . . . 127
Loading and Initializing the
Btrieve Requester for Windows . . . . . . . . 127
Loading and Initializing the
Btrieve Requester for OS/2 . . . . . . . . . . 128
Loading Btrieve in a Windows DOS Box . . . . . . . . . 128
Workstation Mode . . . . . . . . . . . . . . . . . . . 128
Client-Server Mode . . . . . . . . . . . . . . . . . . 129

**Chapter 8: Btrieve Operation Codes . . . . . . . . . . 131**
How to Use This Chapter . . . . . . . . . . . . . . . . . 131
Open (0) . . . . . . . . . . . . . . . . . . . . . . . . . . . 134
Close (1) . . . . . . . . . . . . . . . . . . . . . . . . . . 138
Insert (2) . . . . . . . . . . . . . . . . . . . . . . . . . . 140
Update (3) . . . . . . . . . . . . . . . . . . . . . . . . . . 143
Delete (4) . . . . . . . . . . . . . . . . . . . . . . . . . . 146
Get Equal (5) . . . . . . . . . . . . . . . . . . . . . . . . 149
Get Next (6) . . . . . . . . . . . . . . . . . . . . . . . . . 152

Get Previous (7) . . . . . . . . . . . . . . . . . . . . . . . . 155
Get Greater (8) . . . . . . . . . . . . . . . . . . . . . . . . . 158
Get Greater or Equal (9) . . . . . . . . . . . . . . . . . . . . 161
Get Less Than (10) . . . . . . . . . . . . . . . . . . . . . . . 164
Get Less Than or Equal (11) . . . . . . . . . . . . . . . . . . 167
Get First (12) . . . . . . . . . . . . . . . . . . . . . . . . . 170
Get Last (13) . . . . . . . . . . . . . . . . . . . . . . . . . 173
Create (14) . . . . . . . . . . . . . . . . . . . . . . . . . . 176
Stat (15) . . . . . . . . . . . . . . . . . . . . . . . . . . . 188
Extend (16) . . . . . . . . . . . . . . . . . . . . . . . . . . 191
Set Directory (17) . . . . . . . . . . . . . . . . . . . . . . 193
Get Directory (18) . . . . . . . . . . . . . . . . . . . . . . 194
Begin Transaction (19) . . . . . . . . . . . . . . . . . . . . 195
End Transaction (20) . . . . . . . . . . . . . . . . . . . . . 197
Abort Transaction (21) . . . . . . . . . . . . . . . . . . . . 199
Get Position (22) . . . . . . . . . . . . . . . . . . . . . . . 200
Get Direct (23) . . . . . . . . . . . . . . . . . . . . . . . . 202
Step Next (24) . . . . . . . . . . . . . . . . . . . . . . . . 205
Stop (25) . . . . . . . . . . . . . . . . . . . . . . . . . . . 208
Version (26) . . . . . . . . . . . . . . . . . . . . . . . . . 209
Unlock (27) . . . . . . . . . . . . . . . . . . . . . . . . . . 210
Reset (28) . . . . . . . . . . . . . . . . . . . . . . . . . . . 212
Set Owner (29) . . . . . . . . . . . . . . . . . . . . . . . . 213
Clear Owner (30) . . . . . . . . . . . . . . . . . . . . . . . 215
Create Supplemental Index (31) . . . . . . . . . . . . . . . 216
Drop Supplemental Index (32) . . . . . . . . . . . . . . . . 221
Step First (33) . . . . . . . . . . . . . . . . . . . . . . . . 223
Step Last (34) . . . . . . . . . . . . . . . . . . . . . . . . 225
Step Previous (35) . . . . . . . . . . . . . . . . . . . . . . 227
Get Next Extended (36) . . . . . . . . . . . . . . . . . . . . 229
Get Previous Extended (37) . . . . . . . . . . . . . . . . . . 236
Step Next Extended (38) . . . . . . . . . . . . . . . . . . . 240
Step Previous Extended (39) . . . . . . . . . . . . . . . . . 243
Insert Extended (40) . . . . . . . . . . . . . . . . . . . . . 246

**Appendix A: Btrieve Extended Key Types . . . . . . 251**

String (0) . . . . . . . . . . . . . . . . . . . . . . . . 252

Integer (1) . . . . . . . . . . . . . . . . . . . . . . . . 252

Float (2) . . . . . . . . . . . . . . . . . . . . . . . . 252

Date (3) . . . . . . . . . . . . . . . . . . . . . . . . 253

Time (4) . . . . . . . . . . . . . . . . . . . . . . . . 254

Decimal (5) . . . . . . . . . . . . . . . . . . . . . . . . 254

Money (6) . . . . . . . . . . . . . . . . . . . . . . . . 254

Logical (7) . . . . . . . . . . . . . . . . . . . . . . . . 255

Numeric (8) . . . . . . . . . . . . . . . . . . . . . . . . 255

Bfloat (9) . . . . . . . . . . . . . . . . . . . . . . . . 255

Lstring (10) . . . . . . . . . . . . . . . . . . . . . . . . 256

Zstring (11) . . . . . . . . . . . . . . . . . . . . . . . . 257

Unsigned Binary (12) . . . . . . . . . . . . . . . . . . . . 257

Autoincrement (15) . . . . . . . . . . . . . . . . . . . . 257

**Appendix B: C Language Source Code Examples . . 259**

INCLUDES.C . . . . . . . . . . . . . . . . . . . . . . . . 260

BCREATE.C . . . . . . . . . . . . . . . . . . . . . . . . 261

BINSERT.C . . . . . . . . . . . . . . . . . . . . . . . . 264

BTRAVI.C . . . . . . . . . . . . . . . . . . . . . . . . 268

BTRAVP.C . . . . . . . . . . . . . . . . . . . . . . . . 270

BSEARCH.C . . . . . . . . . . . . . . . . . . . . . . . . 272

BUPDATE.C . . . . . . . . . . . . . . . . . . . . . . . . 274

BGROUP.C . . . . . . . . . . . . . . . . . . . . . . . . 276

BSINDEX.C . . . . . . . . . . . . . . . . . . . . . . . . 279

BXINSERT.C . . . . . . . . . . . . . . . . . . . . . . . . 282

BXGET.C . . . . . . . . . . . . . . . . . . . . . . . . 285

BXGETF.C . . . . . . . . . . . . . . . . . . . . . . . . 289

BUPM.C . . . . . . . . . . . . . . . . . . . . . . . . 293

BUPT.C . . . . . . . . . . . . . . . . . . . . . . . . 296

**Appendix C: Turbo Pascal Source Code Examples . 299**

BCREATE.PAS . . . . . . . . . . . . . . . . . . . . . . . 299

BINSERT.PAS . . . . . . . . . . . . . . . . . . . . . . . 302

BTRAVI.PAS . . . . . . . . . . . . . . . . . . . . . . . 305

**Appendix D: BASIC Source Code Examples . . . . . 309**

BCREATE.BAS . . . . . . . . . . . . . . . . . . . . . . . 309

BINSERT.BAS . . . . . . . . . . . . . . . . . . . . . . . 312

BTRAVI.BAS . . . . . . . . . . . . . . . . . . . . . . . 314

**Appendix E: COBOL Source Code Example . . . . . 315**

CREATE.CBL . . . . . . . . . . . . . . . . . . . . . . . 315

**Appendix F: Btrieve Status Codes . . . . . . . . . . 319**

**Appendix G: Operation Code Quick Reference Tables . . . . . . . . . . . . 337**

Biases (by Bias Value) . . . . . . . . . . . . . . . . . 337

Biases (by Description) . . . . . . . . . . . . . . . . . 337

Operations by OpCode . . . . . . . . . . . . . . . . . 338

Operations by Operation Name . . . . . . . . . . . . 339

*The Illustrated Guide to Btrieve*

# Preface

Welcome to *The Illustrated Guide to Btrieve!* You've probably picked up this book because you either have heard of Btrieve and you want to know what it's all about, or you already use Btrieve and you want to understand more. We think you've found exactly what you need!

While every effort has been made to be sure that this book provides useful and correct information, *The Illustrated Guide to Btrieve* is not intended to be a replacement for Novell's Btrieve manuals or any of the other valuable publications from Novell. What we have tried to do is combine pertinent information about Btrieve and our Btrieve programming experience in one handy and informative book.

All of source code examples in this book are provided in machine-readable format on the optional Tutorial Diskette, available through MIDI America (see the order form on the last page). The Tutorial Diskette also provides two highly valuable utilities that are discussed in Chapter Two.

If you are a programmer, then *The Illustrated Guide to Btrieve* provides the guidance you'll need as you design, develop, and support Btrieve database programs with Btrieve v5.x. If you are a software developer, MIS manager, or computer aficionado considering Btrieve for a possible solution, then this book provides the information you'll need to understand the capabilities of Btrieve. Regardless of your background, *The Illustrated Guide to Btrieve* will teach you how to push this powerful database programming tool to the limit.

*The Illustrated Guide to Btrieve*

# 1 Introduction to Btrieve

## What is Btrieve?

Btrieve was introduced to the database programmer community in 1982 by an Austin, Texas based company called SoftCraft. Borrowing features from existing minicomputer indexing systems, SoftCraft exploited the new capabilities of personal computers and provided programmers a PC-based B-tree indexing utility. This B-tree data retrieval utility (hence "B-tree-ve") was quickly embraced by application programmers as a much needed database utility that would speed up and simplify the process of producing reliable database management applications for PCs.

Around 1984, when DOS 3.1 was introduced with file locking capabilities, SoftCraft made Btrieve available in a multiuser version. By using the new multiuser features of DOS, Btrieve/N became the first true multiuser record manager for the PC LAN. This meant that programmers could easily develop multiuser database software.

By 1987 Novell was becoming established as the leader in Local Area Networking. In the previous year, NetWare 286 had taken the market by storm. The merger with smaller but equally effective companies like Exelan and CXI had given Novell more strength in the computer industry by providing PCs with communications to Apple Macintoshes, UNIX networks, and large mainframe systems. NetWare soon became a viable alternative to minicomputers and a partner with mainframe computing systems.

But NetWare was lacking a database component. If NetWare was to successfully compete in the computer industry, Novell needed to provide an integrated, high-performance, multiuser database engine like the larger computer operating systems.

Novell recognized the importance of Btrieve. It was fast. It required little memory. It supported multiple users. It could be accessed from most programming languages including C Language. It supported large database files. It offered sophisticated fault tolerance. And it had a large and growing user base.

Novell purchased SoftCraft in 1987, incorporating Btrieve into NetWare 286, and establishing Btrieve as the de facto industry standard for record management.

The Btrieve "database" has very little similarity with other popular products that can also be called "databases," such as dBase or Informix and others. Many of these products were initially designed to help non-programmers produce database applications using flexible scripting languages or fourth generation languages (4GLs). These techniques are rapidly evolving and do offer many productivity advantages, but the resulting applications often suffer from many problems, including poor performance, and limited applicability.

Btrieve, on the other hand, is intended to be a general purpose indexing and retrieval mechanism which can be called from more traditional and widely-known third generation languages (3GLs) like COBOL, C, or Pascal, and can be used to implement a variety of application programs. Application programmers will usually tell you that they choose the Btrieve record manager because of its excellent performance characteristics and because it can be used for so many types of complex application system designs.

## Why Use Btrieve?

Performance and flexibility are of primary importance to a programmer writing an effective application program. Fourth generation languages provide the less sophisticated software developer tools to manipulate large amounts of data relatively easily. 4GLs are also useful for prototyping database systems that will then be refined using standard programming tools. And it's worth noting that Btrieve is also accessible from several 4GLs such as dBase and Paradox.

But the programmer who is using a 4GL is making a trade-off: performance and flexibility are usually sacrificed for ease-of-use. In order to master other areas of interest including networking, graphics, communications, MIDI, and high-speed number crunching, programmers will inevitably turn to 3GLs like C Language, Pascal, and COBOL. Here, Btrieve and NetWare are a logical choice.

Btrieve's success can be attributed to the following reasons:

- **Acceptance.** It is a time tested, industry accepted B-tree indexing mechanism suitable to the LAN environment.
- **Performance.** Btrieve is undisputedly one of the fastest performing indexing and retrieval mechanisms overall, when properly configured. Its tunability and LAN features makes Btrieve a particularly fast performer in the high utilization LAN environment.
- **Multi-Language Support.** Btrieve is supported by over fifty programming languages and dialects. With a simple "single function call" interface and straightforward memory management, Btrieve is easy to incorporate into existing programs.

- **True Multitasking.** Btrieve's locking mechanisms allow a variety of multitasking strategies to be implemented.
- **Integrity assurance.** Btrieve provides both automatic and program controlled integrity features (pre-imaging and transaction processing respectively) as well as direct support for NetWare TTS (Transaction Tracking System). These features provide file protection even in a rigorous network environment.
- **Data Format Flexibility.** Btrieve imposes no restrictions on data formats. Btrieve can store both text and binary data in fixed- and variable-length records, which could represent anything from simple names and addresses to statistical data to Morse code.
- **Server-Based Computing.** Novell provides versions of Btrieve that are incorporated into the NetWare operating system. These server-based database processes can cooperate with application processes on workstation clients that require data services. Other server processes can access Btrieve files directly at the file server, as well. Btrieve's server-based architecture eliminates excessive network traffic and supports a variety of database architecture strategies.
- **Novell Support.** Novell is clearly the leader in microcomputer networking technology and provides a solid training and support platform for developers.
- **SQL Access.** Novell offers Structured Query Language access to Btrieve data using a relational data management server process called NetWare SQL. Applications can be written to either the NetWare SQL interface or the Btrieve interface; in either case, the applications store and manipulate data in Btrieve files.

The last bullet raises an important issue. Btrieve's similarity to ISAM/VSAM systems lends itself easily to the relational database model and so Btrieve has often been categorized as a relational database manager.

It is true that Btrieve can be used to implement database designs which involve relational concepts such as "joins" between data files and set-oriented database operations. Further, Btrieve can be coupled with Novell's NetWare SQL relational database server for more complete relational functionality and SQL access.

However, the Btrieve product alone is not a relational database. Btrieve is a "record manager" which manages and indexes data at the physical record level. Btrieve has no need to further divide the data into the logical record level -- the record data structure that specifies the fields or columns required for true Relational Data Modeling.

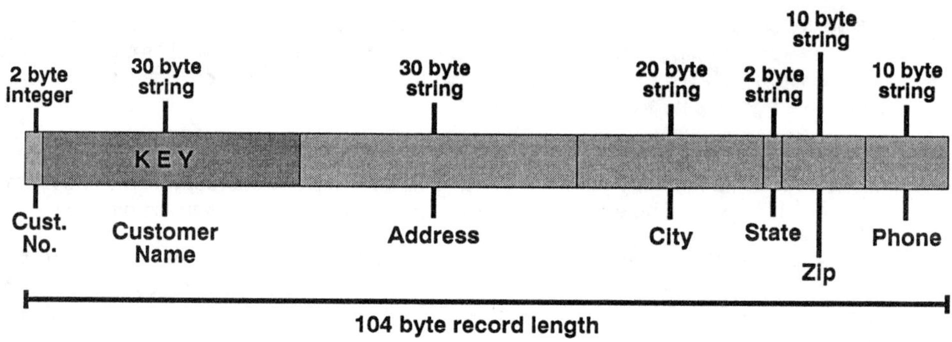


*Figure 1.1: Customer record layout*

## How does Btrieve work?

The definition of a Btrieve file does not require logical field definitions. Btrieve only needs to know about physical record characteristics —the application programmer then builds a record buffer in the program with a data structure that further breaks down the physical record into logical fields.

For example, Figure 1.1 illustrates the logical field layout of a simple customer mailing list database. Each record contains a customer number field, customer name, address fields, and phone number field.

In this example, the sum of the field lengths adds up to 104 bytes. In addition, suppose that you wished to be able to sort and retrieve data based on the customers' names, so an index key must be set up on the customer name field. The customer name field physically begins at the third byte from the beginning of the record and is a 30 byte string (or character array). The basic information to define this Btrieve file is:

| | |
|---|---|
| Record Length | = 104 |
| Key Position | = 3 |
| Key Length | = 30 |
| Key Type | = String |

No further logical field information is required by Btrieve. It is the responsibility of the application program to break each 104 byte record into individual fields.

The application program which processes the customer database simply passes records back and forth between the program's internal record buffer and the Btrieve record manager. The record manager takes care of all the indexing and retrieval and the application program takes care of deciphering and processing the data.

By providing a generic indexing and retrieval mechanism, Btrieve allows the programmer to focus more attention on the application rather than complex indexing algorithms.

## The NetWare Database Product Line

Btrieve is the foundation of an entire product line of database tools and services offered by Novell. All of the products discussed below can be used to access and update information stored in Btrieve data files.

### NetWare Btrieve

NetWare Btrieve is the native record management service component of the NetWare operating system. For NetWare 3.x, Btrieve is written as an NLM (NetWare Loadable Module). For NetWare 2.x, Btrieve is implemented as a VAP (Value-Added Process). In fact, NetWare Btrieve and the associated Btrieve requesters for DOS, OS/2, and Windows are included with every copy of NetWare 2.x and 3.x. Thus, every copy of NetWare comes with everything required to run existing Btrieve applications (this does not include NetWare Lite, but see the discussion of architectural options below).

NetWare Btrieve operates in client-server mode. In this technique, the client (the workstation) issues requests for data reads and writes to the server where NetWare Btrieve is running. Both the Btrieve VAP and NLM monitor the network for workstations requesting access to Btrieve files. Chapter 4, "Btrieve File Architecture," discusses the internal architecture of the NetWare Btrieve system in more detail.

The Btrieve Requester is a communication program that runs in the client machine that intercepts any data access requests from the application program and forwards them on to the Btrieve server. In other words, the Btrieve Requester does not perform any database operations itself but is capable of communicating to both the Btrieve VAP and NLM.

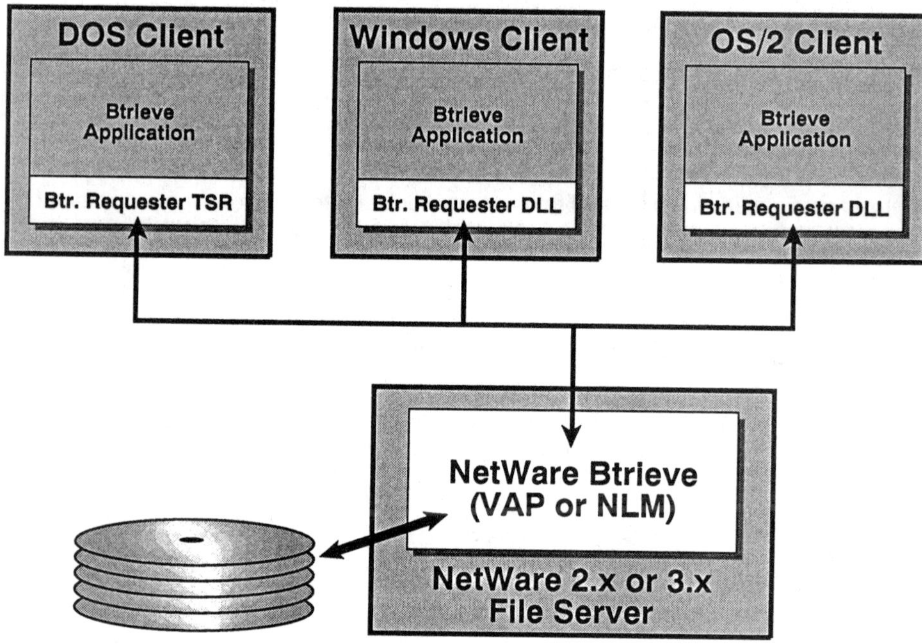


*Figure 1.2: Client/Server NetWare Btrieve configuration*

In addition, NetWare Btrieve comes with a monitoring program, BCONSOLE, and a setup program, BSETUP (these two programs are discussed in Chapter 2, "Tools for Btrieve Programming"). Figure 1.2 illustrates NetWare Btrieve servicing several workstations.

## Btrieve Developer's Kits

Developers who are writing Btrieve applications must purchase a Btrieve Developers Kit in order to obtain the proper software license. These software developers kits are available for DOS, Windows, and OS/2. The products are referred to as Btrieve for OS where OS is either DOS, Windows, or OS/2. These kits are currently priced at $595.

Each developer's kit comes with a version of the Btrieve record management engine referred to as Workstation Btrieve. The term Workstation Btrieve is used because all of an application's Btrieve data processing is performed by a Btrieve engine running on the workstation. This type of database processing is often referred to as client-based processing (as opposed to client/

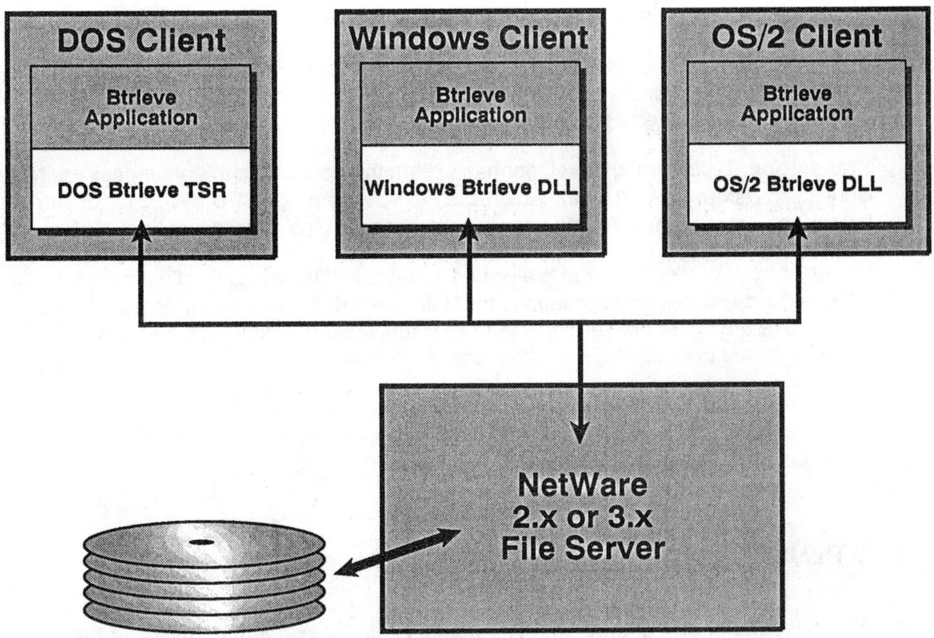


***Figure 1.3: Client-based Workstation Btrieve configuration***

server processing). Workstation Btrieve has had several other names over the years, including Client Btrieve, Btrieve/N, and Btrieve for DOS.

Workstation Btrieve for DOS was essentially the original version of Btrieve once offered by SoftCraft. Workstation Btrieve for DOS is loaded as a TSR and communicates to the local operating system to perform database access functions.

Workstation Btrieve is available for Windows and OS/2 as a DLL (dynamic link library) and like Btrieve for DOS, the local operating system carries out all disk access.

Btrieve Developer's Kits also come with a set of interface modules which allow Btrieve to be called from various programming languages. Interface modules are discussed in Chapter 3, "Calling Btrieve."

In addition, developers kits come with utilities to aid in testing and developing Btrieve applications. These utilities are also discussed in Chapter 3.

Workstation Btrieve allows developers to write and test applications on a standalone PC, then easily load them on a network and have true multiuser applications.

Because Novell does not charge a royalty or licensing fee for distributing Workstation Btrieve, commercial software developers usually include this engine with their applications. Users who purchase these Btrieve-based applications then have three architectural options.

- **Standalone.** Typically the developer has written the application to encompass multiuser issues like record-locking, workstation Btrieve spends a few CPU cycles locking and unlocking records that only one user is accessing, but it all works just fine.
- **Client-based.** Workstation Btrieve issues standard DOS 3.1-compatible calls for multiuser record-locking, so applications that talk to Workstation Btrieve can operate on NetWare or any other network operating systems that understand those DOS calls. This is the best way to run Btrieve applications on NetWare Lite.
- **Client/Server.** In a NetWare 2.x or 3.x environment, the best option is to replace Workstation Btrieve with the appropriate Btrieve Requester. The Btrieve Requester will then pass along data access requests to the Btrieve VAP or NLM.

## Xtrieve PLUS

Xtrieve PLUS was originally offered as menu-based Btrieve development utility for programmers. It allowed the user to define the fields in a Btrieve file so records could be accessed with full screen editing. So many features have been added to Xtrieve PLUS that it has eventually been adopted by the user community as an end user tool. Currently priced at $995 for a network license for either DOS or OS/2 workstations, Xtrieve PLUS offers the following capabilities:

- Define and create files with field definitions
- Access Btrieve records with a spreadsheet-like interface
- Define views that contain fields from several related files
- Search for records and set filter conditions
- Define reports with a report generator
- Operate with a menu or from command scripts

Some software developers bundle Xtrieve PLUS with their Btrieve database applications. For example, Xtrieve PLUS is available with IBM's Platinum Accounting software and provides ad-hoc reporting and easy access to the data files.

Xtrieve PLUS uses a data dictionary to define certain characteristics of each Btrieve file. The Xtrieve PLUS data dictionary is nothing more than a collection of related Btrieve files. The following files are included in the data dictionary:

**X$FILE Data dictionary files**

This file contains one record for each file defined in the data dictionary with a file name, the directory location of the file, and a file identifier.

**X$FIELD Field definitions**

This file contains one record for each field in each file identified in X$FILE and defines a field's name, type, length, and other characteristics.

**X$INDEX Index Key Definitions**

This file contains one record for each index segment in each file and defines the index name, which field is associated with the index, and other characteristics.

**X$ATTRIB Field Attributes**

This file contains one record for each field attribute defined on a field. An attribute defines the display characteristics of a field (e.g., display dates in the DD/MM/YYYY format). Field attributes are optional.

**X$VIEW File views**

This file contains one record for each "view" defined to the data dictionary. A view describes the relationships between different files and the fields in the same application system.

## NetWare SQL and XQL

NetWare SQL is a server-based relational database engine that makes Btrieve calls to provide Structured Query Language access to Btrieve files on a local area and wide area network. The SQL language itself was developed by IBM in the 70's as a standard language for accessing relational database files -- *NetWare* SQL is Novell's implementation of a SQL-based database server. Current pricing for the NetWare SQL NLM for NetWare 3.x is $1495; the VAP version for NetWare 2.x is $595.

XQL is the workstation-based developer's utility required to write NetWare SQL applications. XQL allows the programmer to incorporate SQL statements in an application program for high-level relational database functionality. In addition, XQL comes with an interactive SQL interpreter that allow SQL statements to be executed, stored and recalled. Versions are available for DOS or OS/2 and are currently priced at $795.

NetWare SQL shares the same data dictionary as Xtrieve PLUS. Thus, files created with Xtrieve PLUS can be accessed through NetWare XQL and vice-versa.

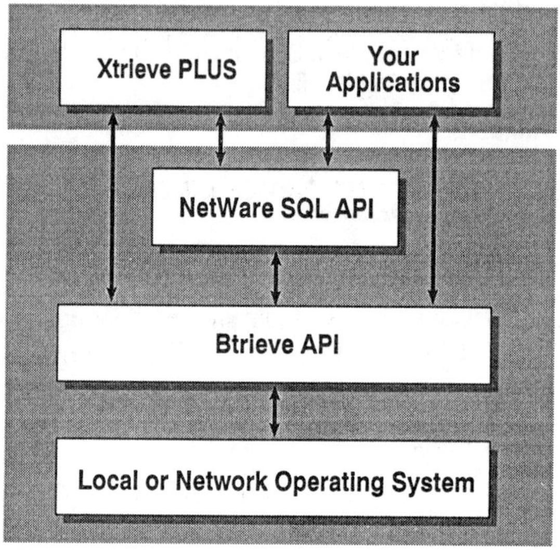


***Figure 1.4: Relationship Between Btrieve, Xtrieve PLUS, and NetWare SQL***

A NetWare SQL file is simply a Btrieve file with an accompanying data dictionary which describes the characteristics of the file and its relationships to other files in the application system. The data dictionary system can be created using Xtrieve PLUS, Structured Query Language, or the XQL interface to NetWare SQL.

Figure 1.4 shows the relationship between Btrieve, Xtrieve PLUS, and NetWare XQL and illustrates that a programmer has several "entry points" or methods of interacting with Btrieve files:

- From a menu-based user interface with Xtrieve PLUS
- From high-level relational operations with XQL
- From low-level record manipulation calls with Btrieve

These products are all engineered, marketed, and supported by the Novell Database Products Division. For sales information and up-to-date pricing call 1-800-RED-WORD (800-733-9673).

Btrieve offers the greatest flexibility at minimal cost in terms of dollars, memory requirements, and performance. Btrieve does not impose any "rules of conduct" on a program such as those imposed SQL and Btrieve is not required to use the data dictionary for database access. However, the use of Btrieve, Xtrieve PLUS, and NetWare SQL are not mutually exclusive. A large application might use each of these products for different functions. The real advantage of Novell's database product line is that they all can share the same database files at the same time.

## Novell's Developer Support Services

Btrieve is supported out of Novell's Austin, Texas site. Btrieve is a relatively support-intensive product due to the sophisticated database operations provided and the fact that Btrieve is available to many different languages, compilers, and operating systems.

### Bug Patches

Bugs in Btrieve are corrected by patches. A patch is a debug script that modifies the existing executable code. Novell generally uses patches as opposed to a "source fix" which is simply a replacement to the original program.

If there is a problem in the current version of Btrieve that you are using, it is important to obtain the patches and apply them to Btrieve. Novell will mail you a free patch diskette if you are currently under a support contract. Patches are also available over CompuServe and are announced in *Bullets,* Novell's newsletter for developers. Novell will not contact users when bugs are discovered; it is up to you to request patches.

### Phone Support

The Btrieve developer's kits come with thirty days of free and unlimited phone support which begins the first time you contact Novell for support. The support number is 1-800-NETWARE (the old 1-800-SAY-HELP number is being phased out). If a company has purchased several developer's kits, thirty days of phone support is provided for each product. After thirty days, extended support can be purchased for $500 per year or $50 per incident.

### Fax Support

Free fax support is available by faxing in your problem at (1-512-345-7478). Novell attempts to respond to all support faxes within 48 hours.

## CompuServe Support

Perhaps the best method of Btrieve support Novell offers is on CompuServe. CompuServe is a bulletin board service available to anyone with a computer and modem. CompuServe offers "forums" for various topics ranging from stock quotations to Btrieve support. "NetWire" is the name of Novell's collection of forums on CompuServe. NetWire is comprised of the following forums:

| | |
|---|---|
| **NOVA** | Topics on NetWire platforms including Btrieve |
| **NOVB** | Communications and Topologies |
| **NOVC** | Development Products |
| **NetWare 2.x** | NetWare Operating System for 286 |
| **NetWare 3.x** | NetWare Operating System for 386 |

The NOVA forum (type GO NETWIRE and select NOVA) provides access to latest Btrieve patches, public domain utilities, Novell Austin's FYI files, and other Btrieve related information. For more information on CompuServe call 1-800-848-8199 or simply purchase a good modem. Most modems come with a CompuServe brochure inside.

## Professional Developers' Program

Novell wants software developers to write Btrieve applications. This gives an easy migration path into a number of other Novell database products (especially NetWare SQL) and further growth of the network computing industry. The Professional Developer's Program is there to help software developers be successful in producing and marketing their software products.

Novell's partnership with third-party developers through the Professional Developer's Program offers big discounts on software products including NetWare v3.x, free seminars, and a free subscription to *Bullets* -- an excellent source of information published by the tech support group in Austin. *Bullets* provides a wealth of information about Btrieve and other Novell Development Products including latest patches, coding examples, release information, and much more. For more information on the Professional Developer's Program, call 1-800-RED-WORD (1-800-733-9673).

## Novell Education

Novell offers a full complement of database educational classes held at various NECs (Novell Education Centers) around the country. These classes provide the best training for programming in Btrieve. Novell offers the following classes for database developers:

- Programming with Btrieve: Introduction
- Programming with Btrieve: Advanced Features
- Xtrieve PLUS
- Programming with XQL for NetWare SQL

Novell's Education department has made Btrieve an area of specialty in the CNE (Certified NetWare Engineer) and CNI (Certified NetWare Instructor) programs. For class scheduling information and an education catalog, call 1-800-233-3382.

It is easy to see why Btrieve is such a popular database mechanism and the record manager of choice to over 30,000 software developers. Btrieve's power and flexibility combined with Novell's lead in the network computing industry make Btrieve an easy choice when choosing a database engine.

# 2 Tools for Btrieve Programming

Btrieve is a low-level file access mechanism, known as a "record manager." In other words, there is no user interface portion of the Btrieve program itself. Btrieve interfaces directly with a compiler. A good compiler, therefore, is a Btrieve programmer's most useful tool; it turns human-readable programming language source code into machine-readable executable programs. However, if additional tools or utilities were not available, you would have to write a program to perform each little chore. Fortunately, Novell supplies several handy utilities and many others are available from third-party software developers. Having the right utilities will make your job as a Btrieve programmer much easier.

## Choosing the Right Compiler

When Btrieve was first introduced, it was one of the first database utilities to support interpreted BASIC. At that time, BASIC was being included with every personal computer sold by IBM. All you needed was a PC and Btrieve and you could develop a relatively high-performance database program that could be sold to a large targeted market (PC owners). Other languages were added to the list: Pascal, FORTRAN, C Language, assembly --all the major programming languages. As soon each new compiler came on the market, SoftCraft's Btrieve would support it. Btrieve's adaptability from language to language soon developed a loyal user base of programmers, many of whom took Btrieve with them whenever they switched to a higher-performance language.

Today, Btrieve supports over 40 compilers. This wide selection of compilers allows the developer to pick the best compiler for any given application.

## Choosing the Best Language

Identifying the right language (and more specifically, the right compiler) for a program largely depends on the nature of the application itself. Certain languages lend themselves to particular applications.

## C Language

C language exploded in popularity during the late 1980s. It was popularized by AT&T as part of the UNIX Compiler. C language allowed programmers to directly access the operating system.

For many advanced programmers, C language is considered to be the language of choice. Many operating systems (including UNIX and NetWare) provide easy entry points via C language libraries. C language offers low-level assembly functionality as well as high-level, complex structures, pointer arithmetic, and memory allocation. Novell publishes an exhaustive API Library (Application Program Interface to NetWare functionality —not to be confused with the solitary Btrieve API) for developers wishing to communicate directly with NetWare.

Novell's own C compiler for DOS comes with Btrieve for DOS and the WATCOM interface. In addition, Novell's C compiler for NLMs can turn client programs into server-based NLMs. With operating system functionality and the fact that there are hundreds of C Language libraries providing a multitude of functions, C Language is a logical choice.

Novell currently supplies Btrieve interfaces for the following C Language compilers:

- Borland Turbo C
- Ci-C86 v1.0
- Ci-C86 v2.0
- DeSmet C
- IBM C/2 for OS/2
- IBM C/2 for OS/2
- Lattice C v6.0
- Lattice C v3.0
- Lattice C v2.0
- Lattice C v1.0
- Mark Williams C
- Microsoft C
- Novell WATCOM C

## BASIC

BASIC (Beginning All-purpose Symbolic Instruction Code) was the first programming language available for the PC. A BASIC interpreter was provided with DOS and provided programmers with many features that were made available by the personal computer. It was quite easy, for example, to write a user input screen or generate graphic images in BASIC. Software solutions could be developed rapidly. Since the original PC BASIC interpreter, many BASIC compilers have been developed that have proved to allow sophisticated, structured programming.

Novell currently supports the following versions of BASIC:

- Borland Turbo Basic
- DR CBASIC (CB-86)
- Generic BASIC compiler
- Generic BASIC interpreter
- IBM BASIC v1.0
- IBM BASIC v2.0
- IBM BASIC v3.0
- IBM BASIC/2 for OS/2
- MS BASIC v7.0
- MS BASIC v6.0
- MS QuickBasic v6.0
- MS QuickBasic v4.0
- MS QuickBasic v3.0
- TI BASIC Compiler
- TI BASIC

## Pascal

The Pascal programming language was named after Blaise Pascal, a 17th century French mathematician. Since the release of Turbo Pascal, Borland has made Pascal the language of choice for many programmers. Early in the evolution of the personal computer the Turbo Pascal Compiler provided programmers (many of whom learned Pascal in college) with a fast and easy-to-write language offering simple control of the video screen. Currently, an abundance of libraries from dozens of vendors are available including multimedia data manipulation. The result is full screen editing and graphics, pop-up windows, and fast scrolling database programs.

Novell currently supports the following Pascal compilers:

- Borland Turbo Pascal v5.0
- Borland Turbo Pascal v4.0

- Metaware Pascal
- SBB Pascal

## COBOL

COBOL (COmmon Business Oriented Language) is widely used by large companies for data processing. Many companies are "bringing their applications down" from a mainframe or minicomputer to a LAN platform. A data processing manager involved in the already difficult conversion from the mainframe to the micro LAN may find it easier to continue to use COBOL on the PCs and modify the database access subroutines to use Btrieve.

As an NLM, Btrieve provides a solid multi-user database platform for COBOL applications. In addition, Btrieve provides a stepping stone to eventually convert to other languages. Novell currently supports the following COBOL compilers:

- MBP COBOL-85
- MBP COBOL
- MS COBOL v3.0
- Micro Focus COBOL/2
- Micro Focus COBOL
- Microsoft COBOL
- RM COBOL
- RM/COBOL-8X
- Realia COBOL

## FORTRAN

A scientist with extensive quantities of measurement data to process may choose FORTRAN (FORmula TRANslation) because most of his or her programs were originally written on a minicomputer in FORTRAN. In addition, FORTRAN offers high performance in floating point arithmetic. Currently, Microsoft FORTRAN is the only supported compiler.

## Other Languages

There are a number of other languages and application development systems that support interfaces to Btrieve data, although Novell does not provide interfaces to these languages. The companies who have developed these languages have written and support their own interface to Btrieve. The following languages offer support for Btrieve:

- CLARION
- FoxPro
- Clipper / dBase
- Visual BASIC
- GUPTA SQLWindows

There are several other packages that offer either direct interfaces to Btrieve, or that enable the manipulation of Btrieve data via NetWare SQL. Contact Novell at 1-800-RED-WORD for the latest information about these third-party products.

## The Btrieve Interface

Most programming utilities come in the form of a library. However, Btrieve can support new languages easily because it is *not* a function call library. A library is a set of functions or subroutines written in a particular language which can be included or linked to a program. Libraries save you from having to write your own subroutines. Libraries often involve thousands of lines of source code. It is very difficult to rewrite these subroutines for just one additional language, let alone for each new language that comes on the market.

Btrieve introduced a unique technique: a single-function TSR (Terminate and Stay Resident program) with B-tree operations which is activated by a DOS interrupt vector. Btrieve is invoked by a single function containing an operation code parameter which tells Btrieve what to do. Because Btrieve involves only one function, it is relatively simple to define this function to multiple languages. Instead of a library of subroutines, Btrieve comes with a set of interface programs, one interface program for each compiler supported.

An interface is a small program (about 100 lines of code) which is included as source code or linked as an object module to the program making Btrieve calls, depending on the language.

## Compiler Independence

An interface program defines the Btrieve function or subroutine call and makes it *callable* from the language. When called, the DOS interface program performs the following tasks:

- Makes sure that Btrieve is loaded.
- Transfers the parameters from the complier specific parameter stack to a common location in memory where Btrieve will find them.
- Generates an interrupt 7B to active the Btrieve TSR
- Transfers the parameters back to the program's parameter stack.

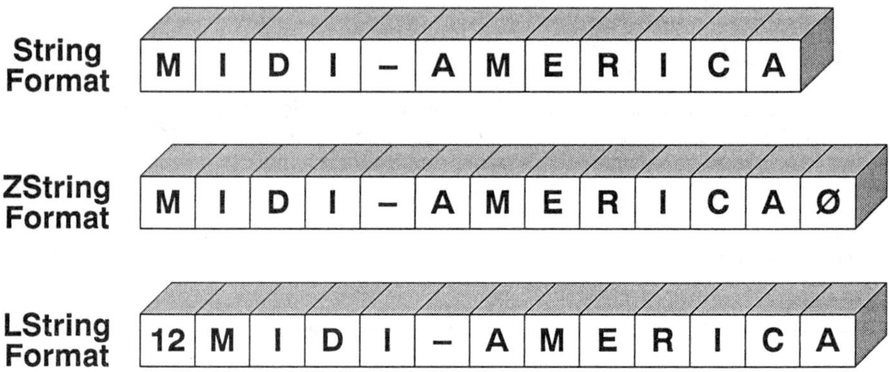


***Figure 2.1: String formats***

This method is very effective in making Btrieve transparent to the programming language. Since only Btrieve itself ever modifies a Btrieve file, it makes no difference which programming language is used to create or add records to a file. A program in any other language can access that file. There is only one type of Btrieve file and that file is compiler independent.

While Btrieve files are compiler independent, there are certain data formats that are compiler specific. For example, C Language uses binary zeros to terminate strings (known as Zstrings), while other languages do not. When comparing two Zstrings, only the values before the binary zero are considered. Turbo Pascal, on the other hand, uses a length byte as the first byte in the string.

Although Btrieve does not require information about the data format of the record, it must know data types when defining keys. When a portion of a record contains a key value, Btrieve must know the data format in order to collate properly.

Figure 2.1 shows three string formats that can be properly indexed with Btrieve. The string key type uses no delimiter. A Zstring uses a binary zero to delimit the end of the string. The Lstring key type is used by Turbo Pascal where the first byte specifies the string length.

Key types are standard data formats (sometimes compiler specific) that can be properly collated by Btrieve. Btrieve currently supports 13 different key types. See Appendix A for more information on Btrieve's key types.

## Btrieve Utilities

Although Btrieve is a powerful database engine, developing efficient and effective database applications is a complex task. A few good Btrieve utilities can make your job a lot easier. While Novell's monitoring utility for the Btrieve NLM (BCONSOLE) is a good tool for network or database administrators, the programming utilities that come with the Btrieve Developer's Kit do not provide all the tools that a Btrieve programmer should have.

For example, one product that provides a number of extremely useful functions for Btrieve programmers is Novell's own Xtrieve PLUS. Xtrieve PLUS provides data dictionary support, data access screens, and a report generator for Btrieve files. However at $995 per copy of Xtrieve PLUS, you might look to shareware and third-party vendors for Btrieve utilities beyond those provided by Novell (shareware programs are available free of charge —a small optional fee is usually requested). Many shareware utilities are available on CompuServe and through Novell. Figure 2.2 shows other commercially available support products for Btrieve developers.

***Figure 2.2: Third-party Btrieve support products***

| Product | Company | Description |
|---|---|---|
| Bee_Util | Service Success Inc. | File utilities |
| Btrap | OMNI Computer Services | TSR debugger |
| Btrieve Starter Kit | Norcom | Programming utilities for COBOL |
| BUtility | Smithware, Inc. | Data dictionary utility for Btrieve |
| Clarion Professional Developer with Btrieve LEM | Clarion Software | 4GL application development |
| Data Junction | Tools & Techniques | File formatting utilities |
| EZedit | First Choice | Function executor/file utilities |
| Magic PC | Aker | Menu driven application developer |
| ProPrint & C Code Generator | Conquest Data | C code generator for report programs |
| WindowBase | Software Products International | GUI interface tools |

There are four basic categories of Btrieve utilities:

- Function executors
- Debuggers
- File utilities
- Data dictionary and development systems

## Btrieve Function Executors

A good function executor is a necessary item for understanding Btrieve. A function executor allows Btrieve operations to be performed from an input screen without having to write a program. Each Btrieve function parameter is displayed and the user interacts with Btrieve just as a program would –one operation at a time. When you need to know how Btrieve will behave in certain situations, it is much easier to go into a function executor and find out for yourself than it is to search for the answer in the manual or write a test program or call technical support.

The B.EXE program is a function executor which is bundled with Btrieve. The BX program included with the optional Tutorial Diskette is another function executor. BX.EXE provides all of the capabilities of B.EXE with the addition of allowing the user to examine and modify the contents of all Btrieve parameters including the Data Buffer, Key Buffer, and Position Block. These parameters can be edited as ASCII characters and as hex values. Multiple position blocks are available to open several files at the same time, allowing you to test record locking from one workstation.

## Btrieve Debuggers

A programmer uses a debugger to find out what values are being passed to Btrieve. BDEBUG, the original Btrieve debugger, is a popular shareware utility. BDEBUG is a DOS TSR that intercepts Btrieve calls and displays the parameters being passed to and from Btrieve. It is used to view Btrieve calls made by an executing program.

## File Utilities

Novell includes BUTIL with Btrieve for DOS, Btrieve for Windows, and Btrieve for OS/2. BUTIL provides several high-level procedures which perform tasks like creating files, and loading and writing to sequential files. BUTIL is also used to unload the Btrieve TSR, display information about a Btrieve file, and close all open files (the Reset procedure). BUTIL provides the following functions:

```
BUTIL -CLONE <OUTPUT-FILE> <SOURCE-FILE> [-O<OWNER1>]

BUTIL -COPY <INPUT-FILE> <OUTPUT-FILE> [-O<OWNER1> [-O<OWNER2>]]

BUTIL -CREATE <FILE-NAME> <DESCRIPTION FILE>

BUTIL -DROP <BTRIEVE-FILE> <KEY NUMBER> [-O<OWNER>]

BUTIL -EXTEND <BTRIEVE-FILE> <EXTENSION-FILE> [<IMMEDIATE(Y/N)>] [-O<OWNER>]

BUTIL -INDEX <BTRIEVE-FILE> <INDEX-FILE> <DESCRIPTION-FILE> [-O<OWNER>]

BUTIL -LOAD <INPUT-FILE> <BTRIEVE-FILE> [-O<OWNER>]

BUTIL -RECOVER <BTRIEVE-FILE> <OUTPUT-FILE> [-O<OWNER>]

BUTIL -RESET [<STATION NAME> | <USER NAME> | <PROCESS ID>]

BUTIL -SAVE <BTRIEVE-FILE> <OUTPUT-FILE> [<INDEX(Y/N)> <INDEX-FILE> | <KEY
NUMBER>] [-O<OWNER>]

BUTIL -SINDEX <BTRIEVE-FILE> <DESCRIPTION-FILE> [-O<OWNER>]

BUTIL -STAT <FILE-NAME> [-O<OWNER>]

BUTIL -STOP

BUTIL -VER
```

BUTIL is especially useful for recovering data from a damaged Btrieve file. The following procedure is recommended by Novell to recover data from a file with a damaged index:

- Create a new Btrieve file from its description file or clone the existing Btrieve file

  ```
  BUTIL -CREATE NEWFILE.BTR NEWFILE.DES
  ```

  or

  ```
  BUTIL -CLONE NEWFILE.BTR OLDFILE.BTR
  ```

- Produce a data-only sequential file from a damaged file

  ```
  BUTIL -RECOVER OLDFILE.BTR OLDFILE.SEQ
  ```

- Load the sequential file into the new file

  ```
  BUTIL -LOAD OLDFILE.SEQ NEWFILE.BTR
  ```

Run BUTIL with no parameters for on-line help with BUTIL.

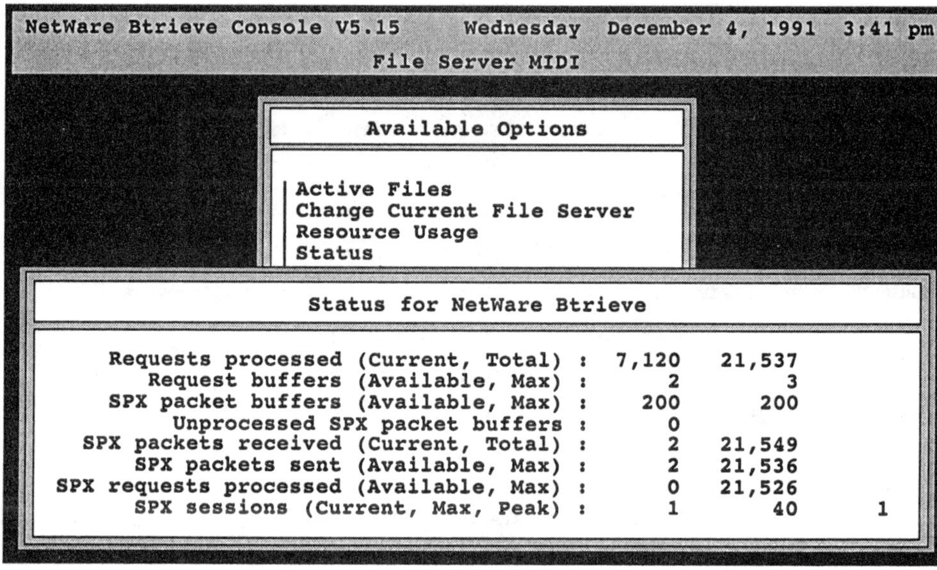


***Figure 2.3: BCONSOLE viewing Btrieve traffic***

BUTIL is also available as an NLM to be executed at the file server. A three-fold performance increase on lengthy operations (such as loading an input file) is often observed on heavy traffic networks.

The optional Tutorial Diskette includes a program called BUTL (similar to BUTIL) which also provides high-level file manipulation procedures. The BUTL program performs many of the same functions as Novell's BUTIL and comes with C Language source code. The NLM version of BUTL demonstrates server-based programming.

## Monitoring Btrieve

BCONSOLE is Novell's excellent server-based monitoring program designed to view the status of a Btrieve server. BCONSOLE is available as a DOS program (run from a workstation) and as an NLM (run from NetWare v3.x). BCONSOLE is less a developer utility than a database administrator's, but it does offer a way to monitor network traffic resulting from Btrieve operations. In addition, BCONSOLE can be used to display information about users currently connected to Btrieve, currently open files, and lock information. The NLM version of BCONSOLE allows the operator to reset connections, in effect, knocking users out of Btrieve. Figure 2.3 shows the Traffic Status Screen of BCONSOLE.

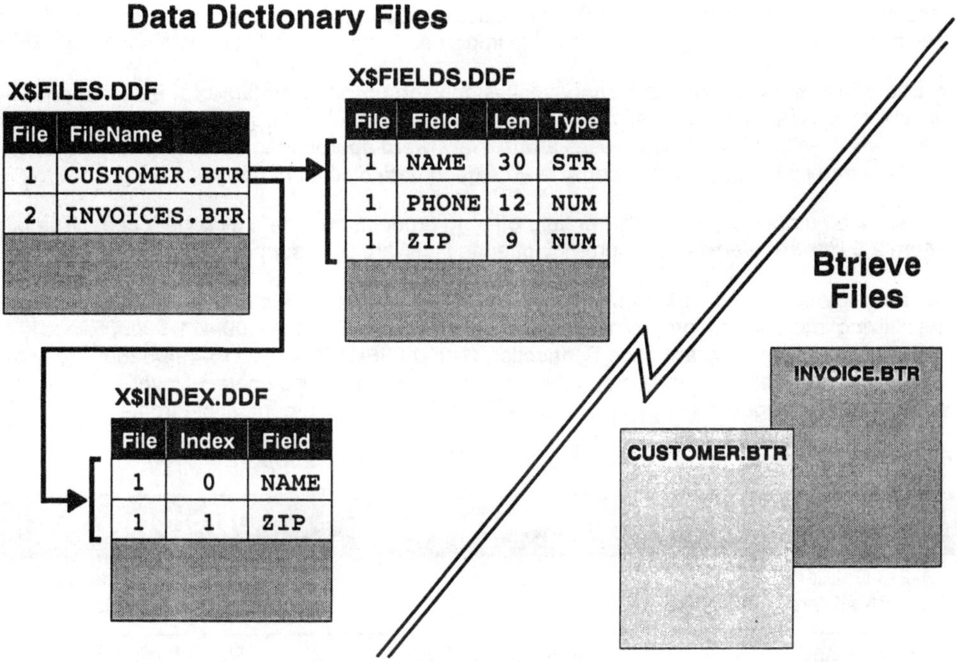


***Figure 2.4: Xtrieve PLUS/NetWare SQL data dictionary layout***

## Data Dictionary and Development Systems

A data dictionary is a set of files that describe the logical structure of a database including field definitions. Since the Btrieve record manager does not recognize fields by itself, a Btrieve data dictionary must be present to provide higher than record-level database access. Novell's Xtrieve PLUS began as a data dictionary utility for Btrieve programmers. Later versions of Xtrieve PLUS have provided enhanced end-user functionality, such as the ability to construct relational database "views" and report generation. NetWare SQL shares the same data dictionaries as Xtrieve PLUS. NetWare SQL uses the data dictionary to support SQL statements against Btrieve files. Figure 2.4 illustrates the Xtrieve PLUS/NetWare SQL data dictionary layout.

While both Xtrieve PLUS and NetWare SQL allow programmers to create files, import and export data, and define logical views of the data, neither one is primarily a programmer utility.

Xtrieve PLUS's utility value is in its relatively easy-to-use data dictionary user interface and its capability to perform quick fixes on Btrieve database files. However, it lacks features like file modification and rebuilding, multi-format file import and export, and file trouble shooting.

NetWare SQL supports data dictionary access only through SQL statements. SQL is a powerful data access language that allows programmers to manipulate large amounts of data with only a few lines of code. SQL imposes a rather awkward approach to data dictionary access, however, and so is not generally considered a good data dictionary utility.

There are a number of third-party vendors offering products with data dictionary capabilities. Figure 2.5 lists several vendors currently offering NetWare SQL support.

The best source of information on the products listed in Figure 2.5 is from a software vendor specializing in utilities for programmers. The Programmer's Shop (1-800-421-8006, FAX 617-749-2018) and The Programmer's Connection (1-800-336-1166, FAX 216-494-5260) are two excellent sources of third-party programming utilities. You can also contact Novell (1-800-RED-WORD) to request a copy of their catalog of NetWare SQL-compatible front-ends.

***Figure 2.5: Some vendors currently offering NetWare SQL support***

| Product | Company | Description |
|---|---|---|
| 1-2-3 Datalens Driver for NetWare SQL | Novell/Lotus | Translator for spreadsheet access to SQL files |
| Forest and Trees | Channel Computing | Report writer |
| JAM/DBi for NetWare SQL | JYACC | 4GL application development |
| MicroSTEP | SYSCORP International | 3GL application development environment |
| Paradox SQL Link for NetWare SQL | Borland | Translator for Paradox access |
| Planet | Network Communications and Techniques | Application development |
| R&R Report Writer for NetWare SQL | Concentric Data Systems | Report writer |
| RaSQL/X for Clipper | Pinnacle Software | Clipper access to NetWare SQL files |

***Figure 2.5: Some vendors currently offering NetWare SQL support***

| Product | Company | Description |
| --- | --- | --- |
| SQLWindows for NetWare SQL | Gupta Technologies | Application development |
| Visual Basic | Microsoft Corp. | BASIC access to NetWare SQL files |

### Utilities for Windows

Btrieve for Windows is relatively new and has a smaller (but expanding) user base. Novell offers a utility package called BTRTOOLS for Windows. BTRTOOLS is a windows-based function executor similar to the B.EXE program. In addition, BTRTOOLS has some of the functionality of BUTIL. BTRTOOLS is in an early stage of development, but it represents a positive move in the direction of a common graphical user interface (GUI) for Btrieve development.

## The Tutorial Diskette

The Tutorial Diskette offered as an optional addition to this book (available through MIDI America, see order form at back of book) provides step-by-step exercises that introduce you to using Btrieve, as well as two excellent utilities you can use to experiment with Btrieve operations and explore typical maintenance procedures associated with developing and maintaining Btrieve applications.

**BX – Btrieve Function Executor.** With BX, you can issue Btrieve operations from a simple user interface screen. Discover how the various Btrieve operations work by making Btrieve calls and examining and updating the contents of each Btrieve parameter.

- Discover how Btrieve operations work
- Simulate a working program in multiuser scenarios
- Examine and edit Btrieve's parameters in ASCII and Hex format
- Make modifications or "quick fixes" to Btrieve files
- Create files and view statistics on Btrieve files

**BUTL – Btrieve File Utility.** Perform high-level file operations on Btrieve files for many useful procedures. The BUTL source code is included, so you can understand how these operations are performed in C Language. In addition, an NLM version of BUTL is provided to demonstrate basic concepts of server-based application development.

- Create, Clone, and Show statistics on Btrieve files
- Load and Extract data to and from Btrieve files using Extended operations
- Copy records between files
- Add and Drop Supplemental Indexes
- Reset a workstation
- Generate a Description file (for use with the Create procedure) from an existing Btrieve file

# 3 Calling Btrieve

One of Btrieve's primary advantages is that it can be called from almost any programming language. From the point of view of an application program, Btrieve is simply a service that performs basic database operations. This service is independent of any given programming language. As long as a program can interface with Btrieve, it has full access to Btrieve database files.

The Btrieve file format is also independent of the programming language. There is only one Btrieve file format and the interface is generic enough that any programming language can easily access Btrieve files. On a DOS workstation, when a call is made to Btrieve, the resident Btrieve TSR (Terminate and Stay Resident program) is activated. The TSR provides all database services to the application program. Under the OS/2 and Windows operating systems, a dynamic link library (DLL) is employed rather than a TSR.

## Flow of Control

In workstation Btrieve, the TSR (or DLL) contains all of the B-tree file access functionality. Workstation Btrieve operates like a traditional database library where the workstation performs all of the database access functions and communicates with the local operating system for file access.

Btrieve is unlike traditional database libraries since it is loaded into the operating system before the program is executed rather than linked to and included in the application program's executable code. For this reason, the executable code of a Btrieve application can be substantially smaller than that of a similar program which is linked to a database library. Figure 3.1 illustrates the flow of control of a call to workstation Btrieve.

With NetWare Btrieve accessed from a DOS workstation, the TSR (BREQUEST.EXE) is a data requester program that sends requests for data over the network to the Btrieve file server

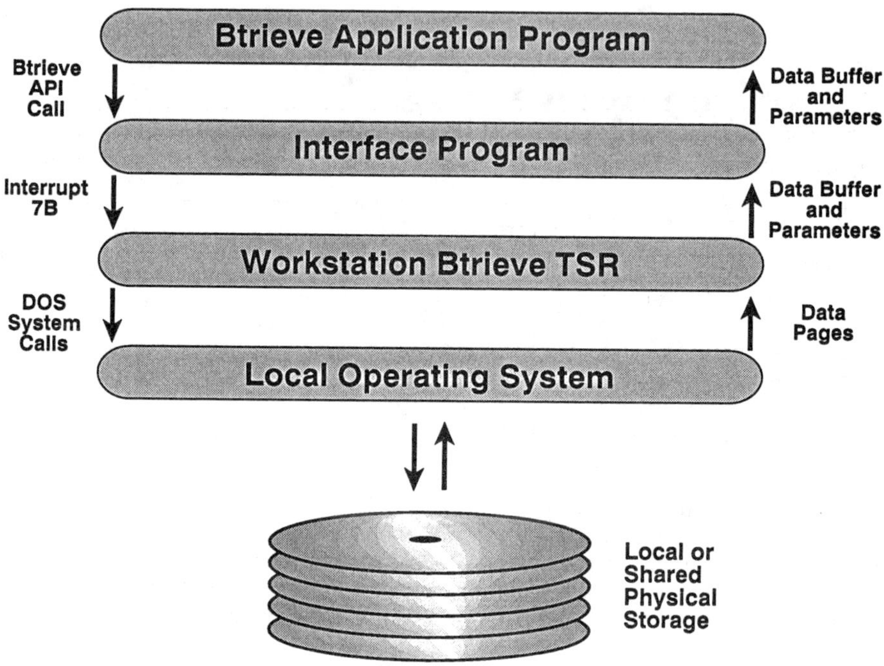


*Figure 3.1: Flow of control for workstation Btrieve on a DOS workstation*

(either the VAP or the NLM). The requester contains no B-tree data access functionality and is comprised primarily of buffer space and network optimization code. Figure 3.2 shows the flow of control of a call to NetWare Btrieve.

With client/server and workstation Btrieve, the workstation process is halted until a response from the file server is received.

The call to Btrieve is the same whether you are working with the workstation version of Btrieve or with the requester —with the TSR or the DLL.

## Btrieve Operations

Btrieve is called via a single function call to perform all database operations. This approach differs from a traditional database library that contain one function or procedure per operation.

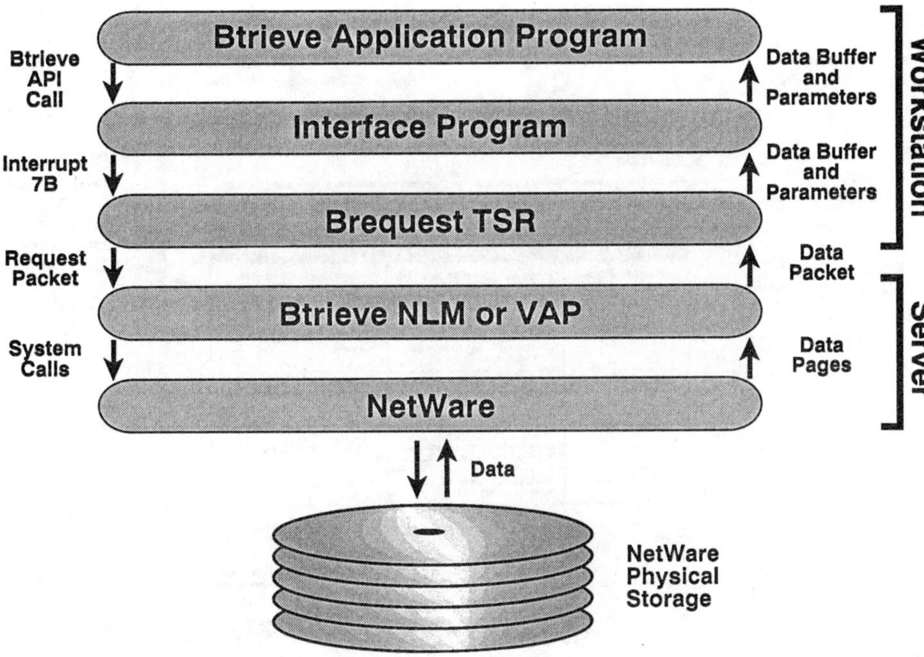


***Figure 3.2: Flow of control with client-server Btrieve***

The Btrieve function call is comprised of seven parameters:

- Operation Code (OpCode)
- Status Code
- Position Block
- Data Buffer
- Data Buffer Length
- Key Buffer
- Key Number

The OpCode tells Btrieve which operation to perform. There are currently forty Btrieve operations which do everything from creating files to deleting records. Another important parameter in the Btrieve call is the status code. The status code indicates to the calling program whether or not the operation was successful, and if not, the reason why the operation failed. A zero status code indicates that the operation was successful. If Btrieve returns a nonzero status code, the calling program must evaluate it in the context of the operation to determine what

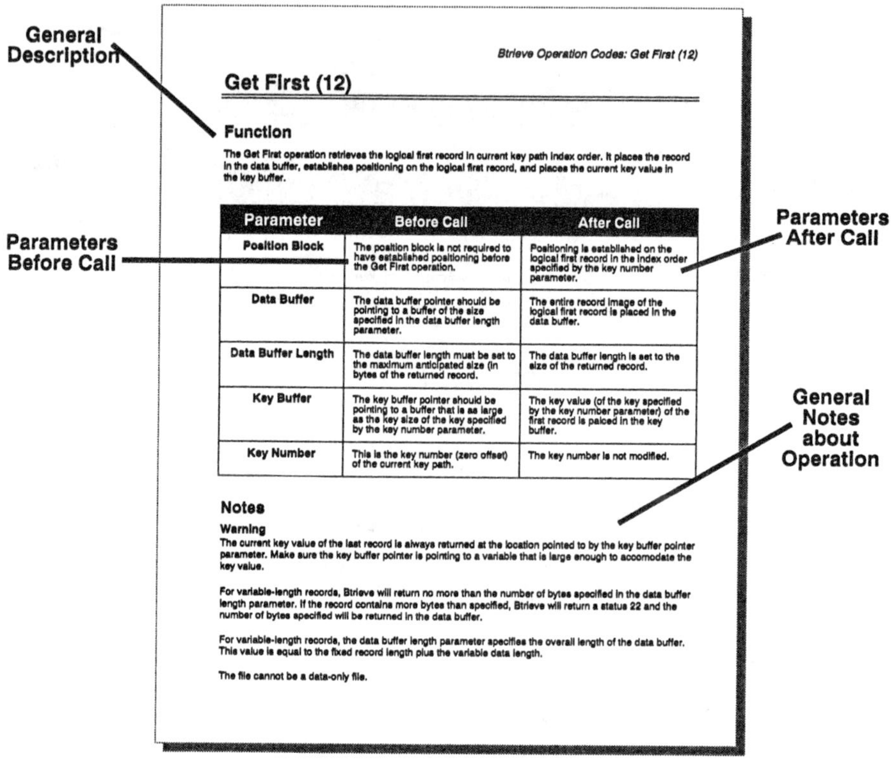


*Btrieve Operation Codes: Get First (12)*

Get First (12)

Function

The Get First operation retrieves the logical first record in current key path index order. It places the record in the data buffer, establishes positioning on the logical first record, and places the current key value in the key buffer.

| Parameter | Before Call | After Call |
|---|---|---|
| Position Block | The position block is not required to have established positioning before the Get First operation. | Positioning is established on the logical first record in the index order specified by the key number parameter. |
| Data Buffer | The data buffer pointer should be pointing to a buffer of the size specified in the data buffer length parameter. | The entire record image of the logical first record is placed in the data buffer. |
| Data Buffer Length | The data buffer length must be set to the maximum anticipated size (in bytes of the returned record. | The data buffer length is set to the size of the returned record. |
| Key Buffer | The key buffer pointer should be pointing to a buffer that is as large as the key size of the key specified by the key number parameter. | The key value (of the key specified by the key number parameter) of the first record is palced in the key buffer. |
| Key Number | This is the key number (zero offset) of the current key path. | The key number is not modified. |

Notes

Warning

The current key value of the last record is always returned at the location pointed to by the key buffer pointer parameter. Make sure the key buffer pointer is pointing to a variable that is large enough to accomodate the key value.

For variable-length records, Btrieve will return no more than the number of bytes specified in the data buffer length parameter. If the record contains more bytes than specified, Btrieve will return a status 22 and the number of bytes specified will be returned in the data buffer.

For variable-length records, the data buffer length parameter specifies the overall length of the data buffer. This value is equal to the fixed record length plus the variable data length.

The file cannot be a data-only file.

***Figure 3.3: Operation code definition from Chapter 8***

corrective action should be taken, if any. The calling program should check the status code after every Btrieve call in order to trap for unexpected conditions.

All forty Btrieve operations are defined in Chapter 8. Included with each definition is a detailed description of the operation, the proper parameter settings before the Btrieve call, the information returned by Btrieve after the call, and other important details about the operation. These operation code definitions are the most detailed source of information pertaining to each operation provided in this book. Figures 3.3 and 3.4 show an example opcode definition from Chapter 8 (the Get First operation), and illustrate the type of information available for each operation.

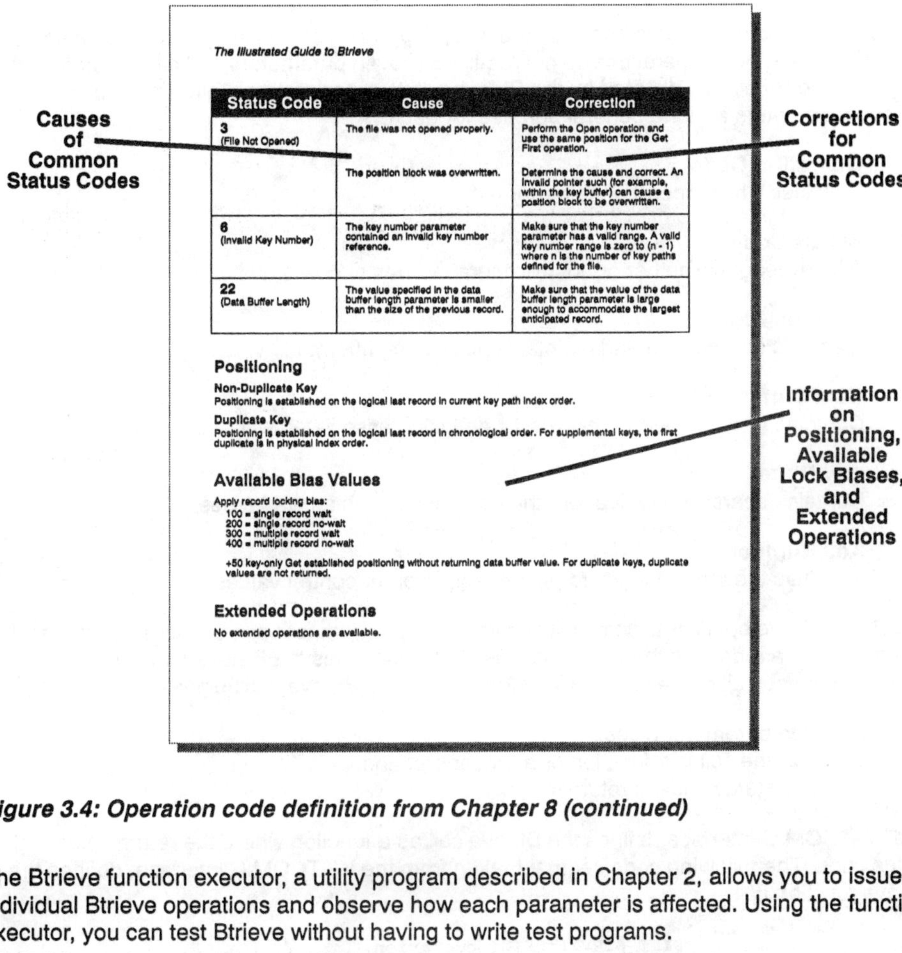


*The Illustrated Guide to Btrieve*

| Status Code | Cause | Correction |
|---|---|---|
| **3** (File Not Opened) | The file was not opened properly. | Perform the Open operation and use the same position for the Get First operation. |
| | The position block was overwritten. | Determine the cause and correct. An invalid pointer such (for example, within the key buffer) can cause a position block to be overwritten. |
| **6** (Invalid Key Number) | The key number parameter contained an invalid key number reference. | Make sure that the key number parameter has a valid range. A valid key number range is zero to (n - 1) where n is the number of key paths defined for the file. |
| **22** (Data Buffer Length) | The value specified in the data buffer length parameter is smaller than the size of the previous record. | Make sure that the value of the data buffer length parameter is large enough to accommodate the largest anticipated record. |

**Positioning**

**Non-Duplicate Key**
Positioning is established on the logical last record in current key path index order.

**Duplicate Key**
Positioning is established on the logical last record in chronological order. For supplemental keys, the first duplicate is in physical index order.

**Available Bias Values**

Apply record locking bias:
100 = single record wait
200 = single record no-wait
300 = multiple record wait
400 = multiple record no-wait

+50 key-only Get established positioning without returning data buffer value. For duplicate keys, duplicate values are not returned.

**Extended Operations**

No extended operations are available.

***Figure 3.4: Operation code definition from Chapter 8 (continued)***

The Btrieve function executor, a utility program described in Chapter 2, allows you to issue individual Btrieve operations and observe how each parameter is affected. Using the function executor, you can test Btrieve without having to write test programs.

## The Btrieve Function Call

With some languages, such as C and Pascal, the Btrieve call is defined as a function which returns the Status Code. Some compilers pass the Status code as an argument along with the other parameters. Some versions of COBOL place the status code in a special system-defined variable.

The seven parameters serve specific purposes, depending on which operation is being performed. Some Btrieve operations do not require all seven parameters, but all parameters must be passed to Btrieve as dictated by the Btrieve function declaration. Following is a list of Btrieve parameters and the general purpose for each.

- **Operation Code**
  Specifies which operation to perform

- **Status Code**
  Acknowledges whether or not the operation was successful.

- **Position Block**
  Identifies an open file and maintains positioning information.

- **Data Buffer**
  Contains a record, set of records, or definition associated with a file.

- **Key Buffer**
  Contains search key value, or other identifiers such as file names.

- **Key Number**
  Identifies the current index for searching, or other control values.

The Btrieve Developer's Kits come with an interface program for each supported compiler. The interface program defines the Btrieve call. Because it defines the Btrieve function call, the interface imposes all of the rules associated with calling Btrieve, including:

- Function parameter types,
- Whether the call is a function or a procedure, and
- How the status code is returned.

The WATCOM C interface defines the Btrieve call as a function where the return value is the status code. The following code segment taken from the WATCOM C interface, defines the Btrieve function call.

```
SINT BTRV (  SINT operation,
             char  *posBlock,
             char  *dataBuf,
             INT   *dataLen,
             char  *keyBuf,
             SINT  keyNum
          )
```

Notice that the posBlock, dataBuf, and dataLen parameters are defined as pointers to character arrays. If a non-character variable, such as an integer, is to be passed for one of these variables, they should be *casted* as pointers to character arrays. This method will enable you to avoid excess warning messages from the compiler.

The Turbo Pascal interface comes as Pascal source code that can be compiled into a Turbo Pascal Unit (TPU). A TPU is an object module that is linked during compilation. Pascal, like C Language, calls Btrieve as a function where the status code is returned.

```
function BTRV (    OP          :integer;
               VAR POS,
                   DATA;
               VAR DATALEN     :integer;
               VAR KBUF;
                   KEY         :integer):  integer;
```

Notice that the POS (Position Block), DATA (Data Buffer), and KBUF (Key Buffer) parameters are non-typed, thus any type of pointer value can be passed.

## Interfacing with Btrieve for DOS

The interface program allows a programming language to communicate with Btrieve. For most languages, Novell provides source code (written in the language of the supported compiler) that is included in the application source code and compiled along with the application program. For a few languages, the interface is only available as a linkable object module. In this case the interface is linked with the application.

The interface is a relatively short program (usually 100 lines of code). Thus, to support a new compiler, Novell only has to provide an interface program for the new compiler. When the Btrieve function is called on a DOS workstation, it does the following:

- Makes sure that Btrieve is loaded
- Transfers the parameters from the compiler specific parameter stack to a common location where Btrieve will find them
- Generates an interrupt 7B to active the Btrieve TSR
- Transfers the parameters back to the program's parameter stack

Any mystery associated with a Btrieve interface can be dispelled by simply examining the interface source code.

To determine which interface to use with a given compiler, see the INTRFACE.DOC file which is supplied with Btrieve. This file lists each interface and provides important instructions.

The table in Figure 3.5 is a condensed version of INTRFACE.DOC and lists each supported compiler and its associated interface.Once you have identified the proper interface, simply pull up INTRFACE.DOC in a text editor and search for the interface name.The information in INTRFACE.DOC plays a crucial role in interfacing your compiler with Btrieve and is often not available in any other Novell document.

***Figure 3.5: Supported compilers and associated interfaces for DOS***

| Language | Compiler | Associated Interface |
|---|---|---|
| BASIC | MS BASIC v7.0 | BC7RBTRV.OBJ |
| BASIC | MS BASIC v6.0 | QB6PBTRV.OBJ |
| BASIC | MS QuickBasic v6.0 | QB6PBTRV.OBJ |
| BASIC | MS QuickBasic v4.0 | QB6PBTRV.OBJ |
| BASIC | MS QuickBasic v3.0 | QBIXBTRV.OBJ |
| BASIC | IBM BASIC v1.0 | QB6PBTRV.OBJ |
| BASIC | IBM BASIC v2.0 | QB6PBTRV.OBJ |
| BASIC | IBM BASIC v3.0 | QB6PBTRV.OBJ |
| BASIC | IBM BASIC/2 for OS/2 | QB6PBTRV.OBJ |
| BASIC | TI BASIC Compiler | BTIXBTRV.OBJ |
| BASIC | TI BASIC interpretive | BTIXBTRV.EXE |
| BASIC | Borland Turbo Basic | TURBBTRV.BAS |
| BASIC | DR CBASIC (CB-86) | CBXBTRV.OBJ |
| BASIC | Generic BASIC compiler | B86XBTRV.OBJ |
| BASIC | Generic BASIC interpreter | B86XBTRV.EXE |
| C | Borland Turbo C | TURCBTRV.C |
| C | IBM C/2 for OS/2 | *C2XBTRV.C |
| C | IBM C/2 for OS/2 | C2FXBTRV.C |

***Figure 3.5: Supported compilers and associated interfaces for DOS***

| Language | Compiler | Associated Interface |
|---|---|---|
| C | Lattice C v6.0 | LCXBTRV3.C |
| C | Lattice C v3.0 | LCXBTRV3.C |
| C | Lattice C v2.0 | LCXBTRV2.C |
| C | Lattice C v1.0 | LCXBTRV.OBJ |
| C | Microsoft C | MSCXBTRV.C |
| C | WATCOM C | WAT2BTRV.C |
| C | Ci-C86 v1.0 | C86XBTRV.C |
| C | Ci-C86 v2.0 | C86XBTV2.C |
| C | DeSmet C | DESXBTRV.C |
| C | Mark Williams C | MWCXBTRV.C |
| COBOL | MBP COBOL-85 | MBP85BTV.OBJ |
| COBOL | MBP COBOL-85 | MBP85FAC.OBJ |
| COBOL | MBP COBOL | MBPXBTRV.OBJ |
| COBOL | Micro Focus COBOL/2 | COBRBTRV.OBJ |
| COBOL | Micro Focus COBOL | MFXBTRV.BIN |
| COBOL | MS COBOL v3.0 | COBRBTRV.OBJ |
| COBOL | Realia COBOL | COBRBTRV.OBJ |
| COBOL | Microsoft COBOL | COBXBTRV.OBJ |
| COBOL | RM COBOL | RMXBTRV.EXE |
| COBOL | RM/COBOL-8X | RM8XBTRV.EXE |
| FORTRAN | Microsoft FORTRAN | FORXBTRV.OBJ |
| Pascal | Borland Turbo Pascal v5.0 | TUR5BTRV.PAS |

***Figure 3.5: Supported compilers and associated interfaces for DOS***

| Language | Compiler | Associated Interface |
|---|---|---|
| Pascal | Borland Turbo Pascal v4.0 | TUR4BTRV.PAS |
| Pascal | Metaware Pascal | MPMXBTRV.OBJ |
| Pascal | SBB Pascal | SBBXBTRV.OBJ |

You only need to learn the rules for each Btrieve operation and they can be applied to virtually any programming language and operating environment. The unique architecture of the Btrieve Record Manager provides a modular approach to building applications. A single application can actually be written in several different programming languages to exploit the various strengths of the languages.

## Interfacing with Btrieve for Windows

Workstation Btrieve for Windows is a DLL (dynamic link library). A DLL differs from a TSR in that it is not loaded until the application makes a call to it. All Windows compilers can communicate with DLLs. Therefore, it is not necessary to have a separate interface for each programming language.

Novell provides two interfaces, for C Language (WBTRINF.C) and Turbo Pascal (TPWBTR.-PAS), that are compatible with the function call for Btrieve for DOS. This allows an easy migration of DOS Btrieve applications to Windows.

There are two ways to call Btrieve for Windows:

- Call the WBTRCALL DLL (dynamic link library)
- Call the interface with a Btrieve for DOS Compatible API

However, it is recommended that a programmer writing a new application should always call the DLL directly, rather than use the interface. The DLL function call is defined in the code segment below.

```
BTRCALL(int                opcode,
        (char far *)       PosBlk,
        (char far *)       DataBuf,
        (unsigned far *)   DataBufLen,
        (char far *)       KeyBuf,
        (unsigned char)    KeyBufLen
        (int               KeyNum );
```

The interface function call is defined as:

```
extern unsigned BTRV (int,
                      char far *,
                      char far *,
                      unsigned far *,
                      char far *, int);
```

Workstation Btrieve for Windows and the NetWare Btrieve Requester for Windows share the same name (WBTRCALL.DLL). Therefore, when using the requester and workstation Btrieve at the same time, workstation Btrieve must be renamed to WBTRLOCL.DLL. This is known as mixed mode. Which ever DLL is called WBTRCALL will respond to a Btrieve function call first. If operating in mixed mode the l: option must be set for the requester. In mixed mode, the requester will pass calls for local data to workstation Btrieve.

In addition to the Btrieve function call, there are three other function calls available in Windows.

1) The BTRVINIT function is used to initialize workstation Btrieve.

```
BTRVINIT(char far *)
extern int BTRVINIT (char far *);
.
.
int       btrInitStat;
.
.
if (BtrStat = BTRVINIT ((char far *) "/m:48 /p:2048 /t:c:\\tmp\\btrieve.trn"))
     printf ("Error on BTRVINIT : %x", BtrStat);
```

2) The BTRVSTOP function must be called upon program termination. If BTRVSTOP is not issued and a program is allowed to close, the task will not be removed from the task table and memory will not be returned to Windows. If a non-zero status is returned, this means that a file is still open or a transaction is in progress.

```
BTRVSTOP (void)
```

3) The RQSHELLINIT function is used to determine if the Windows requester is present. If the requester is not present. A value of (-1) is returned if the requester is not present.

```
RQSHELLINIT (char far *)
```

## Interfacing with Btrieve for OS/2

Btrieve for OS/2 offers several interface programs that support the languages listed in Figure 3.6. These interfaces support the DOS API call.

***Figure 3.6: Interface programs for Btrieve for OS/2***

| File | Description |
|---|---|
| BTRCALLS.LIB | Import Library |
| C2XBTRV.C | OS/2 Btrieve C interface |
| C2FXBTRV.C | OS/2 FAPI Btrieve C interface |
| QB6PBTRV.OBJ | MS-BASIC and IBM BASIC for OS/2 Protected Mode |
| QB6RBTRV.OBJ | MS-BASIC and IBM BASIC for OS/2 Real Mode |
| BC7PBTRV.OBJ | MS-BASIC v7.0 Protected Mode |
| BC7RBTRV.OBJ | MS-BASIC v7.0 Real Mode |
| COBRBTRV.OBJ | Microfocus COBOL/2 Real Mode |
| COBPBTRV.OBJ | Microfocus COBOL/2 Protected Mode |

The Btrieve DLL for OS/2 can be called directly. The function call is defined in the code segment below.

```
return (btrcall (operation,
        (char far *) posblock,
        (char far *) databuf,
        (int far *) datalen,
        (char far *) keybuf,
        (unsigned char) keylen
        (char ckeynum ));
```

In addition to the Btrieve function call, Btrieve for OS/2 supports two other functions: BTRVINIT and BTRVSTOP.

1) The BTRVINIT function initializes the Btrieve DLL. With this function, applications can easily reset the Btrieve load options. In the following example call, the only parameter for this function is a string containing the load options as they would be set with the BTRPARMS variable (BTRPARMS is discussed in "Loading Btrieve for OS/2" -- Chapter 7).

```
int far pascal BTRVINIT (char far *);
.
.
.
Status = BTRVINIT ("/m:32 /f:20 /b:16 /l:20 /t:c:\btrieve.trn");
```

2) The BTRVSTOP function terminates a Btrieve session. It is called by the application either as a part of the program termination process or prior to reinitializing the Btrieve DLL. The BTR-STOP function restores the DLL to its uninitialized state. All files and transactions must be closed before making the call to BTRVSTOP(). If a file is open or a transaction is active, a status1014 is returned. A successful termination returns a zero status. The function is defined as follows:

```
int far pascal BTRVSTOP (void);
```

## Multiple Thread Support

Previous versions of the Btrieve for OS/2 required applications to implement semaphore control to the Btrieve DLL by placing semaphore locks around the call to Btrieve. This is no longer necessary as thread-level control is now implemented by Btrieve. Btrieve for OS/2 also offers a trace file feature that creates a log of Btrieve operations.

The best source of information on calling Btrieve for OS/2 is in the README.DOC file provided with the product. The monthly *Bullets* newsletter also provides up-to-date information on Btrieve for OS/2.

# 4 Btrieve File Architecture

The design philosophy of Btrieve is simple: provide one file format that contains record data and all index structures, and that is common to most popular operating systems and programming languages. A Btrieve file created by a DOS Pascal program, for example, can be shared with an OS/2 C language program; one file contains data and indexes that are independent of the operating system and language.

Details of the internal structure of a Btrieve file is proprietary information and Novell does not provide documentation which fully describes the format of a Btrieve file. Novell's reasoning for this is that a programmer generally does not need to know the internal format of a Btrieve file in order to access data using most languages or operating systems.

It is important, however, to have a general knowledge of the internal architecture of Btrieve files in order to design efficient files and develop programs which fully exploit the potential of Btrieve. Novell does publish some information as to the structure of a Btrieve file. The best sources of this information are Novell Education classes (there are currently two classes, an introduction and advanced), the *Bullets* newsletter (a good source of up to date information about Btrieve), and the red programmer's manual that comes with the product. This chapter contains a compilation of released information about Btrieve's internal file structure but stops short of giving a byte by byte definition.

## Btrieve Pages

A Btrieve file is divided into pages. Pages can contain records, indexes, and control information. The first page of a Btrieve file is the file control record (FCR) page which is the master header page of the file. If the file uses an alternate-collating sequence, the second page contains the alternate-collating sequence definition. All of the remaining pages are either index pages, fixed-length data pages, or variable-length data pages.

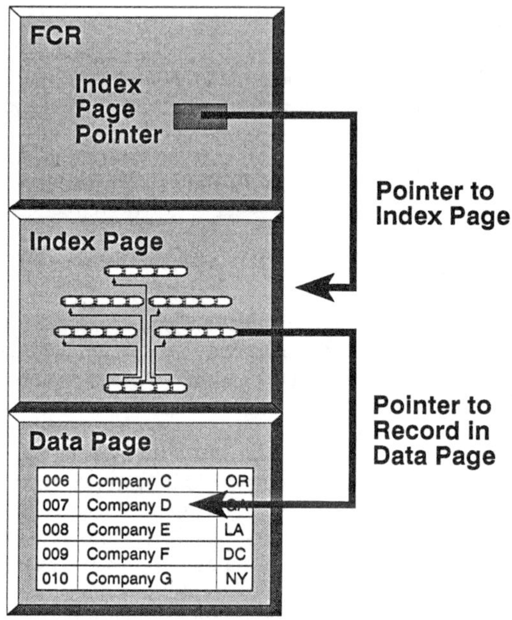


*Figure 4.1: Btrieve File Pages*

All pages in a Btrieve file are the same size. A page must be between 512 and 4096 bytes and a multiple of 512, and must be as large as, or larger than the record length. The right page size sometimes has a dramatic effect on disk utilization and performance (choosing the optimal page size is discussed in further detail later in this chapter).

When the file is created, it contains an FCR page, one page per index, and one data page. As data is added to the file, new pages are appended to the end of the file as they are needed. Thus, data pages and index pages are scattered throughout the file an almost random fashion. Pages can be pre-allocated when a file is created, and a specified number of pages, which can be used as index or data pages, are reserved. Figure 4.1 illustrates a simple Btrieve file.

The page is the smallest unit of data transferred from the disk to Btrieve's cache memory. Thus, when a record is retrieved, the entire page is first loaded into cache, and then the record image is placed in the Data Buffer available to the application program. As records are deleted and pages become empty, those empty pages are placed on a free space list. When Btrieve inserts a new record, it first checks the free space list. If no free space is available, a new page is added to the end of the file.

### Packing Files and Re-indexing

Free pages are placed on the free space list rather than being deallocated from the file. Thus, a Btrieve file will never become smaller. In addition, Btrieve does not rearrange fixed-length records to pack or compress the database file (variable-length record data is rearranged within a given page to provide contiguous record storage). The procedure for packing or condensing a database is as follows:

- Create a new, empty Btrieve file identical to the file to compress
- Copy records from the old file to the new file
- Delete the old file
- Rename the new file to the old file name

***This procedure also re-indexes the Btrieve file.*** This can be done with the BUTIL or BUTL utilities. In the following BUTIL example, the CUSTOMER.BTR file is packed and re-indexed.

```
BUTIL —CLONE TEMP.BTR CUSTOMER.BTR
BUTIL —COPY CUSTOMER.BTR TEMP.BTR
DEL CUSTOMER.BTR
REN TEMP.BTR CUSTOMER.BTR
```

## File Control Record (FCR)

The FCR page is the first and most important page in a Btrieve file. Btrieve must go through the FCR before it can access any other page. If the FCR is damaged, the data often cannot be recovered by Btrieve. (Novell Austin's technical support group (1-800-NETWARE) does provide a utility called BCLEAN that, in certain cases, can reconstruct FCRs and recover damaged files.) The FCR contains the following information:

- The file identifier with version number
- The page size used for the file
- Number of available pages on the free space list
- Control flags
- Free space linked-list pointer
- Number of pages in file
- Number of keys segments defined in the file
- Pre-imaging information for automatic data recovery
- Security password

The FCR also contains a definition of key segments and index pointers consisting of one of the following for each key segment defined to the file.

- Root page of index
- Number of key values in B-tree
- Key definition flags
- Key length
- Number of key entries per B-tree node
- Location of key segment in record
- Length of key segment
- Supplemental key page ID
- Key segment data type
- Null character for key

An application program does not access the FCR directly. There are no Btrieve operations designed to directly manipulate the FCR. All updates to the FCR are made by Btrieve as the result of Btrieve operations rather than through direct manipulation.

## Data Pages

There are two types of data pages: fixed-length record pages, and variable-length data pages. Variable-length records always contain a fixed portion and a variable portion. The fixed record portion is stored in fixed-length record pages (usually referred to as data pages) and the variable portion is stored in variable-length data pages (usually referred to as variable data pages).

### Fixed-Length Record Pages

All records in fixed-length data pages are of the same size. All fixed-length records must fit entirely into a page; they do not span pages (although variable-length records *can* span pages). For variable-length records, all keys are contained in the fixed-length record portion.

Unless fixed-length records fit exactly in the page, there will be some leftover or unused space in each page. It is important to choose a page size that best fits records with a minimum amount of leftover space.

The term *record image* describes the actual data that an application program stores in a record. Btrieve will add other information to a record in certain cases. The physical record consists of the record image followed by additional information Btrieve stores with the record. Btrieve may add the following information to a record image:

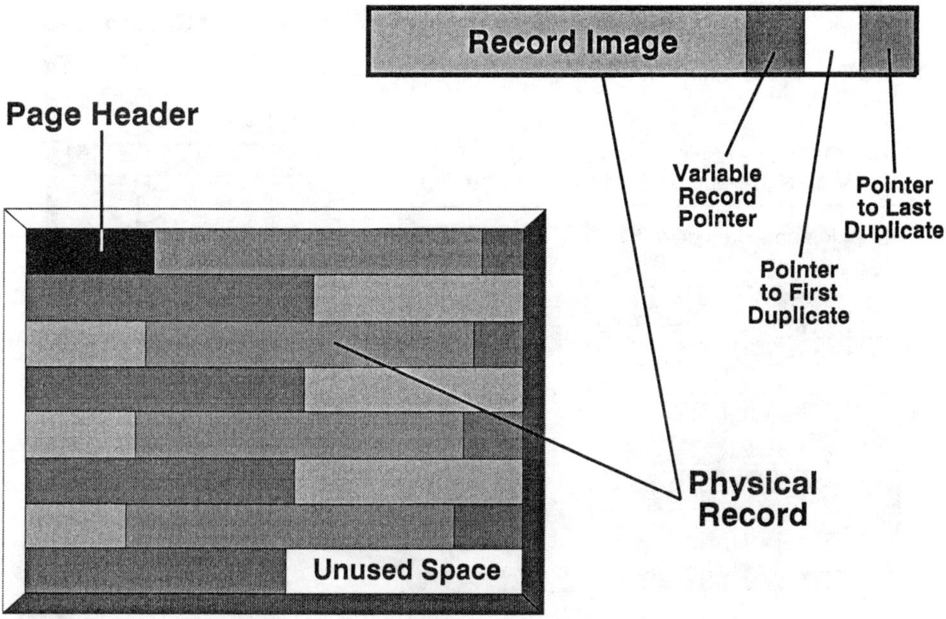


*Figure 4.2: A typical fixed-length record data page*

- Pointer to variable portion of record for variable-length files = 4 bytes
- Number of truncated blanks selected for variable-length file = 2 bytes
- Pointer pair to next and previous duplicate records = 8 bytes, 4 bytes each (one set of pointers for each index supporting duplicate keys)

Figure 4.2 illustrates that fixed-length records are packed into the data page. The physical record is made up of three components:

- The record image or logical record from the application
- A pointer to variable-length data (for variable-length records only)
- Pointer pair to next and previous duplicate key (for duplicate keys only)

The advantage of not allowing fixed records to span data pages is that only one page must be loaded into cache in order retrieve a record, thus reducing retrieval time. The disadvantage is that if an inefficient page size is selected, the file will contain a significant amount of wasted space.

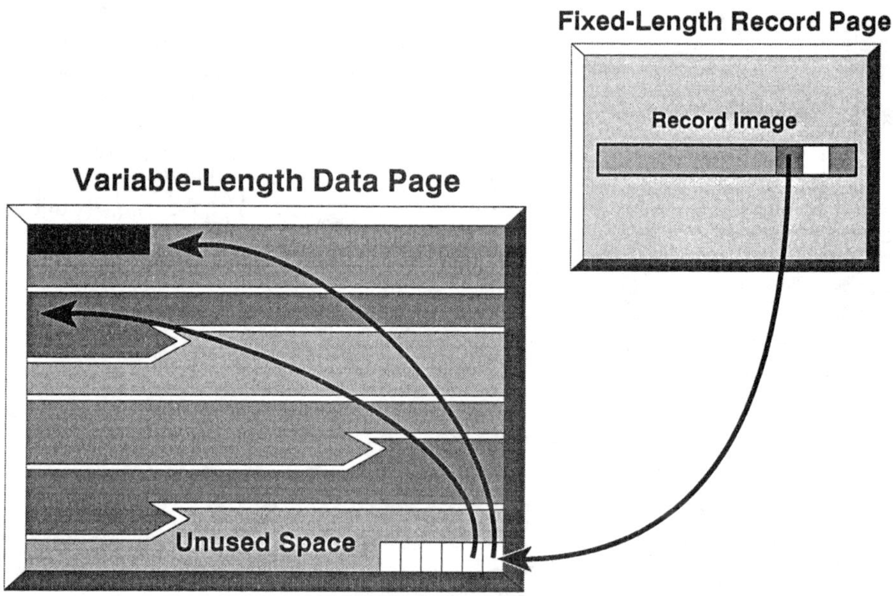


*Figure 4.3: A variable-length record page*

## Record Addressing

Btrieve addresses records by their physical offset (number of bytes from the beginning of the file). The physical record address is a four byte unsigned integer that can address up to four gigabytes. Retrieving records by their physical record address is the most efficient method of retrieval. The Get Position operation (22) retrieves the address of the current record (the current record's physical address can also be obtained at offset 43 of the Position Block). This address can later be used to retrieve the record directly (without traversing or using an index) with the Get Direct operation (23).

The maximum number of records that can be stored in a file is a function of the size of the file. Therefore there are no restrictions on the number of records in a file as long as the file does not exceed four gigabytes in size and the record can be addressed with a four byte integer.

## Variable-Length Record Pages

Variable-length data pages store the variable portion of a record. For files supporting variable-length records, a four-byte variable record pointer is stored along with the record image in the fixed-length record page. This points to a variable record pointer located at the end of the variable page which in turn points to the actual variable-length portion of the record. This scheme of a pointer to a pointer allows Btrieve to rearrange data in the variable data page without having to modify the pointer in the fixed-length record page. Free space in a variable record page occupies one contiguous block of space and data is rearranged within the variable page as records are modified. Figure 4.3 illustrates the general layout of a variable-length record page.

Unlike fixed-length records, the variable-length portion of a record may span several pages. A record spanning several pages is said to be fragmented. Retrieving a fragmented record causes a slight performance degradation because Btrieve must load several pages to retrieve the record.

## Free Space Threshold

The tendency to fragment records can be controlled to some degree by the free space threshold setting specified when the file is created. The free space threshold defines when a variable-length record page is considered free. Thresholds of 10, 20, and 30 percent can be selected. The threshold represents the percentage of a page that must be available as free space, in order for Btrieve to place the page on the free space list. If a page is not on the free space list, no new records will be inserted into the page and the remaining free space on a page is reserved for record expansion. A file with a high free space threshold will tend to reduce fragmentation by reserving more space for record expansion. However, it will not utilize space as efficiently as a low free space threshold which tends to increase fragmentation.

## Blank Truncation

When a file is created with blank truncation turned on, Btrieve does not store trailing blanks on a variable-length record and denotes the number of removed or truncated blank characters with a two byte integer inserted after the variable record pointer in the fixed-length record page. When a record is retrieved, trailing blanks are restored to the record image and returned to the application program.

## Data Compression

Data Compression is a feature of Btrieve used for reducing file size by storing records in a compressed format. The compression format consists of a two-byte integer denoting the number of repeating characters or binary values. Files with a lot of repeating values will benefit from compression more than file with few repeating values (In some cases compression can result in a larger file). Compressed fixed-length records are stored as variable-length records. This results in an additional space savings by reducing unused space in fixed record data pages.

Compression will result in a slight performance degradation (approximately 10 to 20 percent) and should only be used when the need for disk space outweighs the need for better access performance.

Data compression does require additional buffer space to accommodate the compressed and uncompressed record. For workstation Btrieve the /U parameter must be set to the size of the largest record that will be retrieved. Values range from 1 to 64 KB. For NetWare Btrieve the compression buffer size must be specified in the BSETUP program.

## Index Pages

Index information is stored in index pages. An index pages contains one B-tree node (see the next section, "Fundamentals of Indexing" for a description). An entire B-tree index structure may occupy many different index pages throughout the file. The following information is stored with each key in the index page:

- Pointer to page containing key values less than the key value
- The key value
- Data record pointer for first record with the key value
- Data record pointer for last record with the key value

In addition, Btrieve stores 12 bytes of header information at the beginning of each index page. Btrieve requires that the page be large enough to hold at least eight keys. A larger page size may have to be used on files with large key values.

## Data-Only Files

Data-only files have no indexes. Only the Step operations can be used to traverse the database in physical record address order (See Chapter 5, Basic File Access Techniques). Data-only files are created by setting the "Number of Indexes" file specification parameter to zero.

Data-only files are usually used for log files where each record represents a sequential event. Data-only files offer the benefit of high-speed insertion while still maintaining Btrieve's automatic concurrency control.

## Choosing the Optimal Page Size

There are two considerations involved in choosing the best page size: file size and access performance. By picking a page size, one can optimize to gain better performance or optimize to conserve disk space. The optimal page size usually is a compromise where a page is selected that provides adequate performance and still makes efficient use of disk space. See Chapter 6 for formulas that will help you calculate the optimal page size for your application.

### Performance Considerations

For retrieving fixed-length records and small variable-length records (small being a size significantly smaller than the page size), the smaller the page size the better. A page is the smallest unit of the file that is loaded into Btrieve's cache buffer.

Accessing any given record in a Btrieve file will require that at least one data page (the page containing the record image) be loaded into Btrieve's cache memory. If the index pages that contain the index you are using to find the record are not loaded, then one or more index pages may need to be loaded as well. Therefore, smaller pages mean that less data is transferred from the disk into memory.

For workstation Btrieve accessing data on a network drive, the entire page is transferred over the network which can reduce performance significantly. For NetWare Btrieve, a page is loaded into the cache of the server and is not transferred over the network, but can still effect performance. Further, because NetWare's own cache memory loads in 1K increments, it is recommended that you choose a Btrieve page size that is a multiple of 1K. (See Figure 4.4 Btrieve's cache memory architecture.)

### Optimal Page Size for Disk Utilization

An efficient page size can dramatically reduce file size. Optimizing for file size involves choosing a page size which best fits the physical record in the data page with the least amount of unused space. BOPS and PAGEOP are two good utilities freely distributed by Novell's technical support group which easily calculate the optimal page size for disk storage. Refer to Chapter 5, "Creating Files," for an example of calculating the optimal page size for space utilization.

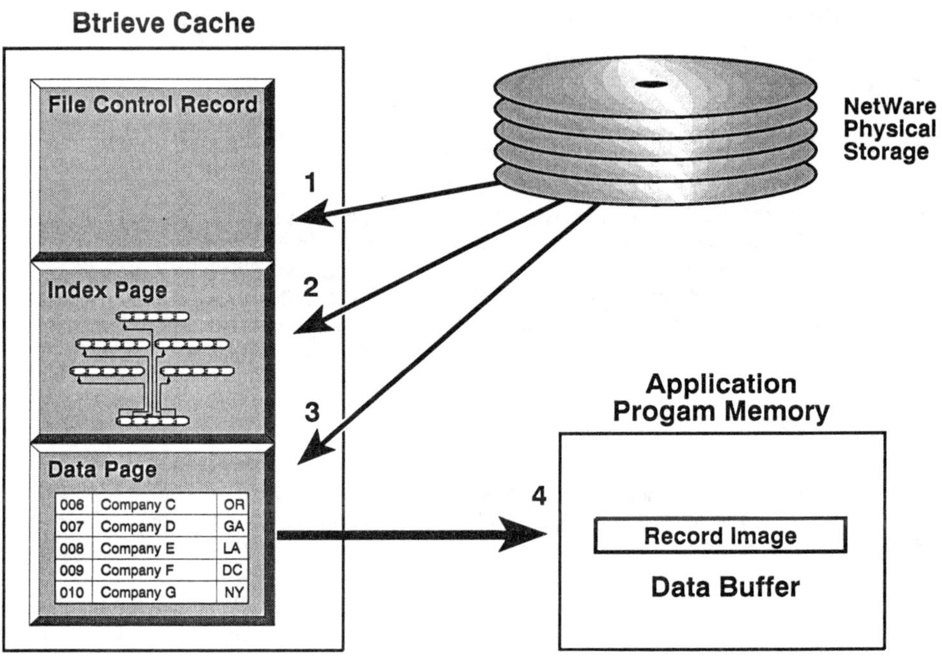


*Figure 4.4: Btrieve's cache memory*

## Btrieve's Memory Scheme

Btrieve maintains its own cache buffers. Figure 4.4 illustrates that when a record is retrieved, the whole data page is loaded into cache, and the record is returned to the application via the data buffer. The Btrieve application, therefore only needs to allocate memory for the record (or set of records with extended operations).

With workstation Btrieve, each workstation on the network maintains its own cache buffers and pages are transferred from disk to cache memory over the network. With NetWare Btrieve, Btrieve's cache is located at the file server and only records are transmitted over the network. Generally, the more memory dedicated to Btrieve's cache buffers, the better the performance. With larger cache memory, more pages can be loaded into memory and the frequency of page swapping is reduced.

The total amount of memory allocated for Btrieve's cache is divided into buffers which are the size of the largest page size load option (/P). The /P load option specifies the largest page size of any file that Btrieve will access. The largest page size must be between 512 bytes and 4096 bytes and a multiple of 512 bytes. By using smaller page sizes, more buffers will be allocated in Btrieve's cache.

For workstation Btrieve, the /M load parameter specifies the total amount of memory (in KB) reserved for Btrieve. This value directly effects the size of the Btrieve TSR. A small amount of the /M memory is utilized for static Btrieve variables, the rest is cache memory. The cache memory is divided into buffers of /P. The /P setting does not effect the size of Btrieve's cache memory but dictates the size of and therefore the number of individual page buffers. The following example loads Btrieve with 48 KB of memory allocated to Btrieve divided into buffers of 512 bytes.

```
BTRIEVE /M:48 /P:512
```

For NetWare Btrieve, the total amount of memory is not specified by the user; rather, it is calculated by Btrieve. Like workstation Btrieve, NetWare Btrieve's cache memory is divided into buffers of size /P. The BSETUP program is used to set NetWare Btrieve's load parameters. Memory for Btrieve's caches is not allocated at the workstation. On the workstation side, the NetWare Btrieve requester allocates buffer space for record transfer (not page transfer) using the /D (Data Buffer Space) load option. This value specifies the largest amount of record data (in bytes) that can be transferred between NetWare Btrieve and the Btrieve requester.

For single record operations, the /D load parameter should be set to the largest record length, including variable-length data, of all files accessed by the application. For multiple record processing with extended operations, the /D buffer must be large enough to transfer the maximum number of records in any extended operation. The /D requester load option corresponds to the "Largest Record Length" parameter in BSETUP, and must be no larger. The following example loads the DOS requester with a 4000 byte record buffer.

```
BREQUEST /D:4000
```

## Pre-Imaging

Pre-imaging is Btrieve's data integrity mechanism. Before a page is updated, it is first copied into Btrieve's pre-image buffer and then flushed to disk as a pre-image file. This creates a "backup" of all modified pages involved in the transaction. Pre-image files have a .PRE extension. For example, a file called CUSTOMER.BTR has an associated CUSTOMER.PRE file. During an update operation, Btrieve stores updated pages in this file. After the operation has completed, the pre-image file is discarded.If a system failure occurs during the update operation, the next time the file is accessed, Btrieve "rolls-back" the pre-image file to restore the data file to its original state before the failed operation.

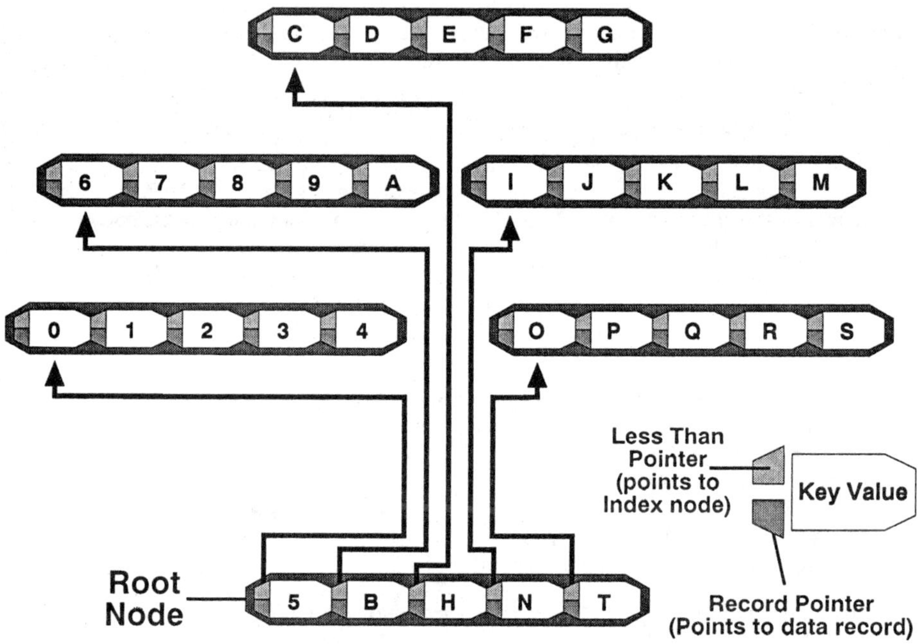


*Figure 4.5: Schematic diagram of a B-tree*

## Fundamentals of Indexing

### Btrieve Indexes

Large database files require efficient indexing for quick data update and retrieval. The B-tree has long been considered to be one of the most efficient indexing structures for large database files where performance and space utilization are a primary concern. This section describes how B-trees are implemented in Btrieve and defines several important terms pertaining to indexing.

While a thorough knowledge of the B-tree indexing technique is not necessary to write Btrieve applications,understanding keys and how they are used in indexing is crucial to developing efficient database programs.

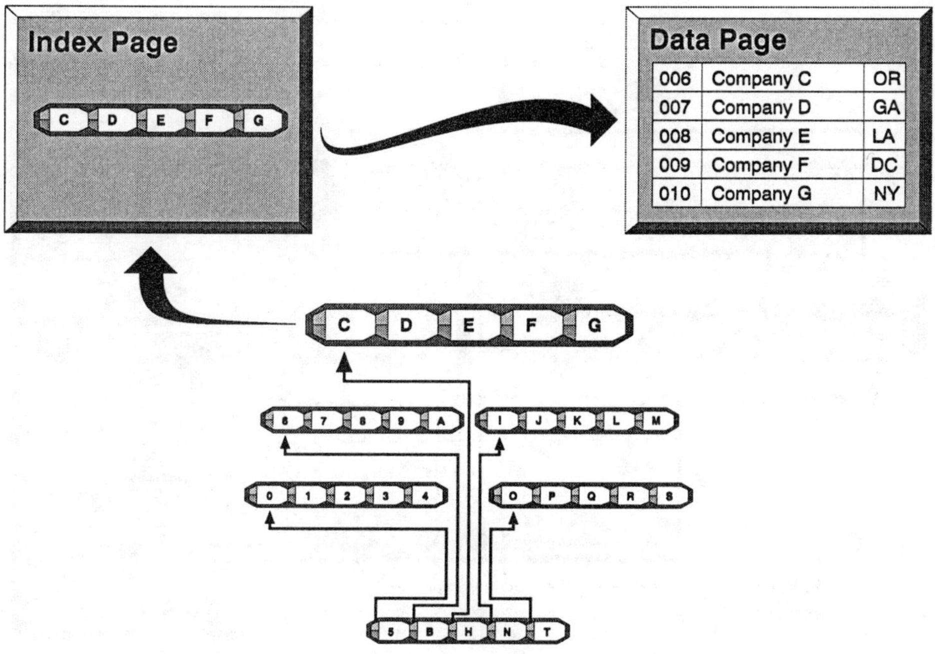


***Figure 4.6: Btrieve's implementation of a B-tree index***

## B-tree Indexes

A B-tree is divided into nodes. Each node contains several key-pointer combinations which are comprised of the following:

- The key value
- A pointer to the node with key values less than the key value
- A pointer to the record which contains the key value

Each of these structural components are represented graphically in Figure 4.5.

When Btrieve searches for a key value in a B-tree, it begins at the first key value in the root node. If Btrieve encounters a value that is greater than the search value, it searches the node pointed to by the less than pointer associated with the higher key value. This process is repeated until the value is found or is determined not to be in the B-tree index.

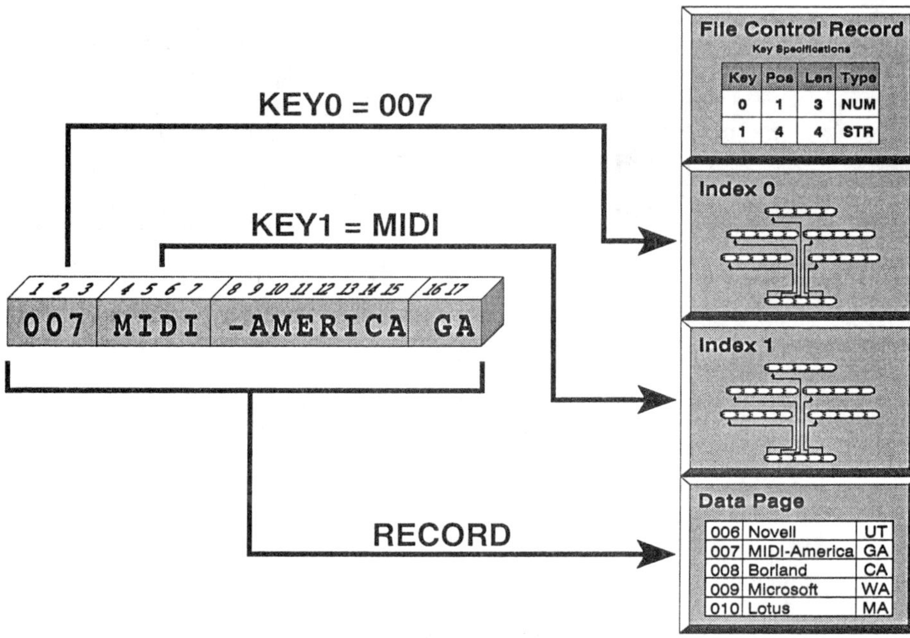


*Figure 4.7: Inserting a record*

## Key Segments

A segment is a contiguous number of bytes within the record. A segmented key is one which contains more than one segment. Segmented keys provide maximum flexibility in key definitions because they allow non-contiguous record data to be combined in a single key.

Segmented keys are often used to perform "sub-level sorting." The example in Figure 4.8 shows a segmented key composed of the state followed by the company name. When records are listed by state, they are ordered by company name within duplicate states.

When a file is created, keys are defined by specifying each segment in the key. A key can have multiple segments, but the total of all segments in all keys of the file must not exceed the maximum number supported by a Btrieve file. For version 5.10 of Btrieve, twenty-four is the limit.

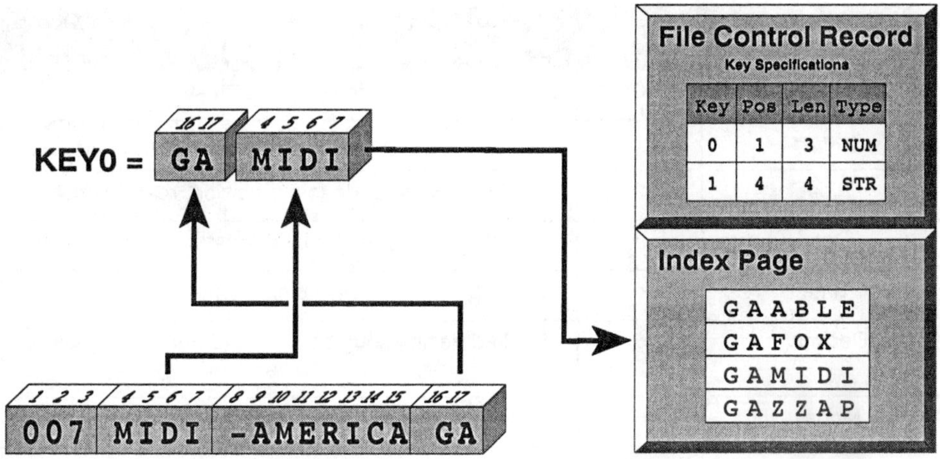


*Figure 4.8: Btrieve Segmented Keys*

There are no restrictions on where a segment can be located in the record and segments of different types can be included in the same key. Be certain that the location of the key data within the record is consistent with the key specification; otherwise, improper collating will result.

## Key Segment Definition Elements

There are four elements that are used in the definition of a key segment: position, length, type and flags. Position refers to the position of the key within the record (one relative). Length refers to the length of the segment including all delimiters. Type refers to the type of data stored at that location in the record. There are 14 key types to choose from; the rest of the data in a Btrieve record may be of any format.

The table in Figure 4.9 lists each Btrieve key type, its code, and its size restrictions. A full specification of each key type is provided in Appendix A.

Flags assign certain characteristics to each key segment. The key flags are assigned as a two-byte integer where each bit assigns a particular characteristic to the key segment. The table in Figure 4.10 lists each key flag.

***Figure 4.9: Btrieve Key Types***

| Extended Key | Code | Description |
|---|---|---|
| String | 0 | Non-delimited ASCII string |
| Integer | 1 | 2- or 4-byte, signed integer |
| Float | 2 | IEEE, single or double precision, real number |
| Date | 3 | 4-byte binary date |
| Time | 4 | 4-byte binary time |
| Decimal | 5 | Packed decimal number with two decimal digits per byte |
| Money | 6 | Same as Decimal type |
| Logical | 7 | 1- or 2-byte string logical value |
| Numeric | 8 | ASCII string with one decimal digit per byte |
| Bfloat | 9 | BASIC floating point representation |
| Lstring | 10 | ASCII string with leading length-byte |
| Zstring | 11 | ASCII string with binary zero terminator |
| Unsigned Binary | 14 | Unsigned binary integer |
| Auto Increment | 15 | 2- or 4-byte integer calculated by Btrieve to be next highest value |

***Figure 4.10: Btrieve Key Flags***

| Key Flag | Decimal Value | Description |
|---|---|---|
| Duplicates | 1 | Allows index to contain duplicate keys |
| Modifiable | 2 | Allows key to be modified |
| Binary | 4 | Maintains backward-compatibility with older files |
| Null | 8 | Allows keys to be omitted based on key value |
| Segmented | 16 | Allows segmented keys |
| Alternate Collating Sequence | 32 | Supports a program-defined, alternate collating sequence (as opposed to ASCII) |
| Descending | 64 | Allows descending key-order |
| Supplemental | 128 | Defines a temporary index |
| Extended Type | 256 | Specifies that the key is one of the (14) extended key types |
| Manual | 512 | Allows keys to be omitted based on key-value |

## Duplicate Key Indexes

In its purest form, a B-tree does not support duplicate key values. Each key in the index must be unique. Therefore there are several methods of handling duplicate key indexes. Btrieve employs two methods. One method is used for permanent indexes, and another is used for supplemental indexes.

## Duplicate Keys on Permanent Indexes

Figure 4.11 illustrates that in permanent index structures, only unique values are stored in the index. The index entry points to the first chronological duplicate record. The record contains

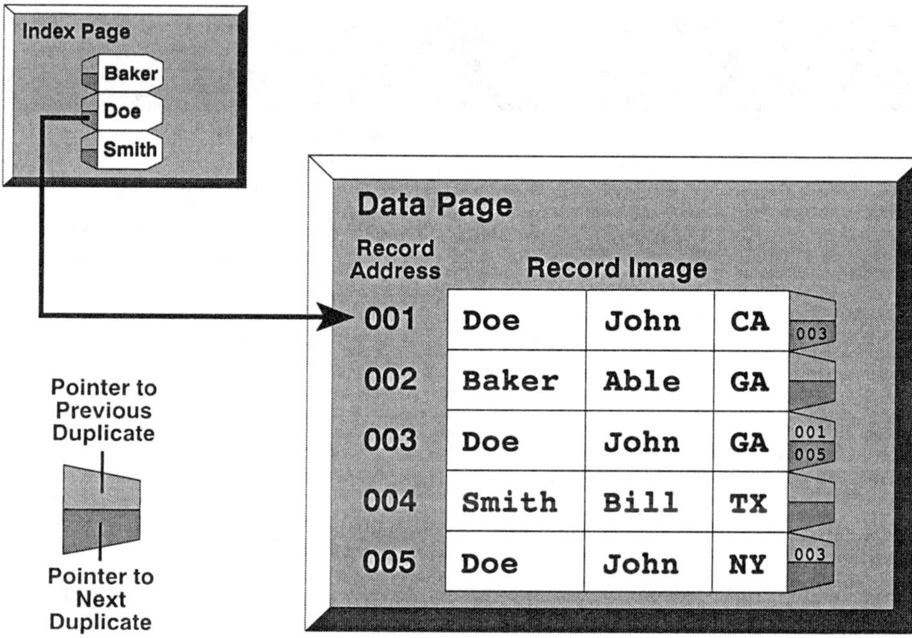


*Figure 4. 11: Btrieve permanent index structure*

two pointers for each key that supports duplicates. These pointers link duplicates to the next and previous chronological duplicate record.

With this doubly-linked list method of handling duplicate key values, chronological order of inserts will dictate the traversal order within duplicate key records. This method of handling duplicate key indexes adds eight additional bytes to the physical record length: two four-byte record pointers.

## Duplicate Keys on Supplemental Indexes

Supplemental index may be added at any time after the creation of a Btrieve file. Therefore, to use the doubly-linked list method would require reformatting all data pages to add the two four-byte pointers. This would be unacceptably slow. Instead, for duplicate key indexes on supplemental indexes, Btrieve concatenates the four-byte record address on the end of each key value to force uniqueness on the key.

This method does not guarantee chronological order within duplicate key records. Deleting records causes new records to be inserted into physical addresses preceding existing records. With this method of indexing, physical position of records will dictate the traversal order within duplicate key records.

# 5 Basic File Access Techniques

This chapter provides an in-depth description of how to perform basic database access operations required to create a database file and insert and retrieve records. An example customer database will be used. Example programs in this section are written in WATCOM C language. Source code examples for Pascal, COBOL, and BASIC are listed in the appendices.

## Creating Files

There are many "front end" programs that can be used to easily create Btrieve files. Xtrieve PLUS, for example, provides an input screen for the user to enter a definition of the Btrieve file and stores the definition in the data dictionary. This data dictionary definition is used to create the Btrieve file. The BUTIL -CREATE procedure creates a Btrieve file from a text description file. Whatever means these tools use to gather the information required to create a file, it is ultimately the Btrieve Create Operation (14) that creates the new file. By using the Create operation, your program will be able to create files on the fly quickly and with little overhead.

The definition of a Btrieve file is surprisingly simple. In Chapter 4, the segment entitled "Fundamentals of Indexing," provides an in-depth description of the role of key segments in defining the index. Chapter 8, "Btrieve Operation Codes," provides a complete description of the Create operation. The following section describes how to define a Btrieve file, given a specific application, and then write a program to create the file.

The definition of any database file is dictated by the user's requirements. The trick to designing a good Btrieve file is translating the user's requirements into the Btrieve Create operation parameters. In this example the user is a sales manager who needs a customer database. The manager's requirements are simple and can be summed up by the following seven statements. The customer database must be able to support the following:

- Maintain the following fields: company, contact name, address (with country and nine digit zip code), phone number, total sales in dollars, and general notes on each customer up to 2000 bytes.

- Allow mailing labels to be printed sorted by zip code and company name within zip code.
- Allow records to be recalled by customer name (last, first) or customer identification number.
- Automatically calculate the customer identification number when records are inserted. The new customer number must be the highest customer number in the database plus one.
- Keep track of the next time a sales rep should contact customer.
- Provide a record flagging mechanism to flag customers for various reasons such as flagging a customer for printing a mailing label. Allow over 500 flag conditions.

The first thing to do is identify all the fields required to fulfill these requirements, then calculate the best page size. For each field specify the field name, size, type, record position, and if the field is part of an index key:

***Figure 5.1: Example database fields***

| Field Name | Type | Size | Position | Key #/ Segment | Flags |
|---|---|---|---|---|---|
| **Customer Number** | Autoinc | 2 | 1 | 0 | — |
| **Customer Name** | String | 30 | 3 | 1 | dup,mod |
| **Company** | String | 60 | 33 | 2/2 | — |
| **Address 1** | String | 30 | 93 | — | — |
| **Address 2** | String | 30 | 123 | — | — |
| **City** | String | 30 | 153 | — | — |
| **State** | String | 2 | 183 | — | — |
| **Zip** | String | 9 | 185 | 2/1 | dup,mod |
| **Country** | String | 3 | 194 | — | — |
| **Phone** | String | 10 | 197 | — | — |

***Figure 5.1: Example database fields***

| Field Name | Type | Size | Position | Key #/ Segment | Flags |
|---|---|---|---|---|---|
| **Sales Representative** | String | 3 | 207 | 3/1 | dup,mod |
| **Next Contact** | Date | 4 | 210 | 3/2 | — |
| **Dollar Volume** | Numeric | 10 | 214 | — | — |
| **Flag** | Integer | 2 | 224 | — | — |
| **Notes** | Lvar | var | 226 | — | — |

The record length is 225 bytes, variable-length records are supported, and there are four keys, three of which support duplicates. An optimal page size can be determined from this information.

In this case, we are interested in conserving disk space as much as possible. We do, however, want to keep the page size as small as possible for performance reasons. Generally speaking, a smaller page size gives better performance since smaller amounts of memory are being moved in and out of Btrieve's cache memory. In addition, for DOS workstation Btrieve a larger page size requires a larger page size load parameter (/P) which increases the size of the TSR. From Chapter 4, "Btrieve File Architecture," we know that the physical record length is calculated as follows:

```
    225 byte record image
     24 bytes for duplicate key pointers (3 keys x 8 bytes per key)
+     4 bytes for variable-length records
    ---------------------------------------------------------------
    253 physical record length
```

We know that the first six bytes of a data page are used by Btrieve for control reasons as a Page Header and that page sizes must be multiples of 512 bytes between 512 and 4096. From this information we can calculate a table of page size options showing us how much unused data page space will result from each page size.

***Figure 5.2: Page size options for example database***

| Page Option | Overhead | Records/ Page | Unused/ Page | Unused/ Record |
|---|---|---|---|---|
| **512** | 506 | 2 | 0 | 0 |
| **1024** | 1018 | 4 | 6 | 1.50 |
| **1536** | 1530 | 6 | 12 | 2.00 |
| **2048** | 2042 | 8 | 18 | 2.25 |
| **2560** | 2554 | 10 | 24 | 2.40 |
| **3072** | 3066 | 12 | 30 | 2.50 |
| **3584** | 3578 | 14 | 36 | 2.57 |
| **4096** | 4090 | 16 | 48 | 3.00 |

The optimal page size for disk utilization with zero unused bytes per page is 512. There is one problem with this -- a key size of 69 is too large (zip code by company key) for a page size of 512. Btrieve requires that each key page in the file be large enough to hold at least eight keys (if an attempt is made to create a file with a page size of 512 and a 69 byte key (9 for zip code and 60 for company name), a status 29 (Invalid Key Length) will result).

Both of these equations must be true:

(length of longest key + length of key pointers) x 8 indexes on a page + index overhead <= page size

-- and --

fixed-record length <= page size

For our database example, the first equation is not true for a page size of 512 bytes:

(69 bytes + 24 bytes) x 8 + 12 bytes <= 512 bytes (not true)

-- and --

225 bytes <= 512 bytes (true)

So, you can either use a page size of 1024 or shorten the key lengths.

Additionally, you should remember that supplemental indexes require a minimum page size of 1024 bytes. If you anticipate that you (or any user of your application) might add a supplemental index, then you should choose a size of 1024 or larger. Later, you will be adding a supplemental index, so for this example, use a page size of 1024.

Btrieve places no restrictions on key lengths. Even though the company field is 60 bytes long, it is possible to index on only the first 10 characters and still meet our indexing requirements. We will index on only the first 10 characters of the customer name field as well. Shortening the customer name key length means that a record can be searched by the first ten characters of the customer name. This is satisfactory for the application. Shortening these keys will also save us index page space and would have allowed us to use a 512 page size, except for the requirements of the supplemental index.

A key segment that is smaller than a logical field is called a sub-field key. Sub-field keys present no difficulty to Btrieve, since Btrieve does not recognize fields in the first place. A sub-field key is not, however, supported by Xtrieve PLUS, or NetWare SQL. In the NetWare SQL data dictionary keys are defined as whole fields. Our departure from the NetWare SQL data dictionary standard is acceptable for this application. A file reorganization may be required to comply with the NetWare SQL data dictionary in the future.

The next decision to make concerns the free space threshold for the variable-length records. Generally, a high free space threshold is appropriate for files with variable-length records that frequently change in size. The large free space threshold allows for record expansion with minimized record fragmentation (see Chapter 4, "Btrieve File Architecture"). A smaller free space threshold makes better use of disk space but increases the likelihood of record fragmentation. Since our records will be fairly static in size, a 5% free space threshold will be used.

The final decisions have to do with data format. Most of the data is string data. There is one field containing a dollar value, one date field, and one field for flagging records. Since this data file will be accessed by several programming languages, primarily C language, we will use string data types for character data. Btrieve's date data type will be used for dates. And dollar amounts will be stored in Btrieve's numeric data type. The flag field will be a two byte integer.

Now we are ready to create the Customer database file. The following source code creates a Btrieve database file according to our specifications. Note: All constants used in this program are defined in the INCLUDES.C include file.

```
//
// BCREATE.C   INSERT EXAMPLE WITH WATCOM C v8.0 AND BTRIEVE 5.10
// AUTHOR:     FRANK A. LEO
// DATE:       OCTOBER 17, 1991
//
#include "includes.c"
#define MAX_NOTE_SIZE  2000
//
// BTRIEVE CREATE STRUCTURES
//
```

```
struct KeySpec
        { int   KeyPos;
          int   KeyLen;
          int   KeyFlags;
          long  KeyTot;
          char  KeyType;
          char  Reserved[5]; };

struct File_Description_Type
        { int   RecLen;
          int   PageSize;
          int   IndxCnt;
          long  RecTot;
          int   FileFlags;
          char  Reserved[2];
          int   Allocation;
          struct KeySpec KeyBuf[24]; };
//
// BTRIEVE DATA TYPE STRUCTURES
//
struct date_type
        {  char  day;
           char  month;
           int   year;   };
//
// APPLICATION STRUCTURE
//
struct  Customer_Record_Type{
        int     cust_number;           // key 0
        char    cust_name[30];         // key 1 (10)
        char    company[60];           // key 2.2 (10)
        char    addr_1[30];
        char    addr_2[30];
        char    city[30];
        char    state[2];
        char    zip[9];                // key 2.1
        char    country[3];
        char    phone[10];
        char    sales_rep[3];          // key 3.1
        struct  date_type next_date;  // key 3.2
        char    dollar_vol[10];
        int     record_flag;
        char    notes[MAX_NOTE_SIZE];   };
//
// BTRIEVE FUNCTION VARIABLES
//
int     Stat;
char    PosBlk[128];
struct  File_Description_Type FileBuf;
struct  Customer_Record_Type  CustRecBuf;
int     BufLen;
char    bFileName[] = {"CUSTOMER.BTR "};
int     Keyno;
//
main()
{
    Create_Customer ();
}
//
//  CREATE CUSTOMER.BTR FILE
```

```
//
void Create_Customer() {
  // FILE SPECIFICATION
  FileBuf.RecLen = sizeof(CustRecBuf) - MAX_NOTE_SIZE;
  FileBuf.PageSize = 1024;
  FileBuf.IndxCnt = 4;
  FileBuf.FileFlags = B_VARIABLE_LENGTH;

  // KEY SPECIFICATIONS
  // KEY 0: BY CUSTOMER NUMBER---------------------------------------------------
  FileBuf.KeyBuf[0].KeyPos = 1;
  FileBuf.KeyBuf[0].KeyLen = 2;
  FileBuf.KeyBuf[0].KeyFlags = B_EXTENDED_KEY_TYPE;
  FileBuf.KeyBuf[0].KeyType = B_AUTOINC;
  // KEY 1: BY FIRST 10 CHARACTERS OF THE CUSTOMER NAME----------------------
  FileBuf.KeyBuf[1].KeyPos = 3;
  FileBuf.KeyBuf[1].KeyLen = 10;
  FileBuf.KeyBuf[1].KeyFlags = B_EXTENDED_KEY_TYPE |
                               B_DUPLICATES |
                               B_MODIFIABLE ;
  FileBuf.KeyBuf[1].KeyType  = B_STRING;
  // KEY 2: BY ZIPCODE BY FIRST 10 CHARACTERS OF THE COMPANY NAME------------
  FileBuf.KeyBuf[2].KeyPos   = 185;       // ZIPCODE
  FileBuf.KeyBuf[2].KeyLen   = 9;
  FileBuf.KeyBuf[2].KeyFlags = B_EXTENDED_KEY_TYPE |
                               B_DUPLICATES |
                               B_MODIFIABLE |
                               B_SEGMENTED;
  FileBuf.KeyBuf[2].KeyType  = B_STRING;
  //
  FileBuf.KeyBuf[3].KeyPos   = 33;        // COMPANY NAME
  FileBuf.KeyBuf[3].KeyLen   = 10;
  FileBuf.KeyBuf[3].KeyFlags = B_EXTENDED_KEY_TYPE |
                               B_DUPLICATES |
                               B_MODIFIABLE;
  FileBuf.KeyBuf[3].KeyType  = B_STRING;
  // KEY 3: BY REP BY NEXT CONTACT DATE---------------------------------------
  FileBuf.KeyBuf[4].KeyPos   = 207;       //REP
  FileBuf.KeyBuf[4].KeyLen   = 3;
  FileBuf.KeyBuf[4].KeyFlags = B_EXTENDED_KEY_TYPE |
                               B_DUPLICATES |
                               B_MODIFIABLE |
                               B_SEGMENTED;
  FileBuf.KeyBuf[4].KeyType  = B_STRING;
  //
  FileBuf.KeyBuf[5].KeyPos   = 210;       //NEXT CONTACT DATE
  FileBuf.KeyBuf[5].KeyLen   = 4;
  FileBuf.KeyBuf[5].KeyFlags = B_EXTENDED_KEY_TYPE |
                               B_DUPLICATES |
                               B_MODIFIABLE;
  FileBuf.KeyBuf[5].KeyType  = B_DATE;
  //---------------------------------------------------------------------------
  BufLen = sizeof(FileBuf);
  Stat = BTRV(B_CREATE, PosBlk, &FileBuf, &BufLen, bFileName, 0);
  if(Stat != 0)
        printf("Error Creating Customer File.  Status = %d\n", Stat);
  else
        printf("Customer File created successfully\n");
  return;
}
```

## Opening and Closing Files

The Open (0) operation must be performed on all files that the application will be accessing. The open operation initializes the Position Block to identify an open file. If there are several open files, there is one Position Block for each file. To access a particular file, pass the Position Block that was used to open the file for the Btrieve operation. A file can be opened several times with several different Position Blocks. This can be done with the function executor, BX, to simulate a multi-user condition where two processes have the same file open. It's much easier to use multiple Position Blocks in BX, than to run back and forth between two workstations to test record locking (The DOS SHARE.EXE program must be loaded for a single user, DOS PC to simulate a network environment).

All files should be closed after they are no longer needed. This ensures that modifications made to the file have been made permanent on disk. Repeated opening of files without closing might result in Btrieve's internal lock table filling up and Btrieve returning a status 47 (Maximum Open Files). Opening and closing files does, however, cause a substantial amount of processing overhead in Btrieve. It is best not to repeatedly open and close files as this may cause a severe performance degradation.

The Open operation sets the access mode using a mode identifier passed in the key number parameter. Chapter 8, "Btrieve Operation Codes," provides a detailed description of the Open operation and the different access modes. In this example we will be opening the file for read/write and allow the file to be shared on the network. This is considered normal mode and the key number value of 0 is passed to Btrieve on the Open operation. The following subroutines open and close the Customer database file.

```
//
// BTRIEVE FUNCTION VARIABLES
//
int     Stat;
char    CustPosBlk[128];
struct  Customer_Record_Type  CustRecBuf;
int     BufLen;
char    bFileName[13];
int     Keyno;
//
main()
{
    Open_Customer ();
    Close_Customer ();
}
//
//
//  OPEN CUSTOMER.BTR FILE
//
void Open_Customer() {
   strcpy(&bFileName, "CUSTOMER.BTR");
   BufLen = sizeof(CustRecBuf) - MAX_NOTE_SIZE;
   Keyno  = 0;
```

```
    Stat    = BTRV(B_OPEN, CustPosBlk, &CustRecBuf, &BufLen, bFileName, Keyno);
    if(Stat != 0)
           printf("Error opening Customer file.  Status = %d\n", Stat);
    else
           printf("Customer file opened successfully\n");
    return;
}
//
//
//  CLOSE CUSTOMER.BTR FILE
//
void Close_Customer() {
    Stat    = BTRV(B_CLOSE, CustPosBlk, &CustRecBuf, &BufLen, bFileName, 0);
    if(Stat != 0)
           printf("Error closing Customer file.  Status = %d\n", Stat);
    else
           printf("Customer file closed\n");
    return;
}
```

# Inserting Records

The real trick to inserting records is formatting each record properly and placing them in the Data Buffer. Once the record (or records) is placed in the Data Buffer, a single Insert (2) or Insert Extended (40) is all that is required to insert the record and update all indexes.

In the following example, records are loaded into the Customer database file from an ASCII text input file that was created in standard data format (SDF). SDF format uses ASCII strings to represent all data, including dates and numerics. SDF files can have fixed-length fields, or comma delimited using quotes (") for string data. Xtrieve PLUS uses a comma separated, SDF file for its SDF format.

In this example, the input file will be an Xtrieve PLUS compatible, comma-separated SDF file created from the following dBase procedure:

```
. USE CUSTOMER
. DISPLAY STRUCTURE

    Structure for database: C:CUSTOMER.dbf
    Number of data records:      100
    Date of last update    : 10/17/91
    Field  Field Name  Type       Width    Dec
        1  CUST_NAME   Character     30
        2  COMPANY     Character     60
        3  ADDR1       Character     30
        4  ADDR2       Character     30
        5  CITY        Character     30
        6  STATE       Character      2
        7  ZIP         Character      9
        8  COUNTRY     Character      3
        9  PHONE       Character     10
```

```
         10 SALES_REP    Character       3
         11 NEXT_DATE    Date            8
         12 DOLLAR_VOL   Numeric        10       2
         13 FLAG         Character       2
         14 NOTES        Memo           10
     ** Total **                       238

 . COPY TO CUSTOMER.SDF DELIMITED WITH "
```

Notice that the input file does not have a customer number field. This will be calculated during the load procedure. The following procedure (INSERT.C) reads the records from the SDF input file, and loads them into the Btrieve Customer file.

The program INSERT.C contains a while loop that reads a record from the SDF input file, places the record in the Data Buffer (CustRecBuf), and executes a Btrieve Insert operation. The fReadSDF_CustRec procedure is a very important procedure (fReadSDF_CustRec is listed in Appendix B, "BINSERT.C"). It reads fields in SDF format and converts these fields into the proper Btrieve field types. If this procedure does not correctly interpret the SDF input file, the fields within each Btrieve record may be misaligned and proper indexing will not be achieved. Remember, Btrieve is a record manager. It is the responsibility of the program to correctly format the data in each record. Btrieve does not "second guess" the calling program. If the date field, for example, is not in the correct position, Btrieve will insert a key value made up of the value that is located where the date field should be (this is dictated by the Create operation). The only warning of this condition is that the dates will be incorrectly collated.

```
//
//  INSERT.C     INSERT EXAMPLE WITH WATCOM C v8.0 AND BTRIEVE 5.10
//  AUTHOR:      FRANK A. LEO
//  DATE:        OCTOBER 17, 1991
//
#include "includes.c"
#define MAX_NOTE_SIZE  2000
#define MAX_FIELD_SIZE 30
//
// FUNCTION PROTOTYPES
//
// Read a CUSTOMER record from an input SDF file
int fReadSDF_CustRec(struct Customer_Record_Type *CustRecBuf,
                     FILE *SDFfile );
//
// BTRIEVE DATA TYPE STRUCTURES
//
struct date_type
        {  char  day;
           char  month;
           int   year;  };
//
// APPLICATION STRUCTURES
//
// Btrieve file CUSTOMER.BTR record format
// Note: Key segments are denoted by "key k.s",
//       where k is the key number and s is the
//      segment. No s means a non segmented key. If the segment length is
```

```
//      smaller than the field, the key segment length is denoted with (l)
//      where l is the segment length.
//
struct  Customer_Record_Type{
        int     cust_number;          // key 0
        char    cust_name[30];        // key 1 (10)
        char    company[60];          // key 2.2 (10)
        char    addr_1[30];
        char    addr_2[30];
        char    city[30];
        char    state[2];
        char    zip[9];               // key 2.1
        char    country[3];
        char    phone[10];
        char    sales_rep[3];         // key 3.1
        struct  date_type next_date;  // key 3.2
        char    dollar_vol[10];
        int     record_flag;
        char    notes[MAX_NOTE_SIZE];  };
//
// BTRIEVE FUNCTION VARIABLES
//
int     Stat;
char    CustPosBlk[128];
struct  Customer_Record_Type  CustRecBuf;
int     BufLen;
char    KeyBuf[255];
char    bFileName[13];
int     Keyno;
// INPUT FILE VARIABLES
FILE    *SDFfile;
char    inChar;
// other variables
char temparr[MAX_FIELD_SIZE];
int  tempint;

main()
{
    Open_Customer ();
    SDFfile  = fopen("CUSTOMER.SDF","r");
    fReadSDF_CustRec(&CustRecBuf, SDFfile);         // Read the first record.
                                                    // Place in Data Buffer
    while ( ! feof(SDFfile) )  {                    // Loop until end of file.
       BufLen = sizeof(CustRecBuf) - MAX_NOTE_SIZE  // Calculate record length.
                + strlen(CustRecBuf.notes) + 1;
       printf(" inserting, recl= %d \n", BufLen);
       Keyno=0;                                //Maintain positioning on key 0.
       Stat   = BTRV( B_INSERT, CustPosBlk, // Insert record into Btrieve file
                      &CustRecBuf, &BufLen,
                      &KeyBuf, Keyno);
       if(Stat != 0)                           // Check for error conditions.
          printf("Error Inserting Customer Record. Status = %d\n",
                  Stat);
       fReadSDF_CustRec(&CustRecBuf, SDFfile); // Read next rec. in input file.
    }
    Close_Customer ();
    fclose( SDFfile );

}
```

## Traversing

Records in a Btrieve file can be traversed in index order as well as physical address order. Traversing involves starting at a record in the file (often times the first record) and continuing to retrieve the next record until a condition stops the traversal (often when the end of the file has been reached). A reverse traversal involves going up the file by continuing to retrieve the previous record. The Btrieve Get operations are used to process records in index order and the Step operations process records based on their physical address. Btrieve supports the following traversal operations:

**Index Traversal Operations**

- Get First (12)
- Get Last (13)
- Get Previous (07)
- Get Next (06)
- Get Next Extended (36)
- Get Previous Extended (37)

**Physical Record Traversal Operations**

- Step First (33)
- Step Last (34)
- Step Next (24)
- Step Next Extended (38)
- Step Previous (35)
- Step Previous Extended (39)

## Positioning

Before a traversal can occur, Btrieve's positioning must be established. The term "establishing positioning" describes the result of a Btrieve operation that modifies the pointers in the Position Block such that the current record pointer contains a valid record address.

The Get First and Get Last operations establish positioning for the first time. They can be used right after the an Open operation. The Get Next and Get Previous operations require that positioning already be established before they can be executed. The term pre-positioning means that positioning must be properly established beforehand. Figure 5.3 illustrates the Position Block's role in index positioning.

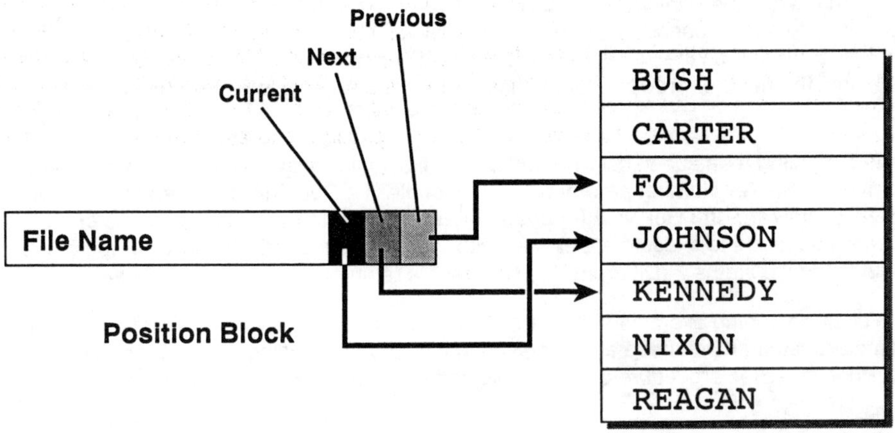


***Figure 5.3: Position Block***

## Index Traversal

Traversal means starting at a particular record (usually the first) and getting the next (or previous) record until a condition is met (usually reaching the end of file). The Get operations are used for indexed traversal--processing records in indexed order as opposed to physical address order. Indexed traversal is also referred to as key path traversal. Any index in a Btrieve file can be used to traverse records. The order in which records are retrieved is dictated by the key type. For example strings are collated from "A" to "Z" and integers are collated from (-9) to (+9). For descending keys, the Get First and Get Next, and Get Last and Get Previous operations are simply reversed.

While traversing on a key path, the Position Block parameter maintains pointers to the current record. The current record is defined as the record who's address is currently stored in the Position Block. For an open file, the Position Block contains the filename and three pointers:

- Current Record address
- Logical Next Record address
- Logical Previous Record address

In addition to the current record, the Position Block maintains pointers to the logical next record and logical previous pointers. The logical next record is defined as the record that would be retrieved by a Get Next (6) operation. The logical previous record is defined as the record that would be retrieved on a Get Previous (7) operation. The logical next and previous record pointers are dependent on the current key (also referred to as the key path). The current key is defined as the key identifier (zero relative) stored in the Key Number parameter. Each time the next (or previous) record is retrieved, positioning is established on the new record.

While traversing a database using an index, positioning is always based on the index key path specified in the Key Number parameter. For example, if a Get First (12) operation is performed with key path zero, the Get Next (6) operation must be performed with key path zero. If an attempt was made to execute a Get Next with the key number other than zero, the operation would fail and a status 7 (Different Key Number) is returned.

The following coding example shows a simple indexed traversal where records from the example Customer Database are displayed in indexed order using the customer name field. The Print_CustRec procedure displays selected fields from the customer record.

```
main()
{
     Open_Customer ();
     Keyno =  1;                                       // Use the name key.
     BufLen = sizeof(CustRecBuf);
     Stat   = BTRV(B_GET_FIRST, CustPosBlk,
             &CustRecBuf, &BufLen, KeyBuf, Keyno);
     if(Stat != 0 )
        printf("Error Getting First Customer Record. Status = %d\n",
                  Stat);
     while (Stat == 0)    {                         // Loop until end of file.
        Print_CustRec(&CustRecBuf);
        BufLen = sizeof(CustRecBuf);                // Reset Buffer length to max.
        Stat   = BTRV( B_GET_NEXT, CustPosBlk,      // Get the next record.
                       &CustRecBuf, &BufLen,
                       &KeyBuf, Keyno);
        if(Stat != 0 && Stat != B_END_OF_FILE)      // Check for error conditions.
           printf("Error Getting Next Customer Record. Status = %d\n", Stat);
     }
     Close_Customer ();
}
```

It is important to note that with the Get operations, Btrieve returns the key value of the record retrieved in the Key Buffer parameter. It is a common programming error to pass a Key Buffer of insufficient size to Btrieve on a Get operation only to have the returning key value overwrite other variables within the program.

For more information on the Get operations, see Chapter 8.

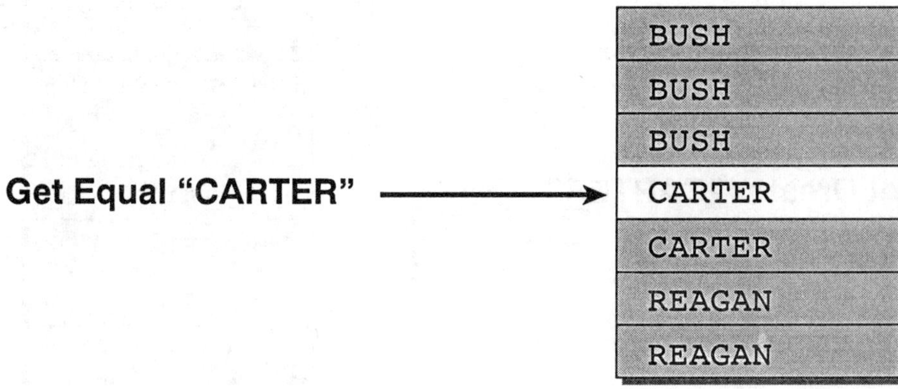


*Figure 5.4: Get Equal*

## Physical Record Traversal

The Step operations are used for physical record traversal. The physical address of a record in Btrieve is a four-byte unsigned integer that is the offset of the first byte in the record from the beginning of the file. A Step First will return the first record in the first data page of the file. A Step Last returns the last record in the data page.

The Step First, Step Last, and Step Next operations will establish positioning without pre-positioning. If a Step Next operation is issued without pre-positioning, Btrieve will issue a Step First operation. This is inconsistent with the Get Next and Step Previous operations in that those operations require pre-positioning.

An attempt to issue a Get Next or Get Previous operation while physical record positioning is established will fail with a status 8 (Invalid Positioning) error. However, a Step Next and Step Previous operation can be performed at any time while index positioning is established.

Physical traversal is the fastest method for Btrieve to process records. With index traversal, Btrieve must load index pages as well as data pages in cache memory in order to traverse records. In addition, the data records are most likely not contiguous within data pages and the data pages can be scattered through the file. This causes more cache swapping. With physi-

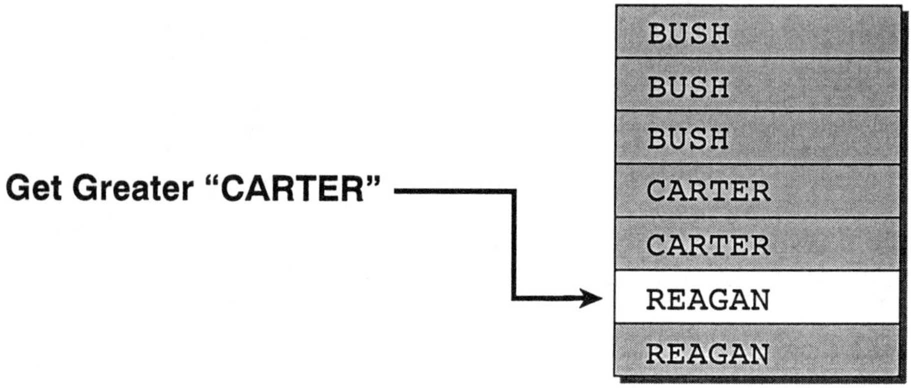


***Figure 5.5: Get Greater***

cal record traversal, index pages are not loaded into memory and records are contiguous within the data page. This is the most efficient use of Btrieve's caching scheme.

The following coding example shows a simple physical record traversal where records from the example Customer Database are displayed in physical record order. Notice that this program is almost identical with the index traversal. The only differences are that the Step First and Step Next operations are used instead of Get First and Get Next. In addition, the Key Number parameter does not have to be set.

```
main()
{
    Open_Customer ();
    BufLen = sizeof(CustRecBuf);
    Stat   = BTRV(B_STEP_FIRST, CustPosBlk,
           &CustRecBuf, &BufLen, &KeyBuf, Keyno);
    if(Stat != 0 )
       printf("Error Getting First Customer Record. Status = %d\n",
                Stat);
    while (Stat == 0)   {                        // Loop until end of file.
       Print_CustRec(&CustRecBuf);
       BufLen = sizeof(CustRecBuf);              // Reset Buffer length to maxi.
       Stat   = BTRV(B_STEP_NEXT, CustPosBlk,         // Get the next record.
                &CustRecBuf, &BufLen,
                &KeyBuf, Keyno);
       if(Stat != 0 && Stat != B_END_OF_FILE)    // Check for error conditions.
```

```
            printf("Error Getting Next Customer Record. Status = %d\n",
                    Stat);
        }
        Close_Customer ();
    }
```

For more information on the Step traversal operations, see Chapter 8.

## Searching

The Btrieve search operations provide quick retrieval of records based on their key values. A record's key value is the value that Btrieve places into the B-tree index when the record is inserted or modified. A record has a key value for each key path and the key number parameter determines which index or key path is searched. The search operations take advantage of the B-tree indexing structure and Btrieve's caching scheme. Btrieve offers the following Search Operations:

- Get Equal (5)
- Get Greater (8)
- Get Greater Equal (9)
- Get Less Than (10)
- Get Less Equal (11)

The search value is placed in the Key Buffer and if the Key Buffer value compares with the key value for the record, the record is returned.

The Get Equal (5) operation returns the first record with a current key value that matches exactly with the value in the Key Buffer. Figure 5.4 illustrates how the Get Equal operation works.

The Get Greater (8) operation returns the first record with a current key value that is greater than the value in the Key Buffer. Figure 5.5 shows how the Get Greater operation works.

Get Greater or Equal (9) returns the first record with a current key value that is greater than or equal to the value in the Key Buffer. The Get Greater or Equal operation is perhaps the most useful search operation. Get Greater or Equal is used for making partial matching searches. Get Greater or Equal is recommended over Get Greater for partial matching searches because if the key value do match exactly, Get Greater or Equal returns the record. Figure 5.6 illustrates the Get Greater or Equal operation.

The Get Less Than (10) operation and Get Less Than or Equal (11) operation return the last record who's key value is less than and less than or equal respectively the value in the Key Buffer. For duplicate keys, Get Less Than and Get Less Than or Equal return the last record in the chain of duplicates. Figure 5.7 illustrates the Get Less Than or Equal operation.

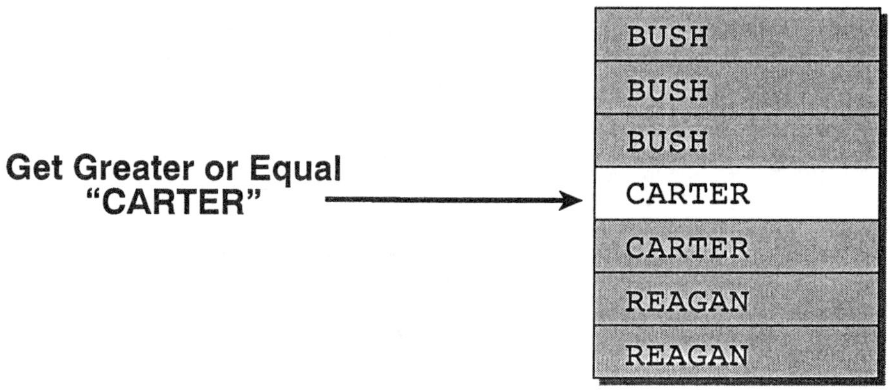


*Figure 5.6 Get Greater or Equal*

The following coding example shows a simple index search from the example Customer Database. A customer record is searched by a customer number entered from the keyboard.

```
main()
{
    Open_Customer ();
    Keyno =  0;                          // Use the customer number key.
    printf("customer number: ");
    scanf("%d", &Cust_No_Key);
    BufLen = sizeof(CustRecBuf);
    Stat   = BTRV(B_GET_EQUAL, CustPosBlk,
            &CustRecBuf, &BufLen, &Cust_No_Key, Keyno);
    if(Stat == 0 )
       Print_CustRec(&CustRecBuf);
    else
       printf("Record not found. Status = %d\n", Stat);
    Close_Customer ();
}
```

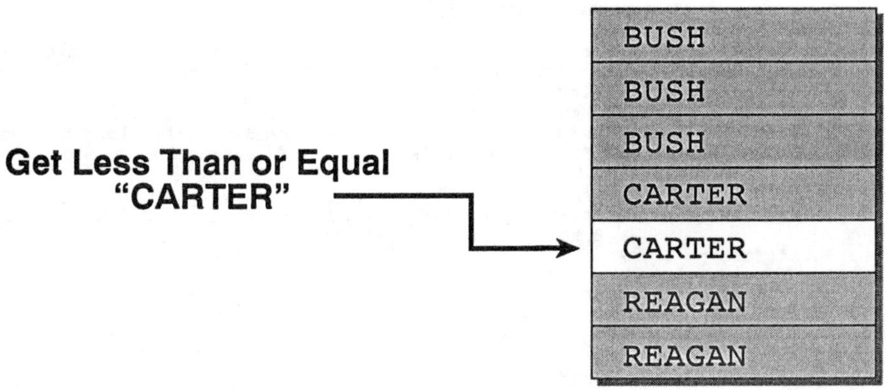


*Figure 5.7: Get Less Than or Equal*

## Updating Records

Updating refers to the Update (3) operation and Delete (4) operation. Both operations work by establishing positioning on the desired record, then updating or deleting the record. Btrieve updates all indexes on Update and Delete operations.

After a record has been updated, positioning is not altered unless the current key value is modified. Thus a correct traversal may not be achieved if the current keypath key value is being modified in the record.

After a record has been deleted, indexed positioning is not effected. Get Next and Get Previous operations will perform just as though the record had not been deleted. A Delete operation will disrupt physical record traversal. Attempting a Step Next or Step Previous operation after a delete will result in a status 8 (Invalid Positioning).

The following example reads customer numbers with sales totals from a text input file, searches for the customer record, adds the sales total to the customer record, and updates the record in the database.

```
main()
{
    Open_Customer ();
    SDFfile  = fopen("UPDATES.SDF","r");            // Open update SDF file.
    fReadSDF_Field( &SDFCust_No, 5,                 // Read the customer number.
                    B_NUMERIC, SDFfile);
    Keyno = 0;
    while ( ! feof(SDFfile) )  {                    // Loop through update file.
       Cust_No_Key = (int) atoi(SDFCust_No);        // Convert cust.# to integer
       printf("Searching for customer: %d.",
                 Cust_No_Key);
       BufLen = sizeof(CustRecBuf);                 // Set buffer length to max.
       Stat = BTRV(B_GET_EQUAL,CustPosBlk,          // Search for Record
              &CustRecBuf,&BufLen,
              &Cust_No_Key, Keyno);
       fReadSDF_Field(&CustRecBuf.dollar_vol, 10,   // Read new dollar amount.
                        B_NUMERIC, SDFfile);
       if(Stat == 0 ) {                             // If record found,
          printf(".record found.");
          Stat = BTRV(B_UPDATE, CustPosBlk,         // update record.
                 &CustRecBuf, &BufLen,
                 &Cust_No_Key, Keyno);
             if(Stat == 0 )
                printf(".updated. \n");
             else
                printf(".error updating, status = %d \n", Stat);
      }
       else {
          printf(".record not found, status = %d, rejecting update.\n", Stat);
       }
       fReadSDF_Field(&SDFCust_No, 5, B_NUMERIC, SDFfile); // Read next cust. #
    }
    Close_Customer ();
    fclose( SDFfile );
}
```

Btrieve provides all the basic file manipulation operations to support a database file. The following chapter describes advanced file operations including making multiple record calls using the extended operations.

# 6 Advanced File Access Techniques

## Advanced Indexing

The Btrieve key-indexed filing system allows a programmer to design almost any type of B-tree Indexing scheme. The definition of a Btrieve index is embodied in the description of each key in the file. The variety of indexing features that Btrieve supports are all defined as key flags in the key segment specifications. These key flags dictate how Btrieve will behave and how the application program will manage the Key Buffer parameter. The Create (14) operation and Create Supplemental Index (31) operation are described in full detail in Chapter 8. Chapter 4, "Btrieve File Architecture," describes how Btrieve performs indexing and how key segments and index structures are related.

## Record Grouping

Record grouping (also referred to as sub-level sorting) is achieved with segmented keys. Segmented keys allow fields to be concatenated into a single key to provide grouping and sub-level grouping. In our example database from Chapter 5, the sales representative's report must list records by next date of contact. A segmented index can be used that is formatted by sales rep by next contact date. The create program uses the following key definition for this key.

```
//--------------------------------------------------------------------------
FileBuf.KeyBuf[4].KeyPos    = 207;        //KEY 3 BY >REP BY NEXT_DATE
FileBuf.KeyBuf[4].KeyLen    = 3;
FileBuf.KeyBuf[4].KeyFlags  = B_EXTENDED_KEY_TYPE |
                              B_DUPLICATES |
                              B_MODIFIABLE |
                              B_SEGMENTED;
FileBuf.KeyBuf[4].KeyType   = B_STRING;
//
FileBuf.KeyBuf[5].KeyPos    = 210;        //KEY 3 BY REP BY >NEXT_DATE
```

```
FileBuf.KeyBuf[5].KeyLen   = 4;
FileBuf.KeyBuf[5].KeyFlags = B_EXTENDED_KEY_TYPE |
                             B_DUPLICATES |
                             B_MODIFIABLE |
FileBuf.KeyBuf[5].KeyType  = B_DATE;
//
```

A Key Buffer must be formatted to contain a string followed by a date. The data structure below includes a Key Buffer for the sales rep key. In addition, it is important to pass Btrieve a Key Buffer that is large enough to contain the returned key value.

Btrieve will return a key value on most operations that involve indexing, including insert and update operations. Failing to accommodate the entire returned key value is one of the most common programming errors. If Btrieve returns a ten-byte key value in a two byte Key Buffer, other variables may be overwritten. If the Position Block is incorrectly overwritten, Btrieve returns either a status 3 (File Not Open) or a status 2 (I/O Error) on the next operations. Bugs like this can be very difficult to track down and may only appear as a problem in certain cases.

An easy way to avoid overwriting other variables with a returned Key Buffer value, is to pass a buffer of maximum key size. The largest key size that Btreive supports is 255 bytes. Since a file may contain several different key types, the "Union" option in C language is used to define the Key Buffer in different manners. A Union is similar to a structure, except that each member of a union is placed starting at the same memory location. By placing a character array, General Buffer, of maximum key size in the union, we are assured that Btrieve will not overwrite other variables with a key value. Variant records can be used in Pascal and the "Redefines" option can be used in COBOL.

In the example customer application, the customer database contains four indexes. The following code shows how to achieve the Union of these key formats in one Key Buffer.

```
//
// Key Buffer STRUCTURES
//

struct ZipCodeKeyType {
        char      zip_code[9];
        char      company[10]; };

struct SalesRepKeyType {
        char                sales_rep[3];
        struct date_type    next_date; };

union {
        int                     CustNo_Key;
        char                    CustName_Key[10];
        struct ZipCodeKeyType   ZipCode_Key;
        struct SalesRepKeyType  SalesRep_Key;
        char                    General_Key[MAX_KEY_SIZE];
      } KeyBuf;
```

In the next example, the sales rep field is segmented with a date field. Thus, with a group of records listing duplicate sales representatives, the dates are ordered chronologically. This example program displays records associated with a particular sales rep in order of next date of contact.

```
main()
{
    Open_Customer ();
    Keyno =  3;                                      // Use Sales Rep Key.
    printf("Enter Rep Code: ");                      // Prompt for Rep Code
    gets(SearchValue);
    BufLen = sizeof(CustRecBuf);
    memcpy(&KeyBuf.SalesRep_Key.sales_rep,           // Copy search value
                                                     // into Key Buffer
                       &SearchValue, 3);
    Stat    = BTRV(B_GET_GREATER_OR_EQ, CustPosBlk,  // Perform Search
             &CustRecBuf, &BufLen, &KeyBuf, Keyno);
    if(Stat != 0 )
       printf("Record not found.
               Status = %d\n", Stat);
    while ((Stat == 0 ) &&                           // Loop while not EOF,
          !memcmp(&KeyBuf, SearchValue, 3)) {        // and the key value matches
       Print_Rep_Report(&CustRecBuf);
       BufLen = sizeof(CustRecBuf);                  // Reset Buffer length to max
       Stat    = BTRV(B_GET_NEXT, CustPosBlk,        // Get the next record
                 &CustRecBuf, &BufLen,
                 &KeyBuf, Keyno);
       if(Stat != 0 && Stat != B_END_OF_FILE)        // Trap for error conditions
          printf("Error Retrieving Customer Record. Status = %d\n", Stat);
    }
    Close_Customer ();
}
```

## Supplemental Indexes

Supplemental indexes can be added and dropped at any time during the life of a Btreive file. After a supplemental index has been created, it operates like a permanent index with the exception that duplicate key values are ordered by physical record address rather than by chronological order of insert. The Create Supplemental Index (31) operation and Drop Supplemental Index (32) operation are described in full detail in Chapter 8.

The following example program adds a supplemental index that is used to find duplicate records. A segmented-key index is created on company name by customer contact name. In addition, an alternate collating sequence is used to avoid case sensitivity.

```
//
//
```

```
// CREATE SUPPLEMENTAL INDEX ON PHONE NUMBER
//
void Create_Supp_Index()

{
   struct KeySpec {
          int   KeyPos;
          int   KeyLen;
          int   KeyFlags;
          long  KeyTot;
          char  KeyType;
          char  Reserved[5];
        };

   struct AltSeq {
          char  ac_const;
          char  ac_name[8];
          char  ac_table[256]; };

   struct SuppIndexSpec {
          struct KeySpec KeyBuf[2];
          struct AltSeq alt_seq_table; };

   struct SuppIndexSpec FileBuf;
   int i;
   //
   // DEFINE SUPPLEMENTAL INDEX
   //
   //-----------------------------------------------------------------------
   FileBuf.KeyBuf[0].KeyPos = 33;          // KEY 4.1 BY >COMPANY *20 BY CONTACT
   FileBuf.KeyBuf[0].KeyLen = 8;
   FileBuf.KeyBuf[0].KeyFlags = B_EXTENDED_KEY_TYPE |
                                B_SUPPLEMENTAL      |
                                B_ALT_COLLATING     |
                                B_DUPLICATES        |
                                B_MODIFIABLE        |
                                B_SEGMENTED;
   FileBuf.KeyBuf[0].KeyType  = B_STRING;
   //-----------------------------------------------------------------------
   FileBuf.KeyBuf[1].KeyPos = 3;           // KEY 4.2 BY COMPANY *20 BY >CONTACT
   FileBuf.KeyBuf[1].KeyLen = 8;
   FileBuf.KeyBuf[1].KeyFlags = B_EXTENDED_KEY_TYPE |
                                B_SUPPLEMENTAL      |
                                B_ALT_COLLATING     |
                                B_DUPLICATES        |
                                B_MODIFIABLE;
   FileBuf.KeyBuf[1].KeyType  = B_STRING;

   // DEFINE ALTERNATE COLLATING SEQUENCE GIVING
   // EQUIVALANCE TO UPPER AND LOWER CASE
   FileBuf.alt_seq_table.ac_const = 0xAC;
   memcpy(FileBuf.alt_seq_table.ac_name,"upper   ",8);
   for(i = 0; i < 256; i++) {
      if (i < 90 || i > 123)
         FileBuf.alt_seq_table.ac_table[i] = i;      // Ignore if not lower case
      else
         FileBuf.alt_seq_table.ac_table[i] = i - 32;// Minus 32 for upper case
   }
   BufLen = sizeof(FileBuf);
   Stat = BTRV(B_CREATE_SUPP_INDEX, CustPosBlk, &FileBuf, &BufLen, KeyBuf, 4);
```

```
    if(Stat != 0)
        printf("\nError Creating Index.  Status = %d\n", Stat);
    else {
        printf("\nIndex created. Press any key... \n");
    }
}
```

When a supplemental index is added, it is referenced by the next highest Key Number. When dropping a supplemental index, the Key Number of the index must be specified. If higher Key Numbers exist, they are decremented so that successive Key Numbers are always contiguous. There can be several supplemental indexes in a file at one time. Additional supplemental indexes can be added as long as the total number of key segments does not exceed 24.

After dropping a supplemental index, the pages occupied by the index are returned to the free space list. Btrieve does not deallocate pages, but maintains empty pages to be reused at a later time. A Btrieve file will not be smaller after dropping a supplemental index. You should generate the supplemental indexes *serially,* or in other words:

- Create the first index
- Run the report
- Drop the first index
- Add the second index

By doing this, you reduce to a minimum the number of empty pages caused by a supplemental index.

## Extended Operations

Extended operations allow Btrieve to process multiple records (or record sets) in a single call. The Insert Extended (40) operation allows you to insert large numbers of records with a single insert operation. The extended Get and Step operations allow filtered traversal to be performed at the file server. Only records passing the filter condition are transmitted back to the workstation. In addition, Btrieve allows sub-records to be retrieved. Selected fields within the record can be specified, and only fields or sub-records are transmitted to the workstation. Btrieve supports the following extended operations:

- Get Next Extended (38)
- Get Previous Extended (37)
- Step Next Extended (38)
- Step Previous Extended (39)
- Insert Extended (40)

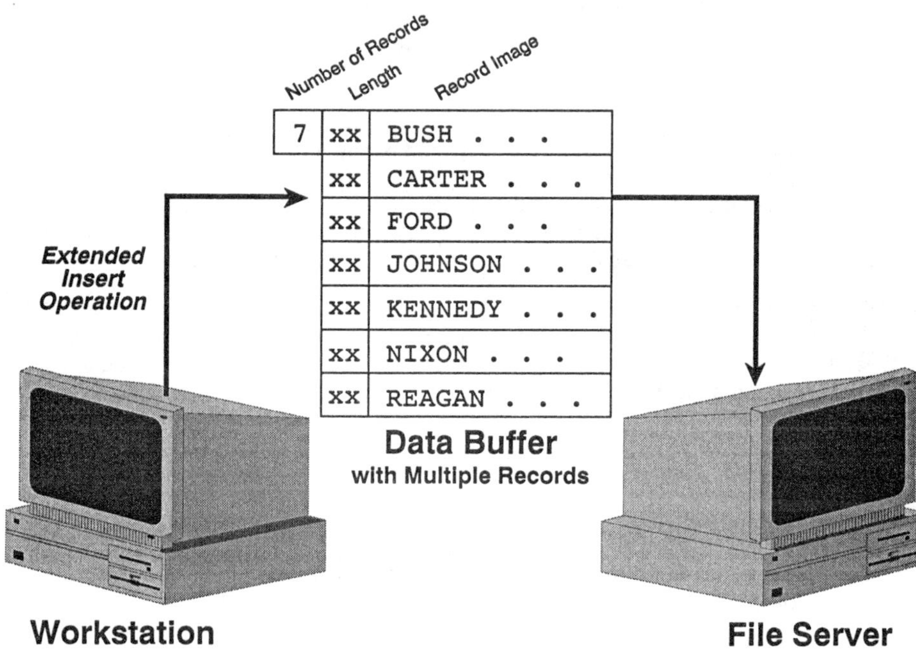


***Figure 6.1: Insert Extended***

Extended operations are Btrieve's latest contribution to high performance network database computing. The overhead of transmitting records between the file server and workstation is dramatically reduced so that no unwanted data has to be transmitted over the network. When using extended retrieval operations on heavy traffic networks, it is common for NetWare Btrieve to show a performance increase of an order of magnitude (compared to the same query performed using single record inserts). The Insert Extended (40) operation will perform from five to ten times faster than single-record inserts. The number of records inserted at a time will also effect performance.

For workstation Btreive, however, the performance improvement is not as dramatic; in some cases, extended operations may even be slower than single record operations. This performance difference is due to the fact that, with NetWare Btrieve, the number of NetWare data packet transmissions is reduced because caching is performed at the file server. With workstation Btrieve, where caching is handled by each workstation over the network, the number of SPX packets may actually *increase* due to excessive cache swapping.

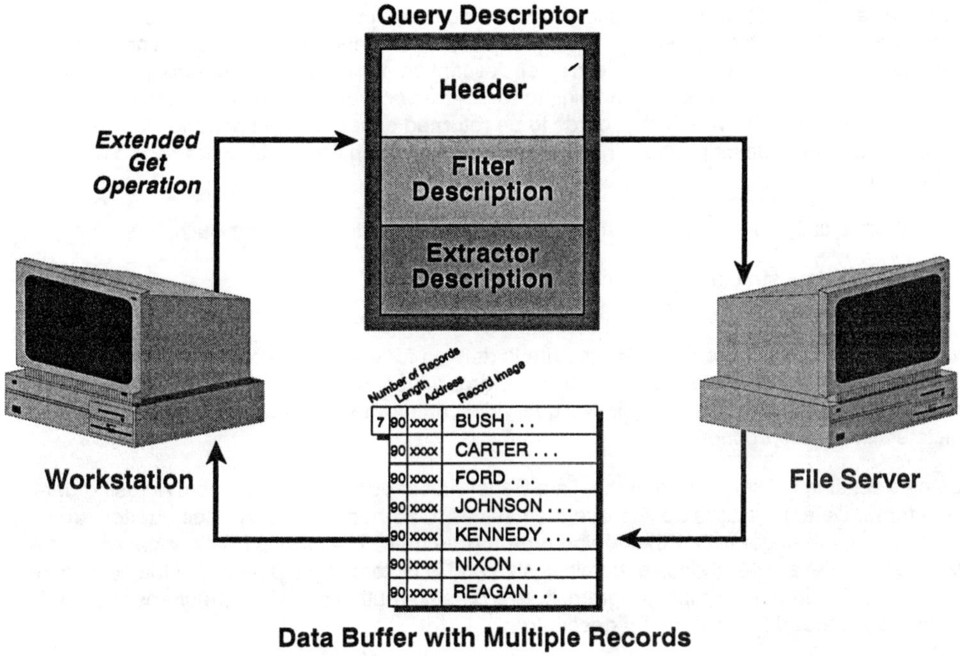


***Figure 6.2: Get Next Extended***

With extended operations, the Data Buffer is much larger. NetWare Btrieve requires that you allocate more buffer space to handle these large Data Buffers. The maximum Data Buffer Length parameter must be increased until it is at least as large as the largest Data Buffer that will be transferred to NetWare Btrieve. The "Largest Data Buffer Length" parameter (/D) for the requester must be increased as well as the "Largest Record Size" option for NetWare Btrieve.

Program complexity is the price you pay for the improved performance of extended operations. Extended operations require more programming. Programs with extended operations are more complicated because you must format the Data Buffer to accommodate multiple records. Also, for extended retrieval operations, you must tell Btrieve how to perform the query. Records in the Data Buffer must be contiguous, and contain the proper header information in a specific format. If the Data Buffer is one byte out of format, the entire extended operation will fail.

Figures 6.1 and 6.2 illustrate the Data Buffer Format for extended operations. The Extended Insert buffer contains the number of records to insert, followed by an array of record images with length bytes.

The Data Buffer serves a dual role in extended retrieval operations. After the extended retrieval is performed, the Data Buffer contains the retrieved data. Before the call, however, the Data Buffer contains a description of the query. The query description contains a control header, a filter description, and an extractor description, which describe control parameters, when to reject a record, and which fields to return respectively. The filter description (which is optional) instructs Btrieve which records to be returned based on the encoded filter description. The extractor description defines the sub-record (which fields within the record are to be returned).

Programmatically, there are two general methods of formatting the Data Buffer:

- Using data structures
- Using a parsing routine

When data structures are used, a structure is defined for each piece of information passed to Btrieve. These structures are combined into a larger query descriptor structure. Alternatively, a parsing routine can be used to fill in the query descriptor one byte at a time from left to right as dictated by the filter condition.

Using a parsing routine to format the Data Buffer has important advantages over using data structures. Data structures do not lend themselves to ad-hoc queries. Ad-hoc queries are entered in by the user rather than being pre-programmed. The Data Buffer Format of an extended retrieval operation is dynamic in size and is dictated by the length of the fields in the filter condition. In our example program, both a parsing routine and data structures are used to build the extended retrieval query descriptor.

## Extended Inserts

The following example program uses Insert Extended (40) operations to load a Customer file. The "MAX_XINSERT_RECS" constant dictates how many records are inserted at a time. This constant can be varied to fine tune the program for better performance. The Insert Extended program uses two internal buffers. The "CustRecBuf" buffer holds one record. One by one, records are read into this buffer and copied into the "XCustRecBuf" buffer which holds all of the records to be inserted. This process continues until all the records have been inserted.

```
#define MAX_XINSERT_RECS20
.
.
//
char XCustRecBuf[5000];
int  RecLen;
int  BufOffs;
int  i;
int  xctr;
long ctr,ictr;
```

```
main()
{
    Open_Customer ();
    SDFfile  = fopen("CUSTOMER.SDF","r");
    BeginTime = (double) clock();
    Keyno      = 0;                          // Maintain positioning on key 0.
    ictr       = 0;                          // Set the counter for records inserted.
    xctr       = 0;                          // Set the counter for records in buffer.
    ctr        = 0;                          // Set the counter for records read.
    BufOffs    = 2;                          // Set buffer pointer beginning of
                                             // data. The first two bytes denote
                                             // the number of records.
    fReadSDF_CustRec(&CustRecBuf,            // Read 1st record place in Data Buffer.
                     SDFfile);
    ctr = 0;
    while ( ! feof(SDFfile) )  {                 // Loop until end of file.
       xctr++;                                   // Count the records in the
                                                 // Insert Extended buffer.
       ctr++;                                    // Count the total # of records.
       RecLen = sizeof(CustRecBuf) - MAX_NOTE_SIZE  // Calc. the record length.
              + strlen(CustRecBuf.notes) + 1;
       printf("%crecord %ld, length = %d", CHR_CAR_RETURN, ctr, RecLen);
       memcpy(&XCustRecBuf[BufOffs],              // Copy length into insert buffer.
            &RecLen, sizeof(RecLen));
       BufOffs += sizeof(RecLen);                 // Set buffer offset to beginning
                                                  // of record image.
       memcpy(&XCustRecBuf[BufOffs],              // Copy the record image into the
              &CustRecBuf, RecLen);               // insert buffer.
       BufOffs += RecLen;                         // Set buffer offset to beginning
                                                  // of next record.
       fReadSDF_CustRec(&CustRecBuf, SDFfile);       // Read the next record
                                                     // from the input file.
       if ((xctr==MAX_XINSERT_RECS)  ||              // If buffer is full or EOF,
                              feof(SDFfile)) {        // insert records/reset counter.
          BufLen = BufOffs;
          memcpy(&XCustRecBuf[0], &xctr, 2);
          Stat   = BTRV(B_INSERT_EXTENDED,    // Insert records into Btrieve file.
                   CustPosBlk, &XCustRecBuf,
                   &BufLen, &KeyBuf, Keyno);
          if(Stat != 0) {                            // Check for error conditions.
              printf(" Error Inserting Customer Record. Status = %d\n", Stat);
              break;
          }
          else {
             memcpy(&i, &XCustRecBuf[0], sizeof(i)); // Count # of rec. inserts
             ictr += (long) i;                        // reported by Btrieve.
          }
          xctr    =0;
          BufOffs = 2;
       }
    }
    EndTime = (double) clock();
    d_time    = (EndTime - BeginTime) / CLK_TCK;
    Close_Customer ();
    fclose( SDFfile );
    RecPerSec = ictr / d_time;
    printf ("inserted %ld records in %6.2f seconds
            or %6.2f records per second\n",
             ictr, d_time, RecPerSec);
}
```

## Extended Retrieval Operations

There are four extended retrieval operations:

- Get Next Extended (36)
- Get Previous Extended (37)
- Step Next Extended (38)
- Step Previous Extended (39)

Before an extended retrieval operation, the Data Buffer contains the query descriptor. After the extended retrieval operation, the Data Buffer contains the data itself. Usually, several extended operations are required to retrieve all the desired data and the Btrieve call is placed in a loop. For example, retrieving a total of 1000 records with a program that only has buffer space for one hundred, you must perform ten extended retrieval operations of 100 records each.

The control parameters of the query descriptor tell Btrieve how to perform the extended retrieval operation. Setting the control parameters in harmony with current positioning is the key to an optimal search. The three control parameters are the header control constant, the reject count, and the maximum number of records.

With the Get Next Extended (36) operation, Btrieve performs a series of Get Next operations, starting at the current record, and traversing through the database until one of the following conditions is met:

- **The maximum number of records is returned.**
  Btrieve has found enough records passing the filter condition to satisfy the maximum number of records parameter value and returns a status 0 (Operation OK). At this point, there still may be records which satisfy the filter condition that have not been returned.

- **The reject count is reached.**
  Based on the filter condition, Btrieve has rejected the number of records specified in the Reject Count parameter and returns a status 60 (Reject Count Reached).

- **The filter limit is reached.**
  Btrieve has determined that no more records in the current path will satisfy the filter condition. If the primary filter condition contains a reference to a field that matches the current key's primary key segment, Btrieve determines that no other records in the database can possibly pass the filter condition and a status 64 (Filter Limit Reached) is returned.

- **The end of the file is reached.**
  When the end of the file has been reached, Btrieve returns a status 9 (End of File).

The control constant is a two-byte string with two valid settings: "EG" (for Extended Get) and "UC" (for Use Current). "EG" instructs Btrieve to begin examining records on the next record after the current record (or the previous record for the Get Previous Extended (37) operation). "UC" instructs Btrieve to include the current record.

In a loop designed to retrieve records, if a Get Equal (5) operation or a Get Greater Than or Equal (9) operation is used to establish positioning, then you should set the control constant on the first extended call to "UC." You are already positioned on one of the records that you want. Use the "EG" control constant on subsequent Get Next Extended (36) calls to avoid returning records that have already been returned. Without the "UC" control constant, the first record of the database could not be retrieved with the Get Next Extended operation.

Sometimes it is useful to return records in such a way that the last record of the previous set is the same as the first record of the next set. Record browsing programs use this method for convenience while paging through records. In such cases, use the "UC" control constant on all calls.

The "UC" control constant was added to NetWare Btrieve v5.15 and is available as a patch for v5.10. It can not be used with workstation Btrieve v5.10.

## Reject Count

The Reject Count parameter tells Btrieve to return control as soon as a specified number of records have been rejected as the result of the filter condition. An optimal search can be performed when the primary search condition contains no other fields besides the field involved in the current key. This occurs, for example, when our current key path is the zip code, and we are extracting records within a zip code range.

During an optimal search, the Reject Count is set to one and positioning is established on the first record that matches the filter condition. This is usually done with a Get Equal (5) operation or a Get Greater Than or Equal (9) operation with the control constant set to "UC." Btrieve will return control on the first record that is rejected.

For a non-optimal search (referred to as a global filtered search), positioning is established on the first record in the database and the Reject Count is set to zero. A zero setting instructs Btrieve to use the maximum Reject Count value.

The Reject Count cannot be disabled during a global filtered search. The retrieval loop must repeat while status equals 60 (Reject Count Reached). The loop ends when the end of the file is reached and a status 9 (End of File) is returned.

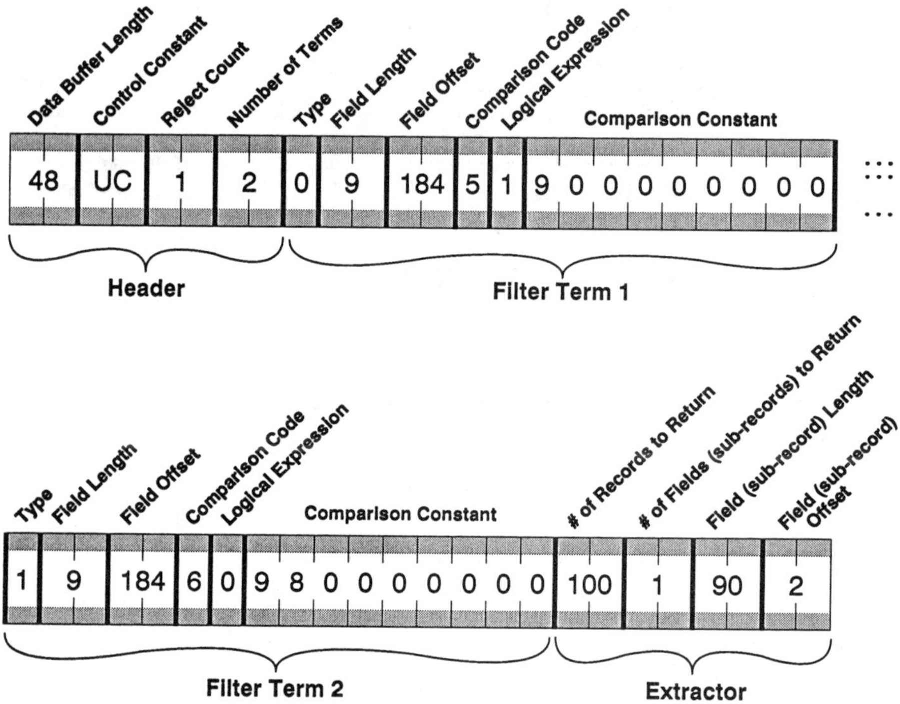


***Figure 6.3: A Data Buffer containing an example query descriptor***

## Maximum Number of Records

The "Maximum Number of Records" parameter sets the buffer limit of the calling program. A calling program has only a finite amount of buffer space. This parameter tells Btrieve to return no more than the specified number of records.

For NetWare Btrieve, the "Maximum Number of Records" value should not exceed the maximum buffer space defined by the /D (Data Buffer Size) load option of the Btrieve requester. The following equation shows the relationship between the "Maximum Number of Records" parameter and the /D requester load option.

maximum number of records X record length <= /D

| Number of Records | Length | Address | Record Image |
|---|---|---|---|
| 7 | 90 | xxxx | BUSH . . . |
| | 90 | xxxx | CARTER . . . |
| | 90 | xxxx | FORD . . . |
| | 90 | xxxx | JOHNSON . . . |
| | 90 | xxxx | KENNEDY . . . |
| | 90 | xxxx | NIXON . . . |
| | 90 | xxxx | REAGAN . . . |

***Figure 6.4: Data Buffer following an Extended Get operation***

The following example program uses extended gets to retrieve address fields for a range of zip codes entered by the user. The "Customer Name," "Company," and "Phone Number" fields are to be returned for customers with zip codes falling between 90000 and 98000. Figure 6.3 illustrates the query descriptor. Note: the Get Next Extended (36) operation is described in detail in Chapter 8. A byte-by-byte definition of the Data Buffer Format is included. Figure 6.4 illustrates the format of the Data Buffer after the call is made.

The retrieval loop is the repeating portion of the program that contains the extended retrieval call (usually a "while" loop, a "perform until" statement, or a "GoTo" statement). Notice that, in the example program, pre-positioning is established with the Get Greater Than or Equal (9) operation. Therefore, the "UC" control constant is used the first time through the loop and subsequent passes through the loop use a "EG" control constant.

```
.
.
#define MAX_XGET_RECS   10
#define MAX_BUFFER_SIZE8000     // This should be the /D value for Btrieve
requester.
//
// FUNCTION PROTOTYPES
//
// Print the customer record.
void BuildXGetDesc(char  CtrlConst[2]);
void Print_CustRecs(struct Customer_Record_Type *CustRecBuf);
//
// EXTENDED RETRIEVAL OPERATION STRUCTURES
//
struct Extended_Retrieval_Header_Type {
       int     DescLen;
       char    CtrlConst[2];
       int     RejectCnt;
       int     NoFilterTerms; };

struct Filter_Term_Type {
       char    FieldType;
       int     FieldLen;
       int     FieldOffs;
       char    CompCode;
       char    LogicalExp; };

struct Extract_Header_Type {
       int     MaxNoRecs;
       int     NoFields; };

struct Extract_Field_Type {
       int     FieldLen;
       int     FieldOffs; };
.
.
//
// APPLICATION STRUCTURES
//
struct View_Record_Image_Type {
        char    cust_name[30];
        char    company[60];
        char    addr_1[30];
        char    addr_2[30];
        char    city[30];
        char    state[2];
        char    zip[9]; };

struct View_Record_Type {
        int                            RecLen;
        long                           RecAddress;
        struct View_Record_Image_Type Image; };

struct View_Type {
        int                            NoRecs;
        struct View_Record_Type        View_Record[MAX_XGET_RECS]; };
.
.
.
.
```

```
//
// BTRIEVE FUNCTION VARIABLES
//
int      Stat;
char     CustPosBlk[128];
union {
         struct Extended_Retrieval_Header_Type XHeader;
         struct View_Type                      XRecords;
         char                                  Data_Buffer[MAX_BUFFER_SIZE];
      }  XDataBuf;
struct   Customer_Record_Type  CustRecBuf;
int      BufLen;
char     KeyBuf[255];
int      Keyno;
.
.
//
char     ZipSrch1[10];
char     ZipSrch2[10];
//
//
main()
{
    Open_Customer ();
    Keyno =  2;                                      // Use the zip code index.
    printf("\nEnter Beginning Zip Code: ");
    gets(&ZipSrch1);
    printf("\nEnter Ending Zip Code   : ");
    gets(&ZipSrch2);
    BufLen = sizeof(CustRecBuf);
    memcpy(&KeyBuf, &ZipSrch1, sizeof(ZipSrch1));
    Stat   = BTRV(B_GET_GREATER_OR_EQ, CustPosBlk,
           &CustRecBuf, &BufLen, &KeyBuf, Keyno);
    if(Stat != 0 )
       printf("No Records Found. Status = %d\n", Stat);
    BuildXGetDesc("EG");
    BufLen = sizeof(XDataBuf);
    Stat   = BTRV(B_GET_NEXT_EXTENDED, CustPosBlk,      // Get the next record.
           &XDataBuf, &BufLen, KeyBuf, Keyno);
    while (TRUE)    {
       if(  Stat == B_END_OF_FILE ||                 // Trap for these conditions.
            Stat == B_REJECT_COUNT_REACHED ||
            Stat == B_FILTER_LIMIT_REACHED  ) {
             Print_CustRecs();
             break;
       }
                 if (Stat != 0) {
          printf("Error Getting Next Extended. Status = %d\n", Stat);
          break;
       }
       Print_CustRecs();
       BufLen = sizeof(XDataBuf);
       BuildXGetDesc("EG");
       Stat   = BTRV(B_GET_NEXT_EXTENDED, CustPosBlk,    // Get the next record.
              &XDataBuf, &BufLen, KeyBuf, Keyno);
       if(Stat != 0 && Stat != B_END_OF_FILE)        // Check for error conditions
          printf("Error Getting Next Extended. Status = %d\n", Stat);
    }
    Close_Customer ();
}
```

```
//
// PLACE EXTENDED GET DESCRIPTION IN BUFFER
//
void BuildXGetDesc(char  CtrlConst[2])
{
        int    ctr;
   struct Filter_Term_Type CurTerm;
   struct Extract_Header_Type CurExtractH;
   struct Extract_Field_Type  CurExtractF;
   // DEFINE HEADER
   memcpy(&XDataBuf.XHeader.CtrlConst[0], CtrlConst, 2);
   XDataBuf.XHeader.RejectCnt        =  1;
   XDataBuf.XHeader.NoFilterTerms    = 2;
   ctr=sizeof(XDataBuf.XHeader);
         //
   // DEFINE FIRST TERM OF FILTER
   CurTerm.FieldType  = B_STRING;
   CurTerm.FieldLen   = 9;
   CurTerm.FieldOffs  =184;
   CurTerm.CompCode   =B_GREATER_OR_EQUAL;
   CurTerm.LogicalExp = B_AND;
   memcpy(&XDataBuf.Data_Buffer[ctr], &CurTerm, sizeof(CurTerm));
   ctr+=sizeof(CurTerm);
   memcpy(&XDataBuf.Data_Buffer[ctr], &ZipSrch1, 9);
   ctr+=9;
   //
   // DEFINE SECOND TERM OF FILTER
   CurTerm.FieldType  = B_STRING;
   CurTerm.FieldLen   = 9;
   CurTerm.FieldOffs  =184;
   CurTerm.CompCode   =B_LESS_OR_EQUAL;
   CurTerm.LogicalExp = B_END_OF_TERM;
   memcpy(&XDataBuf.Data_Buffer[ctr], &CurTerm, sizeof(CurTerm));
   ctr+=sizeof(CurTerm);
   memcpy(&XDataBuf.Data_Buffer[ctr], &ZipSrch2, 9);
   ctr+=9;
   //
   // DEFINE EXTRACTOR
   CurExtractH.MaxNoRecs= MAX_XGET_RECS;
   CurExtractH.NoFields = 1;
   memcpy(&XDataBuf.Data_Buffer[ctr], &CurExtractH, sizeof(CurExtractH));
   CurExtractF.FieldLen  = sizeof(XDataBuf.XRecords.View_Record[0].Image);
   CurExtractF.FieldOffs =2;
   ctr+=sizeof(CurExtractH);
   memcpy(&XDataBuf.Data_Buffer[ctr], &CurExtractF, sizeof(CurExtractF));
   XDataBuf.XHeader.DescLen  = ctr + sizeof(CurExtractF);

}
```

## Multiuser programming

Btrieve began supporting networked or multiuser capabilities when Btrieve\N (N for network) was introduced. Before, running single-user Btrieve on a network could result in severe file damage.

There are several advantages to using Btrieve for multiuser programming:

- Multiuser programs can be executed on a stand-alone PC and operate just as they would on a network.
- Multiuser programs can be tested on a standalone workstation to simulate a network environment (using the DOS share command).
- No extra drivers, libraries, or function calls are required for a multiuser environment.
- The same logic is used for workstations that are not attached to a network as workstations that are on a network.
- Btrieve has automatic multiuser capabilities that take over even if the application does not contain any multiuser logic.

Btrieve applications do not have to be recompiled for each type of network. Applications can run on any network as long as the network adheres to DOS 3.1 file and record locking standards.

You can run a single-user Btrieve application on a network and be assured that files will not be corrupted as the result of two workstations attempting to update the same record simultaneously. Existing single-user programs can be modified to work efficiently in a multiuser environment by making a few logic changes and trapping for additional multiuser status codes.

### Passive Concurrency

The term "concurrency" describes the situation when two or more applications attempt to access the same data at the same time. Passive concurrency is a feature of Btrieve that protects against data corruption as the result of concurrency, even if the application takes no special steps to handle concurrency. For database applications, concurrency only poses a threat during operations that update files. Btrieve's passive concurrency shows itself as a status 80 (Conflict Error). Btrieve returns a conflict error whenever two applications attempt to update the same data at the same time.

With NetWare Btrieve, a conflict error occurs at the record level. For example, if Application One reads a record in order to update the record, and Application Two updates the record after

Application One has read it, Application One will receive a conflict error when it attempts to update the record. Application One must then reread the record before it can successfully update it.

With workstation Btrieve, conflict errors occur at the page level. In this case, if Application One reads a record and Application Two updates a record on the same pages since Application One read the record, Application One will receive a conflict error.

Sometimes, you need to trap for a conflict error. In other cases, it is desirable to eliminate the possibility of a conflict error entirely. This is accomplished with record locking.

## Record Locking

Btrieve supports two basic types of locks that can be placed on a record: Wait and No-Wait locks. Differences between these two types of locks become apparent when you attempt to lock a record that is already locked or to lock a record in a file that has a file lock placed on it.

With No-Wait locks, when an attempt is made to lock an already-locked record, a status code is immediately returned indicating that a lock is in place. A status 84 (Record in Use) is returned if another process has a record lock placed on the record (record locks always work at the record level —never at the page level). A status 85 (File in Use) is returned if the entire file is locked by another process.

There are several situations that can cause a file lock:

- A file is opened in exclusive mode.
- A transaction is initiated on a file (see transaction processing).
- Workstation Btrieve momentarily places a lock on a file during an update operation.
- A supplemental index is being added or dropped.
- A Set Owner operation is encrypting or decrypting a file.

The real trick to multiuser programming with No-Wait locks is deciding what to do when an attempted lock fails. A "Busy-Wait" loop is often used in this case; the application continues attempting to lock the record until the lock is released by the other process or it is decided to abandon the attempt.

With a Wait lock, if an attempt is made to lock a record that is already locked by another process, control is not returned to the calling program until the lock is released by the other process. Wait-locks can result in the workstation itself "locking." The advantage of Wait locks with NetWare Btrieve is that Btrieve performs the "Busy-Wait" logic without causing any excess network traffic. If the application is written so that a lock will never be in place for more than several seconds, workstation lockup can be avoided.

In addition to No-Wait and Wait locks, Btrieve allows single-record locks and multiple-record locks. There are several differences between single- and multiple-record locks.With single-record locks, only one record can be locked in a file at any given time. With multiple-record locks, the "Maximum Number of Locks" load option determines how many records can be locked at any given time.

With single-record locks, attempting to lock another record unlocks the previously locked record. The following operations also unlock a single-record lock:

- Unlock (27)
- Delete (4)
- Update (3)
- Close (1)
- Reset (28)

The following operations unlock a multiple-record lock:

- Unlock (27)
- Close (1)
- Reset (28)

Record locking is achieved by applying a lock bias. Adding a lock bias to a retrieval operation causes the record to be locked. All retrieval operations (with the exception of extended operations) can lock a record.

There is no explicit lock operation. Record locks are always the result of a retrieval operation, guaranteeing that the record in the Data Buffer contains the same data as the record that is locked on the disk. Btrieve supports the following lock biases:

- +100 Single-record Wait lock
- +200 Single-record No-Wait lock
- +300 Multiple-record Wait lock
- +400 Multiple-record No-Wait lock

To perform an operation with a locking bias, you add the opcode to the bias value. So, to perform a Get Equal (5) operation with a single-record No-Wait lock, you would call opcode 205.

**Note:** Wait locks are not supported with Workstation Btrieve for Windows and OS/2.

## Network Simulation with Btrieve

For a Btrieve for DOS multiuser application running on a standalone workstation, the DOS SHARE.EXE command must be loaded. SHARE is a TSR that allows locking to take place at the local level. To simulate a network in single tasking DOS environment:

1) Run SHARE.EXE

2) Use a function executor (i.e. BX, B.EXE) to place a record lock

3) Run your application

The lock will be still in place when your application tries to access the record, just as though it had been placed by another workstation on a network.

The Windows environment provides another excellent way to simulate a network with Btrieve for DOS. To simulate a network with Windows:

1) Run SHARE.EXE

2) Load Windows

3) Activate two DOS boxes and run BTRIEVE.EXE in both

4) Run your multiuser application in each box

In the following code example, the BUPDATE program from Appendix B is modified to work more efficiently in a multiuser environment. This means adding a little persistence to the Get Equal (5) and lock operations by writing a loop that attempts to lock the record before the update. A single-record, No-Wait lock is used. If the record or file is locked, the program delays for several seconds, and then attempts to retrieve and lock the record. This process is repeated until the lock is cleared or the maximum number of retries is exceeded. If the maximum number of retries is exceeded, the program "times out" and the program terminates.

```
.
.
#define MAX_RETRYS      10      //
#define DELAY_MSECS     5000    // Delay five seconds
.
.
.
main()
{
    .
    .
    .
    while ( ! feof(SDFfile) )  {      .
        .
        printf("Searching for customer: %d.",
```

```
            Cust_No_Key);
      retry = 0;
      do {                                                // Multiuser retry loop
         retry++;
         BufLen = sizeof(CustRecBuf);                     // Set buffer length to max
         Stat = BTRV(B_GET_EQUAL+B_SINGLE_NO_WAIT,        // Search for record
                  CustPosBlk, &CustRecBuf,&BufLen,        // and lock.
                  &Cust_No_Key, Keyno);
         if (Stat == 0 ||
            Stat == B_KEY_NOT_FOUND) break;
         if (retry > MAX_RETRYS) break;
         printf("\rFile conatins a lock. Pausing before attempt %d....
", retry);
         delay( DELAY_MSECS );                            // Wait five seconds
       } while (Stat == B_RECORD_IN_USE ||                // Keep trying if one of these
                Stat == B_FILE_IN_USE   ||                // status codes is returned.
                Stat == B_IO_ERROR );
      if (retry >= MAX_RETRYS) {
         printf("\ntime out, program aborted. Status = %d",Stat);
         break;
         .
         .
      }
   }
   Close_Customer ();
   fclose( SDFfile );
}
```

## Transaction Processing

Transaction processing is used to ensure one thing: "If all of the update operations do not occur, then none of the operations will occur."

A transaction is a set of Btrieve operations that are executed after a Begin Transaction (19) operation and before a End Transaction (20) or Abort Transaction (21) operation. Transactions are used to guarantee logical file integrity and avoid conflicting data. Transactions use pre-image files to store updated pages. Updated pages are added to the pre-image file during a transaction until an End Transaction or Abort Transaction operation, or until the program terminates.

If an Abort transaction operation is performed, all of the pages in the pre-image file are inserted back into the Btrieve file, replacing the updated page. This procedure is called a transaction rollback and results in the undoing of all update operations that occurred within the transaction. If a program aborts during a transaction, the "Transaction Pending" flag in the FCR indicates that a transaction must be rolled back. The next process that accesses the file and reads the FCR will initiate a transaction rollback.

## Initiating a Transaction

The Begin Transaction (19) operation does not actually initiate a transaction —the next operation to access a file after the Begin Transaction operation does. Initiating a transaction places a lock on the file. Any Btrieve operation (not just update operations) can prompt Btrieve to attempt to place a lock on a file. Transactions default to a Wait lock, so any operation can potentially place the process in a Wait lock state. Because of this, use a No-Wait lock bias on the Begin Transaction operation. This combination allows you to avoid locking up the workstation with transactions. If an operation attempts to initiate a transaction on a file with a lock, a status 84 (Record in Use) or a status 85 (File in Use) will be returned.

Earlier in this chapter, the update program was modified to handle concurrency. If one of the updates timed out, the program stopped. In the following example, the update program is further modified to use a transaction. A Transaction will be used to roll back or undo previous update operations in the event of a "time out." This procedure assures that, if the program "times out," none of the updates have occurred. The program can be started again without duplicating any previously performed update operation.

```
.
.
.
main()
{
    Open_Customer ();
    SDFfile  = fopen("UPDATES.SDF","r");
    fReadSDF_Field(&SDFCust_No, 5, B_NUMERIC, SDFfile);
    Keyno = 0;
    Stat   = BTRV(B_BEGIN_TRANSACTION+B_SINGLE_NO_WAIT,
                  CustPosBlk, &CustRecBuf, &BufLen, bFileName, Keyno);
    if(Stat != 0)
           printf("Error beginning transaction.  Status = %d \n", Stat);
    else
           printf("Transaction on\n");
    while ( ! feof(SDFfile) )  {
       Cust_No_Key = (int) atoi(SDFCust_No);         // Read customer number
       printf("Searching for customer: %d.",
                 Cust_No_Key);
       retry = 0;
                    do {                             // Multiuser retry loop.
          retry++;
          BufLen = sizeof(CustRecBuf);               // Set buffer length to max.
          Stat = BTRV(B_GET_EQUAL+B_SINGLE_NO_Wait,  // Find record and lock.
                    CustPosBlk, &CustRecBuf,&BufLen,
                    &Cust_No_Key, Keyno);
          if (Stat == 0  ||
              Stat == B_KEY_NOT_FOUND) break;
          if (retry > MAX_RETRYS) break;
          printf("\rFile conatins a lock. Pausing before attempt %d....
", retry);
          delay( DELAY_MSECS );                      // Wait five seconds.
       } while (Stat == B_RECORD_IN_USE  ||          // Keep trying if one of these
                Stat == B_FILE_IN_USE    ||          // status codes is returned.
                Stat == B_IO_ERROR );
```

```
        if (retry >= MAX_RETRYS) {
           printf("\ntime out, program aborted. Status = %d",Stat);
           Stat   = BTRV(B_ABORT_TRANSACTION, CustPosBlk, &CustRecBuf,
                        &BufLen, bFileName, Keyno);
           if(Stat != 0)
                  printf("\nError aborting transaction.  Status = %d \n", Stat);
           else
                  printf("\nTransaction aborted.");
           break;
        }
        .
        .
    }
    Stat    = BTRV(B_END_TRANSACTION, CustPosBlk, &CustRecBuf,
                  &BufLen, bFileName, Keyno);
    if(Stat != 0)
           printf("\nError ending transaction.  Status = %d \n", Stat);
    else
           printf("\nTransaction completed.");
    Close_Customer ();
    fclose( SDFfile );
}
```

## Writing Btrieve NLMs

The compiler provided with Novell's Network C for NLMs Software Developer's Kit can be used to develop NetWare Loadable Modules (NLMs). NLMs are executed at a NetWare file server and become part of the operating system itself. CLIB is an NLM that provides a vast number of function calls to other NLMs. Thus, most NLMs require that CLIB be loaded as well.

Calling Btrieve at the NLM level is just like calling Btrieve from a workstation. All the rules that apply to developing workstation Btrieve applications also apply to server-based applications.

NetWare is a non-preemptive, multi-threaded operating system. Thus, an NLM can have multiple occurrences, or "threads," operating concurrently. For this reason, the Btrieve function call for an NLM supports an additional parameter, Client ID. The following Btrieve function is used for multi-threaded NLMs.

```
#define WORD unsigned short integer
typedef char ClientID_Type[16]
extern WORD btrvID ( WORD OpCode,
                     void *PosBlk,
                     void *DataBuf
                     word *DataLen,
                     void *KeyBuf,
                     short KeyNum,
                     Client_IDType *ClientID };
```

A single task function call is available as well without a client ID.

```
extern WORD btrv    ( WORD OpCode,
                      void *PosBlk,
                      void *DataBuf
                      word *DataLen,
                      void *KeyBuf,
                      short KeyNum      };
```

For the multi-threaded Btrieve call, the ClientID format is shown in Figure 6.5.

***Figure 6.5: Client ID Format***

| Offset | Length | Function |
|---|---|---|
| 0 | 12 | Node ID assigned by the operating system |
| 12 | 4 | Process ID within node assigned by calling NLM |

The Process ID must be greater than or equal to ASCII AA (4141h) and should be a meaningful identification or mnemonic. Each client must have a unique Process ID for concurrency and transaction processing.

The first time a call is made for a specific client, set the Node ID to all zeros. Btrieve will recognize this as a new client and assign a network Node ID. Subsequent calls for this client should pass the assigned Node ID to identify the client.

If a Btrieve request is made to the local NetWare Btrieve NLM, Btrieve calls an exported Btrieve function that uses the same parameters. The operation is processed at the local server and the result is placed directly into the caller's workspace before control is returned to the application.

If BROUTER.NLM is loaded, all Btrieve calls are picked up by BROUTER. If the call is for local data, BROUTER relays the call to NetWare Btrieve. If the request is for data on another file server, BROUTER handles the request in the same manner as a workstation Requester. The request is packaged in an SPX request buffer and transferred to the other server where BSPXCOM services the request, just as though it had been made by a workstation.

Novell encourages developers to write NLMs and offers training for developing NLMs. For information on Novell training, call 1-800-233-3382 and ask for the latest course schedule.

# 7 Loading Btrieve

Btrieve comes in a variety of configurations. The original Btrieve ran on a single-user PC under DOS. When Microsoft introduced network support for DOS, Multiuser Btrieve was released and named Btrieve/N. Novell made Btrieve available as a VAP (Value Added Process) for NetWare v2.x. When NetWare v3.x was introduced, Btrieve was redesigned to run as an NLM (NetWare Loadable Module). Versions of Btrieve for Windows and Btrieve for OS/2 were also introduced. Btrieve can also run in a DOS box inside of Windows and OS/2. (Yet another version of Btrieve, Btrieve for Xenix, was also introduced, but Novell discontinued support for this product).

## Operating Modes

There are many environments or platforms in which Btrieve can operate. In order to understand the different load procedures, consider that there are only two basic modes of operation for Btrieve: client-server mode and workstation mode. Figure 7.1 illustrates that in client-server mode, the application program at the workstation communicates to the Btrieve requester. The requester in turn makes requests through the NetWare shell to NetWare Btrieve (NLM or VAP). NetWare Btrieve performs all of the file I/O and file locking at the server.

The term, "workstation Btrieve," refers to Btrieve for DOS, OS/2, and Windows. Figure 7.2 illustrates that in workstation mode, the application program communicates to workstation Btrieve, which interacts with the local operating system to perform file I/O. If the workstation is attached to a network, Btrieve accesses shared data through the network shell (IPX and NETx) just as it does local data. With workstation Btrieve the local operating system handles all file locking.

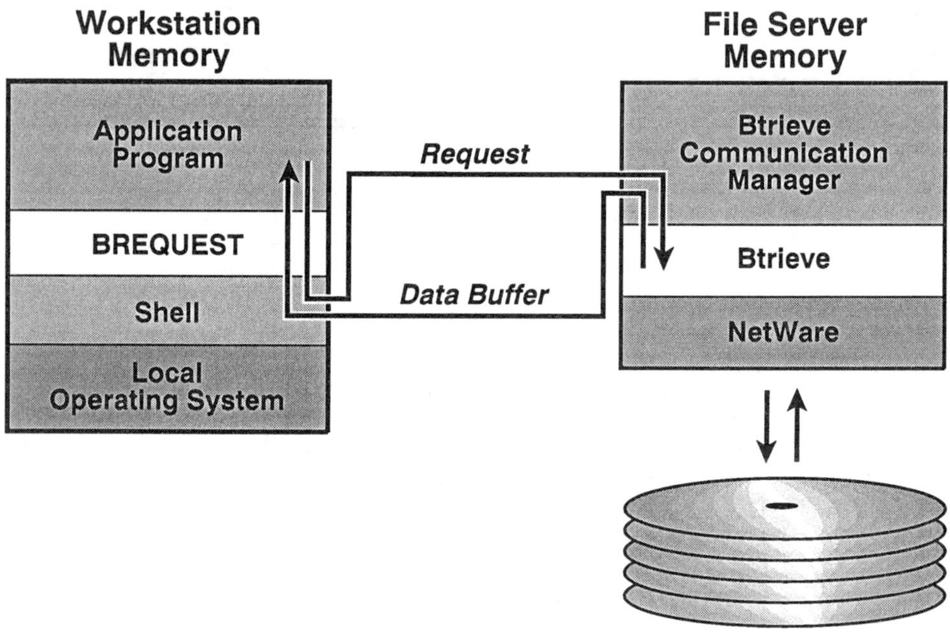


*Figure 7.1: NetWare Btrieve*

## Mixed Mode

For applications that access both shared and local data, operate Btreive in mixed mode. Mixed mode means that you load both workstation Btrieve and the NetWare Btrieve requester into the workstation's memory. In mixed mode, the requester responds first to all calls to Btrieve. If the request is for shared data, it is passed to NetWare Btrieve. If the request is for local data, the request is passed to workstation Btrieve. Figure 7.3 illustrates mixed mode operation.

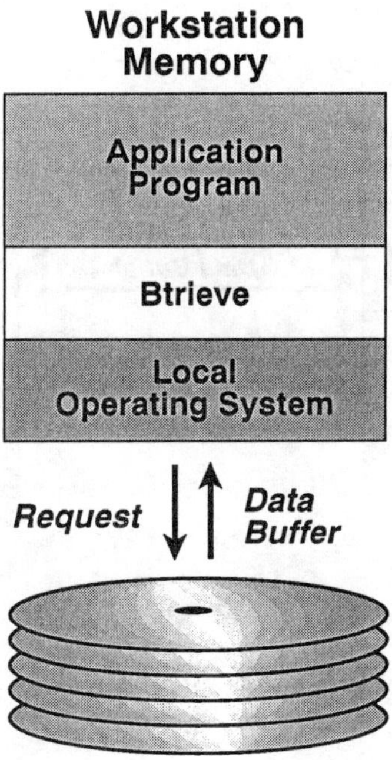


*Figure 7.2: Workstation Btrieve*

## Load Options

Btrieve's load options are use to allocate memory and resources to specific functions. The load parameters for workstation Btrieve and the Btrieve NLM are similar. Further, the load options for DOS, Windows, and OS/2 versions of Btrieve are virtually the same, as well.

With workstation Btrieve, cache buffers are located at each workstation. Therefore, each workstation must specify load options that allocate cache memory. For NetWare Btrieve, the cache buffers are located at the file server. Therefore, the requester (loaded at each workstation) has far fewer load options than workstation Btrieve (3 vs. 13).

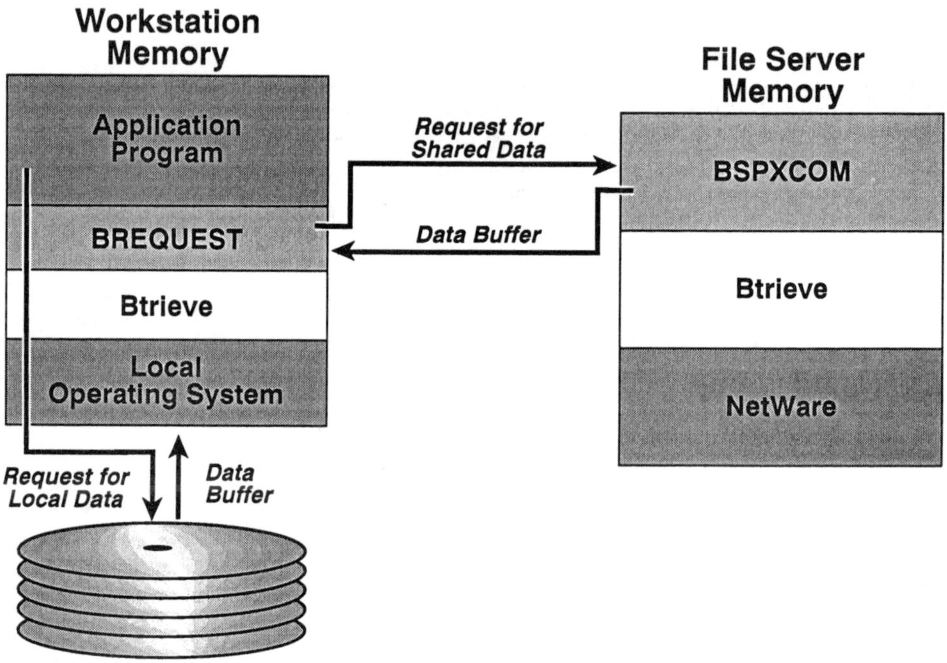


*Figure 7.3: Mixed mode*

## Loading Btrieve for DOS (workstation mode)

With Btrieve for DOS, the load options are specified as command line arguments for the Btrieve TSR executable.

```
BTRIEVE /P:1024 /M:48 /F:35
```

This command loads Btrieve with a maximum page size of 1024 bytes, with 48K for Btrieve's data area, supporting a maximum of 35 Btrieve data files open at any given time. The table in Figure 7.4 lists the load options associated with Btrieve for DOS along with the default, maximum, and minimum values.

***Figure 7.4: Btrieve for DOS load options***

| Parameter | Description | Default | Max. | Min. |
|---|---|---|---|---|
| /M | Total amount of memory allocated to Btrieve in kilobytes (KB) | 32 | 64 | 14 |
| /P | Maximum page size in bytes of any open file | 1024 | 4096 | 512 |
| /T | Transaction control file name (e.g., /T:\DATA\BTRIEVE.TRN) | — | — | — |
| /I | Pre-image file drive | Current | — | — |
| /C | Enable index compaction | — | — | — |
| /B | Pre-image buffer size in KB | 16 | 64 | 1 |
| /F | Maximum number of open files | 20 | 255 | 1 |
| /L | Maximum number of multi-record locks | 8 | 255 | 0 |
| /E | Disable use of expanded memory | — | — | — |
| /O | Override critical error | — | — | — |
| /U | Compression buffer size in KB | — | 64 | 1 |
| /N | Total number of files in a transaction | 12 | 18 | 1 |
| /A | Activate logging for selected files | — | — | — |

To unload Btrieve for DOS, use BUTIL -STOP or issue the Stop (25) operation.

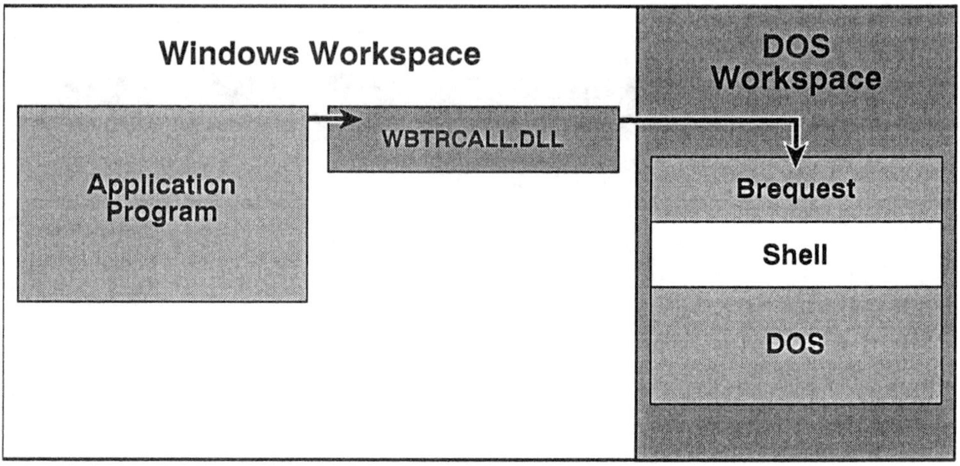


*Figure 7.5: Calling the NetWare Btrieve requester from Windows*

## Loading Btrieve for Windows 3.0 (workstation mode)

With Btrieve for Windows, the Btrieve application communicates with a DLL (dynamic link library) rather than a TSR. The Btrieve DLL, WBTRCALL, is not loaded into memory until it is called. Applications can specify the load options themselves. Therefore, the DLL contains an initialization function, WBTRVINIT() which can be called to initialize Btrieve with the proper load options.

Btrieve for Windows comes with BTRTOOLS.EXE. This utility offers a function executor as well as high-level file manipulation procedures. In addition, BTRTOOLS can be used to set the default load options for WBTRCALL.DLL.

Use the following procedure to load and initialize Btrieve and BTRTOOLS:

- Copy the contents of the distribution diskette into a directory that is included in Window's path.
- Load SHARE.EXE before loading Windows to allow record and file locking to take place between separate tasks running on the same workstation.
- Under the [386Enh] section, modify SYSTEM.INI to include

```
UniqueDOSPSP=true
```

- Link WBTRCALL.LIB to your application
- Initialize Btrieve

Btrieve can be initialized in one of two ways:

- Call the WBTRVINIT(char far *) function when the character pointer is pointing to a string containing the load options
- Set the load option in WIN.INI as follows:

```
[btrieve]
options=/m:32 /f:20 /p:1024
tracefile=btrieve.trc

[btrtools]
msgfile=c:\windows\btrverr.msg
databufsize=1024
textcolor=red
backgroundcolor=blue
```

A Trace file can be specified to keep a log of all Btrieve activity. BTRTOOLS can be used to modify the load options in WIN.INI, as well.

If the WBTRVINIT() function call is not used and the load options are not specified in WIN.INI, then the default load options are used (see Figure 7.4: Btrieve for DOS load options).

There are two methods of calling Btrieve:

- Directly calling the DLL
- Calling Btrieve through the interface

Calling Btrieve through the interface allows applications to call the Btrieve DLL using the DOS API call (refer to Chapter 3, "Interfacing with Btrieve for Windows").

## Loading Btrieve for OS/2 (workstation mode)

Like Btrieve for Windows, Btrieve for OS/2 applications communicate with a DLL rather than with a TSR. The Btrieve DLL, WBTRCALL, is not loaded into memory until it is called.

Use the following procedure to install Btrieve for OS/2:

- Copy the BTRCALLS.DLL files from the distribution diskette into one of the directories specified in the LIBPATH CONFIG.SYS directive.

- Set Btrieve's load options with the BTRPARMS environment variable. The OS/2 load options are the same as those of Btrieve for DOS (Figure 7.4).

```
SET BTRPARMS=/M:48/P:4096
```

# Loading NetWare Btrieve (client-server mode)

## Installing NetWare v3.x Btrieve

The BSETUP program is used to install NetWare Btrieve. For Btrieve v3.x, BSETUP is an NLM that must be executed from the console. BSETUP generates BSTART.NCF. This file contains two load statements that load BTRIEVE and BSPXCOM with their associated load options.

For example, BSTART.NCF may contain the following:

```
LOAD BTRIEVE -p=4096 -f=20 -h=60 -l=20 -t=4 -n=12 -u=0 -s=30
LOAD BSPXCOM -d=8192 -s=15 -w=3
```

NetWare v3.x Btrieve supports load options listed in Figures 7.6 and 7.7.

***Figure 7.6: Load options for BTRIEVE.NLM***

| Option | Description | Default | Maximum |
|---|---|---|---|
| -F | Maximum number of unique open files for Btrieve | 20 | 64K |
| -H | Maximum number of handles for Btrieve | 60 | memory |
| -L | Maximum number of locks for Btrieve | 20 | memory |
| -T | Maximum number of concurrent transactions | 0 | memory |
| -N | Maximum number of files per transaction | 12 | 18 |
| -U | Maximum record length of any compressed record in KB | 0 | 64 |
| -P | Maximum page size in bytes of any open file | 4096 | 4096 |

***Figure 7.6: Load options for BTRIEVE.NLM***

| Option | Description | Default | Maximum |
|---|---|---|---|
| -I | Automatic transaction flagging on Create | — | — |
| -A | Logging of select files | — | — |

***Figure 7.7: Load options for BSPXCOM.NLM***

| Option | Description | Default | Maximum |
|---|---|---|---|
| -D | Maximum Data Buffer size or record length in bytes | 8192 | 55296 |
| -S | Maximum number of concurrent sessions | 15 | 250 |
| -W | Number of work threads or instances of BTRIEVE.NLM | 3 | 16 |

The Btrieve distribution diskette contains two directories, System and Public. To install Btrieve

- Place the distribution diskette in drive A:
- From the console prompt, enter:

```
LOAD A:BSETUP
```

- From the main menu, select:

```
Install Btrieve
```

The files from the distribution diskette's SYSTEM directory are copied into the SYS:SYSTEM directory of the file server, and the files from the distribution diskette's PUBLIC directory are copied into the SYS:PUBLIC directory of the file server.

To load Btrieve, enter BSTART at the console. BSTOP.NCF is supplied to unload Btrieve. To change Btrieve's load parameters, run BSETUP and modify the configuration settings. Then, save these settings and exit BSETUP. Finally, unload Btrieve with BSTOP, and reload Btrieve with BSTART.

Another method of loading NetWare Btrieve v3.x is to copy the contents of the distribution diskette into the SYSTEM and PUBLIC directories yourself. If you are re-installing Btrieve, you may need to flag the Btrieve file to remove the "Delete Inhibited" flag, as shown below.

```
FLAG B*.NLM -D
FLAG B*.HLP -D
FLAG B*.NCF -D
```

In addition, the BSTART.NCF file can be edited with a standard text editor. If you are going to modify BSTART.NCF directly, be careful not to specify erroneous load parameters. This can produce unpredictable results.

The BROUTER.NLM program should also be loaded if other NLMs (such as NetWare SQL) will be communicating with NetWare Btrieve.

## Installing NetWare v2.x Btrieve

The procedure for installing the Btrieve VAP is a somewhat different than installing the BTRIEVE NLM. To install NetWare v2.x Btrieve:

- Create a directory for Btrieve under the root of volume SYS:.
- Copy the contents from the distribution diskette into the Btrieve directory.
- Run BSETUP.EXE from the Btrieve directory that you have created.
- From the BSETUP main menu, select:

  ```
  Set Configuration
  ```

  and set the load options.
- From the BSETUP main menu, select:

  ```
  Install Btrieve
  ```

  Btrieve will ask if BROUTER is to be installed. BROUTER is required only if other VAPs, such as NetWare SQL, will be communicating to Btrieve.
- Reboot the file server to load the Btrieve VAP.

The Install Btrieve procedure actually modifies the Btrieve VAP executable and installs the Btrieve VAP object in the bindery. Every time NetWare v2.x boots, the operator has the option to load the Btrieve VAP. To reconfigure the load option, run BSETUP.EXE, modify the configuration settings, and install. The server must then be rebooted for the modifications to take effect.

## Loading the Btrieve Requester for DOS

In client-server mode, the memory allocation load options are all associated with Btrieve NLM and VAP at the server. The BSETUP program is used to set these options.

With the Btrieve requester for a DOS workstation, the load options are specified as command line arguments for the TSR executable.

```
BREQUEST /D:5000 /S:8 /R:16
```

***Figure 7.8: Btrieve requester load options***

| Option | Description | Default |
|---|---|---|
| /R | Maximum number of mapped drives (Redirection table) | 26 |
| /D | Maximum Data Buffer Length | 4096 |
| /S | Number of attached Btrieve file servers | 8 |

To unload the DOS requester use BUTIL -STOP or issue a Stop (25) operation.

## Loading and Initializing the Btrieve Requester for Windows

Windows is not a true multitasking operating system and is reliant on DOS for file I/O. Therefore Brequest (the Btrieve requester for DOS) must be loaded prior to loading Windows. The Btrieve DLL, WBTRCALL, simply communicates with the Brequest TSR for database operations. Workstation Btrieve for Windows' DLL is also called WBTRCALL. If the requester is to be used with workstation Btrieve, rename workstation Btrieve to WBTRLOCL.

Initialization options for Btrieve are placed WIN.INI as follows:

```
[BREQUESTDPMI]
datalength=4096
tasks=10
local=no
chkparms=no
```

The "datalength" setting corresponds with the Brequest /D option. The "Tasks" option specifies how many concurrent tasks may use WBTRCALL.DLL at one time. Set the "Local" option to "yes" if workstation Btrieve will be used with the requester for accessing local data. The "Chkparms" option instructs the DLL to validate pointers. Pointer validation will cause a performance degradation and is recommended only for use in development.

The WBTRVSTOP() function is used to properly terminate a Btreive task. This function removes the Btreive task from the DLL's task list and terminates the SPX session that the requester has with NetWare Btrieve. A non-zero return code indicates that files are open or transactions are in progress. The Btrieve Reset (28) operation closes all files and aborts all transactions.

### Loading and Initializing the Btrieve Requester for OS/2

To load the OS/2 requester, copy BTRCALLS.DLL into a DLL specified in CONFIG.SYS. The requester's load options are specified with the OS/2 environment variable, "BRQPARMS."

```
SET BRQPARMS=/R:10 /D:2048 /S:2
```

Each load option must be separated with a blank and there must be no space between the BRQPARMS and the equal sign.

If you use workstation Btrieve with the requester, you must use the MAKLOCAL.EXE utility to convert and rename workstation Btrieve to BTRLOCAL.DLL (do not use the "RENAME" command as with the Windows requester). Workstation Btrieve only operate with the requester after running MAKLOCAL.EXE.

## Loading Btrieve in a Windows DOS Box

### Workstation Mode

In order to access database files on a local disk drive from a Windows DOS box, BTRIEVE.-EXE must be loaded in the same manner as BREQUEST for client-server mode. In addition, TBMI and TASKID must be used. The DOS SHARE.EXE program must be loaded before loading Windows in order for multiple DOS application tasks to perform record and file locking at a local level.

## Client-Server Mode

In order to maintain multiple DOS windows that communicate to NetWare Btrieve via BREQUEST.EXE, BREQUEST must be loaded in each window. In addition, the TBMI.EXE TSR program (Task Buffer Manager for IPX) must be used along with TASKID.EXE. TBMI is loaded prior to Windows and each DOS window executes TASKID before loading BREQUEST. The TBMI utility is available as shareware on CompuServe and is freely distributed by Novell technical support. Avoid using versions of TBMI and TASKID that are dated before 12/19/1990.

TBMI and TASKID were developed to synchronize programs running in a multitasking environment that make IPX/SPX calls directly (as opposed to using the NetWare shell). TBMI is located in Windows global memory segment and intercepts calls to IPX/SPX. The TASKID programs running in each window assign task ID information to each communication, allowing TBMI to synchronize communication to NetWare. Only the patched BREQUEST.EXE v5.15 and v5.16 will function properly in a windows DOS box.

A batch file to initialize windows must contain the following:

- TBMI
- WIN
- TBMI /U

Each DOS window is initialized in the following sequence:

- TASKID
- BREQUEST
- Btrieve Program
- TASKID /U

TASKID (with /U option) must be unloaded before closing the DOS session. Failure to unload TASKID before closing a DOS session can result in the system locking up.

# 8 Btrieve Operation Codes

## How to Use This Chapter

In this chapter, each Btrieve operation is described in full detail using a standard format. These descriptions are intended to be used by programmers who are making calls to Btrieve.

Each operation code description contains the following sections:

| | |
|---|---|
| **Function** | A brief description of the operation code. |
| **Parameter Table** | A full description of each Btrieve parameter, including what the parameter should contain before the Btrieve call and what the parameter contains after the Btrieve call. |
| **Notes** | Specific notes describing characteristics that are unique to the operation. |
| **Common Status Codes** | Common status codes associatedwith the operation, along with the cause of the status code and the recommended corrective action. |
| **Positioning** (where applicable) | A description of how the operation effects positioning. |
| **Available Bias Values** | A listing of bias values that can be applied to the operation. |
| **Extended Operation** (where applicable) | If the operation supports an extended (multi-record) version of the operation, it is indicated. |

| Operation Code | Operation | Category |
|---|---|---|
| 1 | Close | Initialize |
| 2 | Insert | File Modification |
| 3 | Update | File Modification |
| 4 | Delete | File Modification |
| 5 | Get Equal | Retrieval/Search |
| 6 | Get Next | Retrieval/Traversal |
| 7 | Get Previous | Retrieval/Traversal |
| 8 | Get Greater Than | Retrieval/Search |
| 9 | Get Greater Than or Equal | Retrieval/Search |
| 10 | Get Less Than | Retrieval/Search |
| 11 | Get Less Than or Equal | Retrieval/Search |
| 12 | Get First | Retrieval/Traversal |
| 13 | Get Last | Retrieval/Traversal |
| 14 | Create | Create |
| 15 | Stat | Status |
| 16 | Extend | Miscellaneous |
| 17 | Set Directory | Miscellaneous |
| 18 | Get Directory | Miscellaneous |
| 19 | Begin Transaction | Transaction |
| 20 | End Transaction | Transaction |
| 21 | Abort Transaction | Transaction |
| 22 | Get Position | Direct Access |
| 23 | Get Direct | Direct Access |
| 24 | Step Next | Retrieval/Traversal |
| 25 | Stop | Initialize |
| 26 | Version | Status |
| 27 | Unlock | Lock Operation |
| 28 | Reset | Initialize |
| 29 | Set Owner | Initialize |
| 30 | Clear Owner | Initialize |
| 31 | Create Supplemental Index | Create |
| 32 | Drop Supplemental Index | Create |
| 33 | Step First | Retrieval/Traversal |
| 34 | Step Last | Retrieval/Traversal |
| 35 | Step Previous | Retrieval/Traversal |
| 36 | Get Next Extended | Retrieval/Traversal |
| 37 | Get Previous Extended | Retrieval/Traversal |
| 38 | Step Next Extended | Retrieval/Traversal |
| 39 | Step Previous Extended | Retrieval/Traversal |
| 40 | Insert Extended | File Modification |

| Operation | Operation Code | Category |
|---|---|---|
| Abort Transaction | 21 | Transaction |
| Begin Transaction | 19 | Transaction |
| Clear Owner | 30 | Initialize |
| Close | 1 | Initialize |
| Create | 14 | Create |
| Create Supplemental Index | 31 | Create |
| Delete | 4 | File Modification |
| Drop Supplemental Index | 32 | Create |
| End Transaction | 20 | Transaction |
| Extend | 16 | Miscellaneous |
| Get Direct | 23 | Direct Access |
| Get Directory | 18 | Miscellaneous |
| Get Equal | 5 | Retrieval/Search |
| Get First | 12 | Retrieval/Traversal |
| Get Greater Than | 8 | Retrieval/Search |
| Get Greater Than or Equal | 9 | Retrieval/Search |
| Get Last | 13 | Retrieval/Traversal |
| Get Less Than | 10 | Retrieval/Search |
| Get Less Than or Equal | 11 | Retrieval/Search |
| Get Next | 6 | Retrieval/Traversal |
| Get Next Extended | 36 | Retrieval/Traversal |
| Get Position | 22 | Direct Access |
| Get Previous | 7 | Retrieval/Traversal |
| Get Previous Extended | 37 | Retrieval/Traversal |
| Insert | 2 | File Modification |
| Insert Extended | 40 | File Modification |
| Reset | 28 | Initialize |
| Set Directory | 17 | Miscellaneous |
| Set Owner | 29 | Initialize |
| Stat | 15 | Status |
| Step First | 33 | Retrieval/Traversal |
| Step Last | 34 | Retrieval/Traversal |
| Step Next | 24 | Retrieval/Traversal |
| Step Next Extended | 38 | Retrieval/Traversal |
| Step Previous | 35 | Retrieval/Traversal |
| Step Previous Extended | 39 | Retrieval/Traversal |
| Stop | 25 | Initialize |
| Unlock | 27 | Lock Operation |
| Update | 3 | File Modification |
| Version | 26 | Status |

# Open (0)

## Function

The Open (0) operation makes a Btrieve file available to access and establishes a connection with the Btrieve record manager. Performing an Open initializes the Position Block parameter to uniquely identify the Btrieve file specified in the Key Buffer parameter.

| Parameter | Before Call | After Call |
|---|---|---|
| **Position Block** | The Position Block must be pointing to a protected 128 byte array. | The Position Block is initialized to identify the opened file. |
| **Data Buffer** | The Data Buffer must contain the owner name for files with owner protection. Owner name must end with a binary zero or a blank space delimiter. | The Data Buffer value is not returned. |
| **Data Buffer Length** | For owner names, the Data Buffer Length must contain the length of the owner name including delimiter. Otherwise, it should be set to a low value, such as zero. | The Data Buffer Length value is not returned. |
| **Key Buffer** | The Key Buffer contains the filename of the file to open, including full pathname, if needed. The filename must be terminated by a blank character or binary zero. | The Key Buffer is not modified. |
| **Key Number** | The Key Number contains the following access modes:<br>1) Accelerated Mode<br>2) Read-Only Mode<br>3) Verify<br>4) Exclusive<br>See Notes for explanation of these modes. | The Key Number is not modified. |

## Notes

The application program cannot perform any Btrieve operations on a file until it is opened.

The Key Buffer parameter can accept full or partial pathnames and drive letters.

Make sure the file name in the Key Buffer is terminated with a blank space or a binary zero.

Specify the owner name in Data Buffer if required.

A file can be opened several times within the same application as long as there is a unique Position Block for each occurrence of the opened file.

File access mode Key Number values do the following:

**0 Normal Mode**
A file opened in normal mode can be modified, shared with other users, and has full pre-imaging data recovery enabled.

**-1 Accelerated Mode**
Accelerated mode disables flushing of the pre-image buffer before every each operation. Thus, automatic data recovery must be considered disabled. Modifications made to a file in accelerated mode are not necessarily written to disk until the file is closed with the Close(1) or Reset (28) operations.

Btrieve locks a buffer in cache for each file opened in accelerated access mode. Thus, fewer files can be opened in accelerated access mode than in non-accelerated access mode (this often results in a status 47 (Maximum Open Files).

**-2 Read-Only Mode**
Files opened in read-only mode cannot be modified with the Insert, Update, or Delete operations. This allows network users with read-only privileges to read data and run reports from Btrieve files.

Btrieve does not attempt to open pre-image files while in read-only mode. This allows damaged files with a missing or damaged pre-image file to be opened. Data can then be recovered using Step operations.

**-3 Verify Mode**
Verify mode applies only to workstation Btrieve for DOS. The DOS verify option is enabled for each operation that modifies the file. Verify mode will cause a performance degradation for update operations.

**-4 Exclusive Mode**
A file opened in exclusive mode becomes locked to other files. No other application can open the file until it is closed.

| Status Code | Cause | Correction |
|---|---|---|
| **2**<br>I/O Error | An error occurred during a disk read or write. This can be the result of hardware failure or the Btrieve file being improperly over written by a non-Btrieve program. | The file must be recreated. |
| **14**<br>Pre-image Open Error | Btrieve attempted to open the pre-image file to restore file integrity. The pre-image file was missing or could not be opened due to insufficient access privileges. | Recover the data by opening the file in read-only mode and using Step operations to recover the records or use the BUTIL recovery procedure. |
| **46**<br>Access to File Denied | The application attempted an Insert, Update, or Delete operation while the file was in read-only mode.<br><br>The application attempted an Insert, Update, or Delete on a file requiring an owner name. | Open the file in normal mode.<br><br>Open the file with the correct owner name (specified in the Data Buffer). |
| **85**<br>File in Use | An attempt was made to open a file while another application had the file locked by opening it in exclusive mode or as the result of a transaction.<br><br>For workstation Btrieve, NetWare Btrieve has the file opened. | Retry the Open operation on the file.<br><br>Use NetWare Btrieve or have the other application use workstation Btrieve. |
| **86**<br>File Table Full | The Open operation would have exceeded the maximum number of opened files configured for Btrieve. | Reload Btrieve with a larger "Maximum Number of Open Files" load option. |
| **87**<br>Handle Table Full | The Open operation would have exceeded the maximum number of file handles configured for Btrieve. | Reload Btrieve with a larger "Maximum Number of File Handles" configuration setting. |

| Status Code | Cause | Correction |
|---|---|---|
| **94**<br>Permission Error | With NetWare Btrieve, the workstation does not have read/write privileges for the file. | Open the file in read-only mode or grant read/write privileges to the workstation. |
| | For NetWare Btrieve, a version of workstation Btrieve has the file opened. | Use workstation Btrieve or have the other application use NetWare Btrieve. |

## Positioning

No positioning is established.

## Available Biases

No lock bias is available. Some versions of Btrieve accept a lock bias on the Open operation; however, the bias is ignored and the file does not become locked. Use exclusive mode to lock the file (see Key Number parameter above).

# Close (1)

## Function

The Close (1) operation closes an open Btrieve file, releases all locks, and flushes all buffers.

| Parameter | Before Call | After Call |
|---|---|---|
| **Position Block** | The Position Block must be initialized for an open file. | All positioning associated with the file is removed. |
| **Data Buffer** | No Data Buffer value is required. | No Data Buffer value is returned. |
| **Data Buffer Length** | No Data Buffer Length value is required. | No Data Buffer Length value is returned. |
| **Key Buffer** | No Key Buffer value is required. | No Key Buffer value is returned. |
| **Key Number** | No Key Number value is required. | No Key Number value is returned. |

## Notes

A file cannot be closed within a transaction.

If an open file is not closed, Btrieve will hold the file opened until a Reset (28) operation is issued or Btrieve is unloaded or, on a network, the workstation looses its connection.

With NetWare Btrieve, a file that remains open by Btrieve cannot be copied or deleted until Btrieve closes the file. This often results in an Access Denied network error. Use the BUTIL - RESET procedure (or the Reset operation) to close all Btrieve opened under a workstation's connection number.

| Status Code | Cause | Correction |
|---|---|---|
| **3**<br>File Not Open | The file was never opened.<br><br>The Position Block was erroneously overwritten. | Only close open files.<br><br>Determine why the Position Block was overwritten and correct. Invalid pointer values from previous Btrieve operations can cause the Position Block to be erroneously overwritten. Check the parameters on previous Btrieve calls. |
| **41**<br>Operation Not Allowed | An attempt was made to close a file within a transaction. | Terminate the transaction with an End Transaction (20), Abort Transaction (21), or Reset (28). |

## Positioning

No positioning is established.

# Insert (2)

## Function

The Insert (2) operation inserts the record image contained in the Data Buffer into the Btrieve file. It updates all indexes and establishes positioning on the inserted record.

| Parameter | Before Call | After Call |
|---|---|---|
| **Position Block** | The Position Block must be initialized by the Open operation. The Position Block is not required to have positioning established before the Insert. | The Position Block contains pointers to the currently inserted record and logical next/previous record in current key path order specified by the Key Number parameter. |
| **Data Buffer** | The Data Buffer must contain the record image to be inserted. | The Data Buffer is modified only for records with an autoincrement key to reflect the calculated autoincrement value. |
| **Data Buffer Length** | The Data Buffer Length must be at least as long and preferably the exact length of the record being inserted. | The Data Buffer Length is set to the number of bytes inserted. |
| **Key Buffer** | The Key Buffer should be as large as the key specified by the Key Number parameter. | The current key value of the inserted record is returned in the Key Buffer. |
| **Key Number** | The Key Number (zero offset) of the current key path. | The Key Number is not modified. |

## Notes

For inserting variable-length records, the Data Buffer Length parameter specifies the number of bytes being inserted.

Calculated autoincrement values are passed back in the Data Buffer as well as the Key Buffer if the Key Number parameter corresponds with the autoincrement key.

When you allow duplicate key values within permanent indexes, duplicate key records will always be retrieved in the chronological order in which they were inserted.

**Warning**
The current key value of the inserted record is always returned at the location pointed to by the Key Buffer pointer parameter. Make sure the Key Buffer pointer is pointing to a variable large enough to accommodate the key value.

| Status Code | Cause | Correction |
|---|---|---|
| **2**<br>I/O Error | An error occurred during a disk write. This can be the result of hardware failure or the Btrieve file being improperly over written by a non-Btrieve program. | The file must be recreated. |
| **3**<br>File Not Opened | The file was not opened properly. | Perform the open operation, and use the same Position Block. |
| **5**<br>Duplicate Key Error | The Position Block was overwritten. | Determine the cause and correct. An invalid pointer such as with the Key Buffer can cause a Position Block to be incorrectly overwritten. |
| **14**<br>Pre-Image Open Error | Btrieve attempted to create the pre-image file and was unable due to the disk being full.<br><br>Btrieve attempted to create the pre-image file and was unable due to insufficient access rights to the directory where the pre-image file is located. | Data integrity cannot be ensured. Issue a reset command and remove files to provide sufficient disk space.<br><br>Data integrity cannot be ensured. Proper access rights must be assigned to the workstation (see "Grant" command, NetWare manual). |
| **15**<br>Pre-image I/O Error | Btrieve attempted to write to the pre-image file and the disk is full.<br><br>The pre-image file was damaged. | Provide more disk space.<br><br>Discontinue insertion. Data integrity cannot be ensured. If the Btrieve file is inaccessible with other indexed access operations, recover the data with the BUTIL recovery and load operations. |
| **18**<br>Disk Full | The disk is full and Btrieve attempted to expand the file. | Provide more disk space. |

| Status Code | Cause | Correction |
|---|---|---|
| **22**<br>Data Buffer Length | The value specified in the Data Buffer Length is smaller than the fixed record length. | Determine the proper record length and specify that value in the Data Buffer Length parameter. |
| **46**<br>Access to File Denied | The file was opened in read-only mode.<br><br>The file requires an owner name to perform the Insert operation. | Open the file in normal mode.<br><br>Open the file with the correct owner name. |

## Positioning

**Non-duplicate key path**

Positioning is established on the inserted record for the key path specified in the Key Number parameter.

**Duplicate key path**

The inserted record becomes the last record in the chain of duplicates. For permanent indexes, this becomes the last record in chronological order of insert. For supplemental indexes, the record becomes the last record in physical address order.

## Available Biases

No lock bias is supported. Some versions accept the Insert operation with a lock bias however the record does not become locked.

## Extended Operations

Insert Extended (40)

# Update (3)

## Function

The Update (3) operation overwrites the current record with the value in the Data Buffer.

It updates all indexes, re-establishes positioning on the modified record for the current key number and returns the current key value in the Key Buffer.

| Parameter | Before Call | After Call |
|---|---|---|
| **Position Block** | The Position Block must have position established on the record to be modified with a positioning operation other than Extended Get/Step and any key-only operation. | The Position Block contains pointers to the currently modified record and logical next and previous record in current key path order. |
| **Data Buffer** | The Data Buffer must contain the record image that will become the modified record image in the file. | No Data Buffer value is returned. |
| **Data Buffer Length** | The Data Buffer Length must be at least as long and preferably the exact length of the record being updated. | The Data Buffer Length is set to the number of bytes updated. |
| **Key Buffer** | The Key Buffer should be as large as the key specified by the Key Number parameter. | The current key value of the updated record is returned in the Key Buffer. |
| **Key Number** | The Key Number (zero offset) of the current key path on which positioning is established. | The Key Number is not modified. |

## Notes

The Update operation will release a single record lock. Update will not release a multiple record lock.

**Warning**
The current key value of the updated record is always returned in the Key Buffer parameter. Make sure the Key Buffer is large enough to accommodate the key value.

| Status Code | Cause | Correction |
|---|---|---|
| **5**<br>Duplicate Key Error | The record contained a key value that already exists in a non-duplicate key index. | Do not attempt to insert record. If a duplicate value is not expected, it is possible that the key definition did not specify the proper location of the key value in the record during the Create operation. |
| **8**<br>Invalid Positioning | An invalid Position Block was used on the Update operation. | Ensure the integrity of the Position Block and pass the same Position Block that was used by the previous retrieval operation. |
| **10**<br>Modifiable Key Value Error | An attempt was made to modify a non-modifiable key. | If this error is unexpected, ensure that the Data Buffer is formatted correctly. |
| **14**<br>Pre-Image Open Error | Btrieve attempted to create the pre-image file and was unable due to the disk being full.<br><br>Btrieve attempted to create the pre-image file and was unable due to insufficient access rights to the directory where the pre-image file is located. | Data integrity cannot be ensured. Issue a reset command and remove files to provide sufficient disk space.<br><br>Data integrity cannot be ensured. Proper access rights must be assigned to the workstation (see "Grant" command, NetWare manual). |
| **15**<br>Pre-image I/O Error | Btrieve attempted to write to the pre-image file and the disk is full.<br><br>The pre-image file was damaged. | Provide more disk space.<br><br>Discontinue insertion. Data integrity cannot be ensured. If the Btrieve file is inaccessible with other indexed access operations, recover the data with the BUTIL recovery and load operations. |

| Status Code | Cause | Correction |
|---|---|---|
| **22**<br>Data Buffer Length | The value specified in the Data Buffer Length parameter is smaller than the fixed record length. | Determine the proper record length and specify that value in the Data Buffer Length parameter. |
| **46**<br>Access to File Denied | The file was opened in read-only mode.<br><br>The file requires an owner name to Insert. | Open the file in normal mode.<br><br>Open the file with the correct owner name in the Data Buffer. |
| **80**<br>Conflict Error | The record or page (NetWare Btrieve record or workstation Btrieve page) was modified by another process since the time it was read from disk. | Reread the record, reapply modifications to the record image, and perform another Update.<br>Use a lock operation to establish positioning before the Update. A Conflict Error will not result from a locked record. |

## Positioning

**Non-duplicate key path**
Positioning is established on the updated record for the key path specified in the Key Number parameter.

**Duplicate key path**
The updated record maintains its original position in the chain of duplicates.

# Delete (4)

## Function

The Delete (4) operation removes the current record from the file. It erases the record image in the data page, removes key values from all indexes, releases record locks, and maintains current positioning.

| Parameter | Before Call | After Call |
|---|---|---|
| **Position Block** | The Position Block must have positioning established on the record to be deleted with any retrieval operation (other than Extended Gets or Step operations and key-only operations), Insert, and Update. | The Position Block contains a null pointer as the current record. Pointers to the logical next and previous record remain unchanged. |
| **Data Buffer** | No Data Buffer value is required. | No Data Buffer value is returned. |
| **Data Buffer Length** | No Data Buffer Length value is required. | No Data Buffer Length value is returned. |
| **Key Buffer** | No Key Buffer value is required. | No Key Buffer value is returned. |
| **Key Number** | No Key Number value is required. | No Key Number value is returned. |

## Notes

Deleted records are returned to the free space list in last-in first-out order. Thus, deleting records may cause a loss of chronological order while traversing with Step operations.

Chronological order is maintained, however, within duplicate key records and is not disturbed by deleting records.

A Get Position (22) operation attempted after a record was deleted will return a status 8 (Invalid Position).

A Get Direct (23) operation with the address of a deleted record in the Data Buffer will return an status 43 (Invalid Record Address).

| Status Code | Cause | Correction |
|---|---|---|
| **8**<br>Invalid Positioning | An invalid Position Block was used on the Delete operation. | Ensure the integrity of the Position Block and pass the same Position Block that was used by the previous retrieval operation. |
| **14**<br>Pre-Image Open Error | Btrieve attempted to create the pre-image file and was unable due to the disk being full. | Data integrity cannot be ensured. Issue a reset command and remove files to provide sufficient disk space. |
| | Btrieve attempted to create the pre-image file and was unable due to insufficient access rights to the directory where the pre-image file is located. | Data integrity cannot be ensured. Proper access rights must be assigned to the workstation (see "Grant" command, NetWare manual). |
| **15**<br>Pre-image I/O Error | Btrieve attempted to write to the pre-image file and the disk is full. | Provide more disk space. |
| | The pre-image file was damaged. | Discontinue insertion. Data integrity cannot be ensured. If the Btrieve file is inaccessible with other indexed access operations, recover the data with the BUTIL recovery and load operations. |
| **46**<br>Access to File Denied | The file was opened in read-only mode. | Open the file in normal mode. |
| | The file requires an owner name to Delete. | Open the file with the correct owner name. |
| **80**<br>Conflict Error | The record or page (NetWare Btrieve record or workstation Btrieve page) has been modified by another process since the time it was read from disk. | Reread the record, then delete. Use a lock operation to establish positioning before the Delete. Conflict errors do not result from a locked record. |

## Positioning

Positioning for the next and previous record is not altered. A Get Next (6) or Get Previous (7) will perform just as though the record was not deleted. A Get Position (22), however, will return a Status Code 8, Invalid Position.

# Get Equal (5)

## Function

The Get Equal (5) operation retrieves the first record with a key value equal to the Key Buffer value for the current key. The Get Equal operation places the record in the Data Buffer and positioning is established on the matching record.

| Parameter | Before Call | After Call |
|---|---|---|
| **Position Block** | The Position Block must have been initialized by the Open operation. It is not required to have established positioning before the Get Greater operation. | Positioning is established on the first record encountered with a key value matching the Key Buffer. |
| **Data Buffer** | The Data Buffer pointer should be as large as the size that is specified in the Data Buffer Length parameter. | The entire record image of the matching record is placed in the Data Buffer. |
| **Data Buffer Length** | The Data Buffer Length must be set to the maximum anticipated size (in bytes) of the returned record. | The Data Buffer Length is set to the size of the returned record. |
| **Key Buffer** | The Key Buffer should be the same type as the current key. All key segments within the Key Buffer must match exactly with the key value in the record. | The Key Buffer is not modified. |
| **Key Number** | The Key Number is the identifier (zero offset) of the index to be searched. | The Key Number is not modified. |

## Notes

For variable-length records, Btrieve will return no more than the number of bytes specified in the Data Buffer Length parameter. If the record contains more bytes than specified, a status 22 is returned and the number of bytes specified is returned in the Data Buffer.

For variable-length records, the Data Buffer Length parameter specifies the overall length of the Data Buffer. This is equal to the fixed record length plus the variable data length.

The file cannot be a data-only file.

| Status Code | Cause | Correction |
|---|---|---|
| **3**<br>File Not Opened | The file was not opened properly.<br><br>The Position Block was overwritten. | Perform the Open again and use the same Position Block for the Get Equal.<br><br>Determine the cause and correct. An invalid pointer (e.g., the Key Buffer pointer) can cause a Position Block to be overwritten. |
| **4**<br>Key Value Not Found | No key value was found in the specified index (by Key Number) that exactly matches the value in the Key Buffer.<br><br>An invalid key type, position, or length was specified at the time the file was created or the record was incorrectly inserted. | Retrieve the record via another key value.<br><br>Recreate the file specifying the proper key type, position, and length and then reload the records. Use the BUTIL recovery and load procedures. |
| **6**<br>Invalid Key Number | The Key Number parameter contained an invalid index number reference. | Make sure the Key Number parameter has a valid value. A valid Key Number range is zero to (n - 1), where n is the number of key paths defined for the file. |
| **22**<br>Data Buffer Length | The value specified in the Data Buffer Length parameter is smaller than the size of the current record. | Make sure that the value of the The Data Buffer Length parameter is large enough to accommodate the largest anticipated record. |

# Positioning

**Non-Duplicate Key**
Positioning is established on the record with a matching key value in the index specified by the Key Number parameter.

**Duplicate Key**
Positioning is established on the chronological first duplicate record with a matching key value. For supplemental keys, positioning is established on the first (physical) duplicate record.

## Available Bias Values

Apply record locking bias:

100 = single record Wait
200 = single record No-Wait
300 = multiple record Wait
400 = multiple record No-Wait

50 = key-only Get. This establishes positioning without returning a Data Buffer value. For duplicate keys, duplicate values are not returned.

# Get Next (6)

## Function

The Get Next (6) operation retrieves the next record in current key path order. It places the record in the Data Buffer, establishes positioning on the next logical record, and places the current key value in the Key Buffer.

| Parameter | Before Call | After Call |
|---|---|---|
| **Position Block** | The Position Block must have position established on the same key path as specified in the Key Number parameter. | Positioning is established on the next record in the order specified by the Key Number parameter. |
| **Data Buffer** | The Data Buffer should be large enough for the returned record. | The entire record image of the next record is placed in the Data Buffer. |
| **Data Buffer Length** | The Data Buffer Length must be set to a value at least as large as the fixed record length of the file. | The Data Buffer Length is set to the size of the returned record. |
| **Key Buffer** | The Key Buffer should be large enough for the returned key. | The current key value of the next record is placed in the Key Buffer. |
| **Key Number** | This is the current Key Number (zero offset) of the current key path. | The Key Number is not modified. |

## Notes

Get Next is used to perform a forward traversal of the database in a particular key path order. Begin traversal with a Get First (12) and specify the same Key Number for the Get Next. For faster non-indexed traversal use the Step Next (24) operation.

**Warning**
The current key value of the next record is always returned at the location pointed to by the Key Buffer pointer parameter. Make sure the Key Buffer pointer is pointing to a variable of large enough to accommodate the key value.

The Key Number parameter must be the same Key Number as the previous operation that established positioning.

To change key paths while traversing, perform a Get Position (22) followed by a Get Direct (23) with the new key path set in the Key Number parameter. Remember to reset the Data Buffer Length parameter to the largest anticipated record length before the performing the Get Direct operation.

For variable-length records, Btrieve will return no more than the number of bytes specified in the Data Buffer Length parameter. If the record contains more bytes than specified, a Status Code 22 is returned and the number of bytes specified is returned in the Data Buffer.

For variable-length records, the Data Buffer Length parameter should specify the overall length of the Data Buffer. This is equal to the fixed record length plus the variable data length.

The file cannot be a data-only file.

| Status Code | Cause | Correction |
|---|---|---|
| **3**<br>File Not Opened | The file was not opened properly. | Perform the Open operation and use the same Position Block. |
| **6**<br>Invalid Key Number | The Key Number parameter contained an invalid Key Number reference. | Make sure the Key Number parameter has a valid value. A valid Key Number range is zero to (n - 1), where n is the number of keys paths defined for the file. |
| **7**<br>Different Key Number | The Key Number value was different from the key path used to establish positioning. | Make sure the Key Number parameter specifies the same key path previously used to establish positioning. To change key paths while traversing, perform a Get Position (22) followed by a Get Direct (23) with the new key path set in the Key Number parameter. |
| **9**<br>End of File | The current record is the last logical record in the file. | Discontinue database traversal. |
| **22**<br>Data Buffer Length | For variable-length records, the value specified in the Data Buffer Length parameter is smaller than the fixed record length. | Make sure that the value of the Data Buffer Length parameter is at least as large as the fixed record length. |

## Positioning

**Non-Duplicate Key**
Positioning is established on the next highest value in the current key path order.

**Duplicate Key**
Positioning is established on the next highest value, or the next duplicate value in chronological order. For supplemental keys, the next duplicate is in physical record order.

## Available Bias Values

Apply record locking bias:

100 = single record Wait
200 = single record No-Wait
300 = multiple record Wait
400 = multiple record No-Wait

50 = key-only Get. This establishes positioning without returning a Data Buffer value.

## Extended Operations

Get Next Extended (36)

# Get Previous (7)

## Function

The Get Previous (7) operation retrieves the previous record in current key path order. It places the record in the Data Buffer, establishes positioning on the previous logical record, and places the current key value in the Key Buffer.

| Parameter | Before Call | After Call |
|---|---|---|
| **Position Block** | The Position Block must have position established on the same key path as specified in the Key Number parameter. | Positioning is established on the previous record in the order specified by the Key Number parameter. |
| **Data Buffer** | The Data Buffer should be large enough for the returned record. | The entire record image of the previous record is placed in the Data Buffer. |
| **Data Buffer Length** | The Data Buffer Length must be set to a value at least as large as the fixed record length of the file. | The Data Buffer Length is set to the size of the returned record. |
| **Key Buffer** | The Key Buffer should be large enough for the returned key. | The current key value parameter of the previous record is placed in the Key Buffer. |
| **Key Number** | This is the current Key Number (zero offset) of the current key path. | The Key Number is not modified. |

## Notes

Get Previous is used to perform a reverse traversal of the database in a particular key path order. Begin traversal with a Get Last (13) and specify the same Key Number for the Get Previous. For faster non-indexed traversal use the Step Previous (35) operation.

**Warning**
The current key value of the previous record is always returned at the location pointed to by the Key Buffer pointer parameter. Make sure the Key Buffer pointer points to a variable that is large enough to accommodate the key value.

The Key Number parameter must be the same Key Number as the previous operation that established positioning.

To change key paths while traversing, perform a Get Position (22) followed by a Get Direct (23) with the new key path set in the Key Number parameter. Remember to reset the Data Buffer Length parameter to the largest anticipated record length before the performing the Get Direct operation.

For variable-length records, Btrieve will return no more than the number of bytes specified in the Data Buffer Length parameter. If the record contains more bytes than specified, a Status Code 22 is returned and the number of bytes specified is returned in the Data Buffer

For variable-length records, the Data Buffer Length parameter should specify the overall length of the Data Buffer. This is equal to the fixed record length plus the variable data length.

The file cannot be a data-only file.

| Status Code | Cause | Correction |
|---|---|---|
| 3<br>File Not Opened | The file was not opened properly. | Perform the open operation, and use the same Position Block. |
| | The Position Block was overwritten. | Determine the cause and correct. An invalid pointer (e.g., the Key Buffer pointer) can cause a Position Block to be overwritten. |
| 6<br>Invalid Key Number | The Key Number parameter contained an invalid Key Number reference. | Make sure the Key Number parameter has a valid value. A valid Key Number range is zero to (n - 1) where n is the number of keys paths defined for the file. |
| 7<br>Different Key Number | The Key Number value was different from the key path used to establish positioning. | Make sure the Key Number parameter specifies the same key path previously used to establish positioning. To change key paths while traversing perform a Get Position (22) followed by a Get Direct (23) with the new key path set in the Key Number parameter. |
| 9<br>End of File | The current record is the first record in the file. | Discontinue database traversal. |

| Status Code | Cause | Correction |
|---|---|---|
| **22**<br>Data Buffer Length | The value specified in the Data Buffer Length parameter is smaller than the size of the record. | Make sure that the value of the Data Buffer Length parameter is set large enough to accommodate the largest anticipated record. |

## Positioning

**Non-Duplicate Key**
Positioning is established on the logical previous record in current key path order.

**Duplicate Key**
Positioning is established on the logical previous record in chronological order. For supplemental keys, the previous duplicate is in physical record order.

## Available Bias Values

Apply record locking bias:

100 = single record Wait
200 = single record No-Wait
300 = multiple record Wait
400 = multiple record No-Wait

50 = key-only Get. This establishes positioning without returning a Data Buffer value.

# Get Greater (8)

## Function

The Get Greater (8) operation retrieves the first record with a current key value greater than the key value specified in the Key Buffer. It places the record in the Data Buffer and establishes positioning on the matching record.

| Parameter | Before Call | After Call |
|---|---|---|
| **Position Block** | The Position Block must have been initialized by the Open operation. It is not required to have established positioning before the Get Greater operation. | Positioning is established on the first record encountered with a key value that is greater than the value specified in the Key Buffer. |
| **Data Buffer** | The Data Buffer should be large enough for the returned record. | The entire record image of the matching record is placed in the Data Buffer. |
| **Data Buffer Length** | The Data Buffer Length must be set to the maximum anticipated size (in bytes) of the returned record. | The Data Buffer Length is set to the size of the returned record. |
| **Key Buffer** | The Key Buffer should be the same type as the key type for the current index. | The current key value of the matching record is placed in the Key Buffer. |
| **Key Number** | The Key Number must be set to the identifier (zero offset) of the current key path. | The Key Number is not modified. |

## Notes

The Get Greater operation is used to perform a "partial match search." Positioning is established on the first record with matching left-most key values. Thus, a match is made on a Key Buffer value containing less than the entire record key value. Get Greater will also position on an exact key match.

The Get Greater operation will not match a record with an identical key value. Use the Get Greater or Equal (9) operation for a partial matching search.

**Warning**
The current key value of the matching record is always returned at the location pointed to by the Key Buffer pointer parameter. This can result in the loss of the original key value.

For variable-length records, the Data Buffer Length parameter specifies the overall length of the Data Buffer. This value is equal to the fixed record length plus the variable data length.

For variable-length records, Btrieve will return no more than the number of bytes specified in the Data Buffer Length parameter. If the record contains more bytes than specified, Btrieve returns a status 22 and the number of bytes specified is returned in the Data Buffer.

The file cannot be a data-only file.

| Status Code | Cause | Correction |
|---|---|---|
| **3**<br>File Not Opened | The file was not opened properly. | Perform the open operation, and use the same Position Block. |
| | The Position Block was over written. | Determine the cause and correct. An invalid pointer (e.g., Key Buffer pointer) can cause a Position Block to be overwritten. |
| **6**<br>Invalid Key Number | The Key Number parameter contained an invalid Key Number reference. | Make sure the Key Number parameter has a valid value. A valid Key Number range is zero to (n - 1) where n is the number of indexed key paths defined for the file. |
| **9**<br>End of File | No key value was found greater than or equal to the Key Buffer. | Retrieve the record via another key value. |
| | An invalid key type, position, or length was specified at the time the file was created or the record was inserted incorrectly. | Recreate the file specifying the proper key type, position, and position and length and reload the records. |

| Status Code | Cause | Correction |
|---|---|---|
| **22**<br>Data Buffer Length | The value specified in the Data Buffer Length parameter is smaller than the current record. | Make sure that the value of the Data Buffer Length parameter is set large enough to accommodate the largest anticipated record. |

## Positioning

**Non-Duplicate Keys**
Positioning is established on the first record who's left-most key value is greater than or equal the value in the Key Buffer.

**Duplicate Keys**
Positioning is established on the chronological first duplicate record whose left-most key value is greater than or equal to the value in the Key Buffer. For supplemental indexes, positioning is established on the physical first duplicate record.

## Available Bias Values

Apply record locking bias:

100 = single record Wait
200 = single record No-Wait
300 = multiple record Wait
400 = multiple record No-Wait

50 = key-only Get. This establishes positioning without returning a Data Buffer value.

# Get Greater or Equal (9)

## Function

The Get Greater or Equal (9) operation retrieves the first record with a key value that is greater than or equal to the key value specified in the Key Buffer. The record is placed in the Data Buffer and positioning is establishes on the matching record.

| Parameter | Before Call | After Call |
|---|---|---|
| **Position Block** | The Position Block must have been initialized by the Open operation. It is not required to have established positioning before the Get Greater or Equal operation. | Positioning is established on the first record encountered with a key value greater than or equal to the value specified in the Key Buffer. |
| **Data Buffer** | The Data Buffer should be the size specified in the Data Buffer Length parameter. | The entire record image of the matching record is placed in the Data Buffer. |
| **Data Buffer Length** | The Data Buffer Length must be set to the maximum anticipated size (in bytes) of the returned record. | The Data Buffer Length is set to the size of the returned record. |
| **Key Buffer** | The Key Buffer should be the same type as the key type of the current index. | The current key value of the matching record is placed in the Key Buffer. |
| **Key Number** | The Key Number must be set to the identifier (zero offset) of the current key path. | The Key Number is not modified. |

## Notes

The Get Greater or Equal operation is used to perform a "partial match search." Positioning is established on the first record with matching left-most key values. Thus, a match is made on a Key Buffer value containing less than the entire record key value. Get Greater or Equal will also position on an exact key match.

**Warning**
The current key value of the matching record is always returned at the location pointed to by the Key Buffer pointer parameter. This can result in the loss of the original key value.

For variable-length records, the Data Buffer Length parameter specifies the overall length of the Data Buffer. This is equal to the fixed record length plus the variable data length.

For variablo-length records, Btrieve will return no more than the number of bytes specified in the Data Buffer Length parameter. If the record contains more bytes than specified, a status 22 is returned and the number of bytes specified is returned in the Data Buffer.

The file cannot be a data-only file.

| Status Code | Cause | Correction |
|---|---|---|
| **3**<br>File Not Opened | The file was not opened properly. | Perform the open operation, and use the same Position Block. |
| | The Position Block was over written. | Determine the cause and correct. An invalid pointer (e.g., Key Buffer pointer) can cause a Position Block to be overwritten. |
| **6**<br>Invalid Key Number | The Key Number parameter contained an invalid Key Number reference. | Make sure the Key Number parameter has a valid value. A valid Key Number range is zero to (n - 1) where n is the number of indexed key paths defined for the file. |
| **9**<br>End of File | No key value was found greater than or equal to the Key Buffer. | Retrieve the record via another key value. |
| | An invalid key type, position, or length was specified at the time the file was created or the record was inserted incorrectly. | Recreate the file specifying the proper key type, position, and position and length and reload the records. |
| **22**<br>Data Buffer Length | The value specified in the Data Buffer Length parameter is smaller than the current record. | Make sure that the value of the Data Buffer Length parameter is set large enough to accommodate the largest anticipated record. |

## Positioning

**Non-Duplicate Keys**
Positioning is established on the first record who's left-most key value is greater than or equal the value in the Key Buffer.

**Duplicate Keys**
Positioning is established on the chronological first duplicate record who's left-most key value is greater than or equal the value in the Key Buffer. For supplemental indexes, positioning is established on the physical first duplicate record.

## Available Bias Values

Apply record locking bias:

100 = single record Wait
200 = single record No-Wait
300 = multiple record Wait
400 = multiple record No-Wait

50 = key-only Get. This establishes positioning without returning a Data Buffer value.

# Get Less Than (10)

## Function

The Get Less Than (10) operation retrieves the last record with a key value that is less than or equal the key value specified in the Key Buffer. It places the record in the Data Buffer and establishes positioning on the matching record.

| Parameter | Before Call | After Call |
|---|---|---|
| **Position Block** | The Position Block must have been initialized by the Open operation. It is not required to have established positioning. | Positioning is established on the last record encountered with a key value less than the value specified in the Key Buffer. |
| **Data Buffer** | The Data Buffer should be as large as the size specified in the Data Buffer Length parameter. | The entire record image of the matching record is placed in the Data Buffer. |
| **Data Buffer Length** | The Data Buffer Length must be set to the maximum anticipated size (in bytes) of the returned record. | The Data Buffer Length is set to the size of the returned record. |
| **Key Buffer** | The Key Buffer should be the same type as the key type for the current index. | The current key value of the matching record is placed in the Key Buffer. |
| **Key Number** | The current Key Number must be set to the identifier (zero offset) of the index key path to search. | The current Key Number is not modified. |

## Notes

The Get Less Than operation is used to position on the last record with a key value less than the Key Buffer. In the case of duplicate keys, Get Less Than begins searching from the bottom up. The operation will always position on the last record in the chain of duplicates. With this, a last-in, first-out algorithm is easy to perform.

**Warning**
The current key value of the matching record is always returned at the location pointed to by the Key Buffer pointer parameter possibly resulting in the loss of the original key value.

For variable-length records, Btrieve will return no more than the number of bytes specified in the Data Buffer Length parameter. If the record contains more bytes than specified, a status 22 is returned and the number of bytes specified is returned in the Data Buffer.

For variable-length records, the Data Buffer Length parameter specifies the overall length of the Data Buffer. This is equal to the fixed record length plus the variable data length.

The file cannot be a data-only file.

| Status Code | Cause | Correction |
|---|---|---|
| **3**<br>File Not Opened | The file was not opened properly. | Perform the Open operation, and use the same Position Block. |
| | The Position Block was overwritten. | Determine the cause and correct. An invalid pointer (e.g., Key Buffer pointer) can cause a Position Block to be overwritten. |
| **6**<br>Invalid Key Number | The Key Number parameter contained an invalid Key Number reference. | Make sure the Key Number parameter has a valid value. A valid Key Number range is zero to (n - 1) where n is the number of indexed key paths defined for the file. |
| **9**<br>End of File | No key value was found with a value less than the value in the Key Buffer. | Retrieve the record via another key value. |
| | An invalid key type, position, or length was specified at the time the file was created or the record was incorrectly inserted. | Recreate the file specifying the proper key type, position, and position and length and reload the records. |
| **22**<br>Data Buffer Length | The value specified in the Data Buffer Length parameter is smaller than the size of the current record. | Make sure that the value of the Data Buffer Length parameter is set large enough to accommodate the largest anticipated record. |

## Positioning

**Non-Duplicate Keys**
Positioning is established on the first record for which the left-most key value is less the value in the Key Buffer.

**Duplicate Keys**
Positioning is established on the chronological last duplicate record for which the left-most key value is less than the value in the Key Buffer. For supplemental indexes, positioning is established on the physical last duplicate record.

## Available Bias Values

Apply record locking bias:

100 = single record Wait
200 = single record No-Wait
300 = multiple record Wait
400 = multiple record No-Wait

50 = key-only Get. This establishes positioning without returning a Data Buffer value.

# Get Less Than or Equal (11)

## Function

The Get Less Than or Equal (11) operation retrieves the last record with a key value that is less than or equal to the key value specified in the Key Buffer. It places the record in the Data Buffer and establishes positioning on the matching record.

| Parameter | Before Call | After Call |
|---|---|---|
| **Position Block** | The Position Block must have been initialized by the Open operation. It is not required to have established positioning. | Positioning is established on the last record encountered with a key value less than the value specified in the Key Buffer. |
| **Data Buffer** | The Data Buffer should be as large as the size specified in the Data Buffer Length parameter. | The entire record image of the matching record is placed in the Data Buffer. |
| **Data Buffer Length** | The Data Buffer Length must be set to the maximum anticipated size (in bytes) of the returned record. | The Data Buffer Length is set to the size of the returned record. |
| **Key Buffer** | The Key Buffer should be the same type as the key type for the current index. | The current key value of the matching record is placed in the Key Buffer. |
| **Key Number** | The current Key Number must be set to the identifier (zero offset) of the index key path to search. | The current Key Number is not modified. |

## Notes

The Get Less Than or Equal operation is used to position on the last record with a key value less than or equal to the Key Buffer. In the case of duplicate keys, Get Less Than or Equal begins searching from the bottom up. This operation will always position on the last record in the chain of duplicates. With this, a last-in, first-out algorithm is easy to perform.

**Warning**
The current key value of the matching record is always returned at the location pointed to by the Key Buffer pointer parameter possibly resulting in the loss of the original key value.

For variable-length records, Btrieve will return no more than the number of bytes specified in the Data Buffer Length parameter. If the record contains more bytes than specified, a status 22 is returned and the number of bytes specified is returned in the Data Buffer.

For variable-length records, the Data Buffer Length parameter specifies the overall length of the Data Buffer. This is equal to the fixed record length plus the variable data length.

The file cannot be a data-only file.

| Status Code | Cause | Correction |
|---|---|---|
| 3<br>File Not Opened | The file was not opened properly.<br><br>The Position Block was overwritten. | Perform the Open operation, and use the same Position Block.<br><br>Determine the cause and correct. An invalid pointer (e.g., Key Buffer pointer) can cause a Position Block to be overwritten. |
| 6<br>Invalid Key Number | The Key Number parameter contained an invalid Key Number reference. | Make sure the Key Number parameter has a valid value. A valid Key Number range is zero to (n - 1) where n is the number of indexed key paths defined for the file. |
| 9<br>End of File | No key value was found with a value less than or equal the value in the Key Buffer.<br><br>An invalid key type, position, or length was specified at the time the file was created or the record was incorrectly inserted. | Retrieve the record via another key value.<br><br>Recreate the file specifying the proper key type, position, and position and length and reload the records. |
| 22<br>Data Buffer Length | The value specified in the Data Buffer Length parameter is smaller than the size of the current record. | Make sure that the value of the Data Buffer Length parameter is set large enough to accommodate the largest anticipated record. |

## Positioning

**Non-Duplicate Keys**
Positioning is established on the first record for which the left–most key value is less than or equal the value in the Key Buffer.

**Duplicate Keys**
Positioning is established on the chronological last duplicate record for which the left-most key value is less than or equal the value in the Key Buffer. For supplemental indexes, positioning is established on the physical last duplicate record.

## Available Bias Values

Apply record locking bias:

100 = single record Wait
200 = single record No-Wait
300 = multiple record Wait
400 = multiple record No-Wait

50 = key-only Get. This establishes positioning without returning a Data Buffer value.

# Get First (12)

## Function

The Get First (12) operation retrieves the logical first record in current key path index order. It places the record in the Data Buffer, establishes positioning on the logical first record, and places the current key value in the Key Buffer.

| Parameter | Before Call | After Call |
|---|---|---|
| **Position Block** | The Position Block must have been initialized by the Open operation. It is not required to have positioning established. | Positioning is established on the first record in the index order specified by the Key Number parameter. |
| **Data Buffer** | The Data Buffer should be as large as the size specified in the Data Buffer Length parameter. | The entire record image of the logical first record is placed in the Data Buffer. |
| **Data Buffer Length** | The Data Buffer Length must be set to the maximum anticipated size (in bytes) of the returned record. | The Data Buffer Length is set to the size of the returned record. |
| **Key Buffer** | The Key Buffer should be as large as the key size of the key specified by the Key Number parameter. | The current key value of the first record is placed in the Key Buffer. |
| **Key Number** | This is the current Key Number (zero offset) of the current key path. | The current Key Number is not modified. |

## Notes

**Warning**
The current key value of the first record is always returned at the location pointed to by the Key Buffer pointer parameter. Make sure the Key Buffer pointer is pointing to a variable that is large enough to accommodate the key value.

For variable-length records, Btrieve will return no more than the number of bytes specified in the Data Buffer Length parameter. If the record contains more bytes than specified, Btrieve returns a status 22 and the number of bytes specified is returned in the Data Buffer.

For variable-length records, the Data Buffer Length parameter specifies the overall length of the Data Buffer. This is equal to the fixed record length plus the variable data length.

The file cannot be a data-only file.

| Status Code | Cause | Correction |
|---|---|---|
| **3**<br>File Not Opened | The file was not opened properly. | Perform the Open operation, and use the same Position Block. |
| | The Position Block was overwritten. | Determine the cause and correct. An invalid pointer (e.g., Key Buffer pointer) can cause a Position Block to be overwritten. |
| **6**<br>Invalid Key Number | The Key Number parameter contained an invalid Key Number reference. | Make sure the Key Number parameter has a valid value. A valid Key Number range is zero to (n - 1) where n is the number of keys paths defined for the file. |
| **22**<br>Data Buffer Length | The value specified in the Data Buffer Length parameter is smaller than the size of the current record. | Make sure that the Data Buffer Length parameter is large enough to accommodate the largest anticipated record. |

## Positioning

**Non-Duplicate Key**
Positioning is established on the logical first record in current key path index order.

**Duplicate Key**
Positioning is established on the logical first record in chronological order. For supplemental keys, the first duplicate is in physical index order.

## Available Bias Values

Apply record locking bias:

100 = single record Wait
200 = single record No-Wait
300 = multiple record Wait
400 = multiple record No-Wait

50 = key-only Get. This establishes positioning without returning a Data Buffer value. For duplicate keys, duplicate values are not returned.

# Get Last (13)

## Function

The Get Last (13) operation retrieves the logical last record in current key path order. It places the record in the Data Buffer, establishes positioning on the logical last record, and place the current key value in the Key Buffer.

| Parameter | Before Call | After Call |
|---|---|---|
| **Position Block** | The Position Block must have been initialized by the Open operation. It is not required to have positioning established before the Get Last operation. | Positioning is established on the logical last record in the index order specified by the Key Number parameter. |
| **Data Buffer** | The Data Buffer should be as large as the size specified in the Data Buffer Length parameter. | The entire record image of the logical last record is placed in the Data Buffer. |
| **Data Buffer Length** | The Data Buffer Length must be set to the maximum anticipated size (in bytes) of the returned record. | The Data Buffer Length is set to the size of the returned record. |
| **Key Buffer** | The Key Buffer should be as large as the key size of the key specified by the Key Number parameter. | The current key value of the last record is placed in the Key Buffer. |
| **Key Number** | This is the current Key Number (zero offset) of the current key path. | The current Key Number is not modified. |

## Notes

**Warning**
The current key value of the last record is always returned at the location pointed to by the Key Buffer pointer parameter. Make sure the Key Buffer pointer is pointing to a variable large enough to accommodate the key value.

For variable-length records, Btrieve will return no more than the number of bytes specified in the Data Buffer Length parameter. If the record contains more bytes than specified, Btrieve returns a status 22 and the number of bytes specified is returned in the Data Buffer.

For variable-length records, the Data Buffer Length parameter specifies the overall length of the Data Buffer. This is equal to the fixed record length plus the variable data length.

The file cannot be a data-only file.

| Status Code | Cause | Correction |
|---|---|---|
| **3**<br>File Not Opened | The file was not opened properly. | Perform the open operation, and use the same Position Block. |
| | The Position Block was over written. | Determine the cause and correct. An invalid pointer (e.g., Key Buffer pointer) can cause a Position Block to be overwritten. |
| **6**<br>Invalid Key Number | The Key Number parameter contained an invalid Key Number reference. | Make sure the Key Number parameter has a valid value. A valid Key Number range is zero to (n - 1) where n is the number of keys paths defined for the file. |
| **22**<br>Data Buffer Length | The value specified in the Data Buffer Length parameter is smaller than the size of the current record. | Make sure that the value of the Data Buffer Length parameter is set large enough to accommodate the largest anticipated record. |

# Positioning

**Non-Duplicate Key**
Positioning is established on the logical last record in current key path index order.

**Duplicate Key**
Positioning is established on the logical last record in chronological order. For supplemental keys, the first duplicate is in physical index order.

## Available Bias Values

Apply record locking bias:

100 = single record Wait
200 = single record No-Wait
300 = multiple record Wait
400 = multiple record No-Wait

50 = key-only Get. This establishes positioning without returning a Data Buffer value. For duplicate keys, duplicate values are not returned.

# Create (14)

## Function

The Create (14) operation creates a Btrieve file from the specification in the Data Buffer.

| Parameters | Before Call | After Call |
|---|---|---|
| **Position Block** | No value is required. | No value is returned. |
| **Data Buffer** | The Data Buffer contains the definition of the file to be created consisting of:<br>• A 16-byte file specification block which defines the characteristics of the file,<br>• A 16-byte key segment specification block for each key segment which defines the characteristics of each key and the file's indexes, and<br>• An alternate collating sequence defined following the file and key specifications. (See notes on the Data Buffer format below.) | No value is returned. |
| **Data Buffer Length** | The Data Buffer Length must be at least the size of the file description, and should be the exact length of the file specification including the file specification block, key segment specification blocks, and the alternate collating sequence definition. | No value is returned. |
| **Key Buffer** | The Key Buffer contains the filename of the file to open, including full pathname, if needed. The filename must be terminated by a blank character or binary zero. | No value is returned. |

| Parameters | Before Call | After Call |
|---|---|---|
| **Key Number** | The Key Number determines whether or not to overwrite a file with the same file name and override the "Create File as Transactional" BSETUP configuration setting. (See notes on the Key Buffer settings below.) | No value is returned. |

## Notes

**Data Buffer Format**

The following tables describe the Data Buffer format for defining a Btrieve file. There must be one file segment specification block followed by one key segment specification block for each key segment. For segmented keys, contiguous key specification blocks define each segment of the key, the segmented key flag specifying that the following block defines the next segment of the current key. A segmented key flag setting of zero marks the last segment for the current key.

**File Specification Block (one per file)**

| Description | Length | Function |
|---|---|---|
| **Record Length** | 2 | Logical record length of fixed record |
| **Page Size** | 2 | Page size of the file |
| **Number of Indexes** | 2 | Number of B-tree index structures |
| **Reserved 1** | 4 | |
| **File Flags** | 2 | Defines file characteristics (see next table) |
| **Reserved 2** | 2 | |
| **Allocation** | 2 | Number of pages to pre-allocate if flagged |

| File Flag | Value | Set to 1 | Set to 0 |
|---|---|---|---|
| **Variable-Length Records** | **1** | Allow variable-length records to be inserted into the file. The record length parameter specifies the fixed-length portion of the record. Data in a record beyond the fixed-length data is stored in variable-length data pages. The file will be created with one variable-length data page. | Do not allow variable-length data. |
| **Blank Truncation** | **2** | If variable-length records, do not store trailing blanks. Specify the number of truncated, blank characters (ASCII 32 Decimal) are stored as a two byte integer at the end of the fixed-length record. Return blank characters in the Data Buffer on retrieval operations. | Do not store records with truncated, blank characters. |
| **Preallocation** | **4** | Create the file containing the number of pages as specified in the Preallocation File specification. These pages are used data and index pages as required. | Create the file with only the minimum number of pages: one FCR page, one alternate collating sequence page (if selected), and one index page per index. |
| **Data Compression** | **8** | Store records (fixed- and variable-length data) in a compressed format where repeating characters are represented by a binary zero followed by a byte representing the number of repeating characters, followed by the character. | Do not store records in compressed format. |

| File Flag | Value | Set to 1 | Set to 0 |
|---|---|---|---|
| **Key-Only** | **16** | Create a key-only file which contains no data pages. Only key value are inserted to the file. Once inserted, keys cannot be deleted or modified. | Allow records to be stored in data pages. |
| **10% Free Space** | **64** | The free space threshold for variable-length records is set to 10% of the size of the variable-length data page. The free space threshold specifies the minimum amount of free space required on a page in order for it to be included in the free space list. This will affect the degree of record fragmentation across data pages. A low free space threshold results in a higher likelihood of record fragmentation. | N/A |
| **20% Free Space** | **128** | The free space threshold for variable-length records is set to 20% of the size of the variable-length data page. | N/A |
| **30% Free Space** | **192** | The free space threshold for variable-length records is set to 30% of the size of the variable-length data page. | N/A |

**Key Segment Specification Block**
(one per key segment defined)

| Description | Length | Function |
|---|---|---|
| Key Position | 2 | Location of key segment in record (1 relative) |
| Key Length | 2 | Length of key segment in bytes |
| Key Flags | 2 | defines key characteristics (see next table) |
| Reserved 1 | 4 | |
| Extended Key Type | 1 | Btrieve key type of segment |
| Null Value | 1 | Character considered to be the null value |
| Reserved 2 | 4 | |

| Key Flag | Value | Set to 1 | Set to 0 |
|---|---|---|---|
| **Duplicates** | **1** | Duplicate keys are accepted in the index. | Duplicate keys are not accepted in the index and attempting to insert a duplicate key results in a status 5 (Duplicate Key Value). All segments of a segmented key must have the same duplicate flag setting. |
| **Modifiable** | **2** | The key value within the record can be modified (with the Update operation) after the record has been Inserted. | The key value within the record cannot be modified. Attempting to do so yields a status 10 (Modifiable Key Error). All segments of a segmented key must have the same modifiable flag setting. |

| Key Flag | Value | Set to 1 | Set to 0 |
|---|---|---|---|
| **Binary** | **4** | The key segment is a binary value if the extended key type flag is set to zero. This flag is only used to maintain backward compatibility to older Btrieve files with only two key types: binary and string. Extended key types replaced the old binary/string key types and new files should set this flag to zero and specify the key type in the one-byte, extended key type variable. | The key segment is of the old string type if the extended key type flag is set to zero. |
| **Null** | **8** | The key is a null key and the Null Value parameter defines a null value. If the entire key, including all key segments, contain the null value, the key is not inserted into the index. The record must be accessed via another key path or by physical address. | The key is not considered a null key, and all key values will be inserted into the index. All segments of a segmented key must have the same Null flag setting. |
| **Segmented** | **16** | The key segment is part of a segmented key and the following key specification block is the next segment of the key. | The key segment is the last segment of the key. A zero value delimits the last segment of a segmented key. A key containing only one segment, is considered a non-segmented key. A key containing more than one segmented is considered a segmented key. |

| Key Flag | Value | Set to 1 | Set to 0 |
|---|---|---|---|
| **Alternate Collating Sequence** | **32** | The key segment uses the alternate collating sequence whose definition follows the file and key specification blocks. This flag is only supported by the String, Lstring, and Zstring types. | The key segment uses the default collating sequence. |
| **Descending** | **64** | Collating is performed in a descending manner (highest to lowest). | Collating is performed in an ascending manner (lowest to highest). |
| **Supplemental** | **128** | The key segment is part of a supplemental index. | The key segment is part of a permanent index. |
| **Extended Key Type** | **256** | The key segment is of an extended key type specified by the Extended Key Type parameter. | The key type is either a binary or string type specified by the Binary flag. This setting is only used for backward compatibility with older Btrieve files. Use extended key types when ever possible. |
| **Manual** | **512** | The key is considered a manual key. A manual key is the same as a null key with the following difference: If any one segment of the key is contains all null values, then the key is not inserted into the index. | The key is not considered a manual key. |

**Extended Key Types**

| Key Type | Value |
|---|---|
| String | 0 |
| Integer | 1 |
| Float | 2 |
| Date | 3 |
| Time | 4 |
| Decimal | 5 |
| Money | 6 |
| Logical | 7 |
| Numeric | 8 |
| Bfloat | 9 |
| Lstring | 10 |
| Zstring | 11 |
| Unsigned Binary | 12 |
| Autoincrement | 15 |

**Key Number Settings**

| Value | Effect |
|---|---|
| 0 | Overwrite existing file and create file with transactional attribute |
| -1 | Return status 59 (File Already Exists) and create file with transactional attribute |
| -2 | Overwrite existing file, but do not create file with transactional attribute |
| -3 | Return status 59 (File Already Exists), but do not create file with transactional attribute |

Note: The Key Number values, 0 and -1, only create files with the transactional flag for NetWare Btrieve with the BSETUP "Create Files as Transactional" option.

### Alternate Collating Sequence

The alternate collating sequence must directly follow the last 16 byte. The alternated collating sequence key flag can be used with String, Lstring, and Zstring types.

### Format for the Alternate Collating Sequence definition

| Parameter | Length | Description |
|---|---|---|
| **Signature Byte** | 1 | Contains constant AC hex |
| **Sequence Identifier** | 8 | Unique sequence name for future multiple sequences |
| **Sequence Table** | 256 | Has table containing ASCII translate values |

| Status Code | Cause | Correction |
|---|---|---|
| **2**<br>File I/O Error | A hardware or network malfunction occurred while the file was being created. | Correct the hardware or network malfunction. |
| **18**<br>Disk Full | There is no disk space available. | Free up disk space.<br><br>Use the Extend operation to use another disk or volume (not supported with NetWare v3.x NetWare). |

| Status Code | Cause | Correction |
|---|---|---|
| **22**<br>Data Buffer Length | The Data Buffer Length value is not long enough to accommodate the entire file specification. | Make sure the Data Buffer Length value is large enough for the size of the file specification including the alternate collating sequence (if present).<br><br>Make sure all file specification parameters are set correctly, especially the Number of Indexes file specification block parameter and the segmented key flag on the last key specification block. |
| **24**<br>Page Size Error | The page size file specification block parameter is not set to a multiple of 512 no larger than 4096 bytes. | Make sure the page size file specification block parameter contains a valid page size.<br><br>Check the file specification structure and the Data Buffer pointer. An improper Data Buffer pointer will often first show up as a status 24 (Page Size Error) |
| **25**<br>Create I/O Error | An attempt to create over an existing file was not allowed by the operating system due to the file being open by Btrieve or a transactional flag. | Issue a Reset (28) operation or a BUTIL -RESET command if the file was opened by the workstation. |
| **26**<br>Number of Keys | The Number of Keys file specification block parameter was set to invalid value. | Set a proper Number of Keys parameter value. For page size of 512, this value must be between 1 and 8. For larger page sizes, this value must be between 1 and 24.<br><br>Check the key specification structures. An improper key specification structure will often show up as a Number of Keys error. |

| Status Code | Cause | Correction |
|---|---|---|
| **27**<br>Invalid Key Position | A key segment definition (position and length) exceeds the record length of the file being defined. | Ensure that each key segment definition defines the key within the record. One way to determine which key specification block is causing the error is to create the file several times decrementing the Number of Indexes parameter value each time until the error does not occur or only one key remains. |
| **28**<br>Invalid Record Length | The record length specified in the file specification block in less than four or greater than the page size specified. | Adjust the record length parameter or page size parameter.<br><br>Check the file specification structure. An improper file specification structure can appear as a status 28 (Invalid Record Length). |
| **29**<br>Invalid Key Length | The key length specified in one of the key specification blocks was less than zero or greater than 255 (the maximum key size). | Adjust the key length parameter in the key specification block causing the error. To determine which key specification block is causing the error, create the file several times decrementing the Number of Indexes parameter value each time until the error does not occur or only one key remains. |
| **48**<br>Invalid Alternate Sequence | The first byte in the alternate collating sequence does not contain a hex AC. | Place a hex AC in the first byte of the definition.<br><br>Make sure that the alternate collating sequence directly follows the last key specification block. |

| Status Code | Cause | Correction |
|---|---|---|
| **49**<br>Key Type Error | The key type specified in one of the key specification blocks contained an invalid key type. | Make sure all key type parameters contain a proper key type. |
| | An attempt was made to assign an alternate collating sequence to a non-string key type. | Only assign an alternate collating sequence to a String, Lstring, or Zstring key type. |
| **59**<br>File Already Exists | A file with the same name exists and the Key Number parameter contains a [-1]. | Overwrite the existing file by placing a value other than -1 in the Key Number parameter or change the file name in the Key Buffer. |

## Positioning

The Create operation does not establish positioning.

# Stat (15)

## Function

The Stat (15) operation retrieves the following information about a Btrieve file:

- The file specification used to create the file,
- The number of records in the file,
- The number of unused pages in the file, and
- The number of unique key value entries for each index.

| Parameter | Before Call | After Call |
|---|---|---|
| **Position Block** | The Position Block must be initialized for an open file. Record positioning is not required. | No value is returned. |
| **Data Buffer** | The Data Buffer contains the same file definition as used by the Create operation, including:<br>• One 16-byte file specification block<br>• One 16-byte key segment specification block for each key segment, and<br>• If an alternate collating sequence is used, the definition follows the file and key specifications.<br>See notes for a definition of the file and key specification blocks. See the Create (14) operation for further details on the file and key specifications. | No value is returned. |
| **Data Buffer Length** | The Data Buffer must be at least the size of the file description, and should be the exact length of the file specification including the file specification block, key segment specification blocks, and the alternate collating sequence definition. | No value is returned. |

| Parameter | Before Call | After Call |
|---|---|---|
| **Key Buffer** | No value is required. | If the file was extended with the Extend operation (16), the name of the extended file is returned with a binary zero terminator. Otherwise a binary zero is returned. |
| **Key Number** | No value is required. | No value is returned. |

## Notes

### Data Buffer Format

The following tables describe the Data Buffer format returned from the Stat (15) operation. The Data Buffer format is the same as the Create operation with the addition of the total number of records and unused pages for the file specification block, and the total number of unique keys for each key definition block.

**File Specification Block** (one per file)

| Description | Length | Function |
|---|---|---|
| **Record Length** | 2 | Logical record length of fixed record |
| **Page Size** | 2 | Page size of the file |
| **Number of Indexes** | 2 | Number of B-tree index structures |
| **Number of Records** | 4 | Number of records in the file |
| **File Flags** | 2 | Defines file characteristics (see below) |
| **Reserved** | 2 | |
| **Unused pages** | 2 | Number of unused pages in the file |

**Key Segment Specification Block Parameters (one for each key segment defined)**

| Description | Length | Function |
|---|---|---|
| **Key Position** | 2 | Location of key segment in record (1 relative) |
| **Key Length** | 2 | Length of key segment in bytes |
| **Key Flags** | 2 | Defines file characteristics (see below) |
| **Number of Keys** | 4 | Number of unique keys |
| **Extended Key Type** | 2 | Btrieve key type of segment |
| **Null Value** | 1 | Character considered to be the null value |
| **Reserved** | 4 | |

If present, a 265-byte alternate collating sequence definition will follow the last key specification block.

See the Create (14) operation for definition of key and file flags and alternate collating sequence definition.

| Status Code | Cause | Correction |
|---|---|---|
| **3**<br>File Not Opened | The Position Block was not initialized for an opened file. | Open the file before performing a Stat operation. |
| **22**<br>Data Buffer Length | The Data Buffer Length parameter is not large enough to accommodate the entire file specification. | Make sure that the Data Buffer Length parameter is large enough to specify the size of the file specification, including the alternate collating sequence (if present). |

## Positioning

The Stat (15) operation does not establish positioning.

# Extend (16)

## Function

The Extend (16) operation extends the file to another logical drive. The Btrieve file will then occupy two separate logical drives. This operation is supported only by workstation Btrieve and Btrieve for NetWare v2.x to overcome size restrictions. The Extend operation (16) is not supported by NetWare Btrieve v3.x.

| Parameters | Before Call | After Call |
|---|---|---|
| **Position Block** | The Position Block must be initialized for an open file. Record positioning is not required. | No value is returned. |
| **Data Buffer** | No value is required. | No value is returned. |
| **Data Buffer Length** | No value is required. | No value is returned. |
| **Key Buffer** | The Key Buffer contains the file name with the drive, volume, and pathname of the extended file. The file name must be terminated with a binary zero. | No value is returned. |
| **Key Number** | A Key Number value of [-1] instructs Btrieve to immediately begin storing new data in the extended file. With values other than [-1], Btrieve will not store new data in the extended file until the original drive becomes full. | No value is returned. |

## Notes

The file must be closed and reopened immediately after the Extend (16) operation in order for the extended file to be accessed.

Both the original drive and the extension drive must be online to access extended data.

The extended file cannot be renamed or moved to another location once it has been created. In addition, the drive mapping or designator must not change.

| Status Code | Cause | Correction |
|---|---|---|
| **3**<br>File Not Opened | The Position Block is not initialized for an opened file. | Open the file before performing a Stat (16) operation. |
| **31**<br>File Already Extended | The file has already been extended. A file can only be extended once. | If all space on both drives has been exhausted, use a more advanced operating system (i.e., NetWare v3.x) that offers greater drive capacity. |
| **32**<br>Extend I/O Error | The file could not be extended due to a full directory or disk, or the drive is write protected. | Extend to a drive with sufficient write capacity. |
| **34**<br>Invalid Extension Name | An invalid file name was specified. | Specify a proper file name terminated with a binary zero. |

## Positioning

The Extend (16) operation does not establish positioning.

# Set Directory (17)

## Function

The Set Directory (17) operation changes the current directory to the specified pathname.

| Parameter | Before Call | After Call |
|---|---|---|
| **Position Block** | No value is required. | No value is returned. |
| **Data Buffer** | No value is required. | No value is returned. |
| **Data Buffer Length** | No value is required. | No value is returned. |
| **Key Buffer** | The Key Buffer contains the drive letter and directory path name which will become the current directory. The path name must be terminated with a binary zero. | No value is returned. |
| **Key Number** | No value is required. | No value is returned. |

## Notes

If a drive name is omitted, the current drive is assumed.

If the complete path name is not specified, the path name is appended onto the current directory.

The local operating system will recognize the new directory path as the current directory.

If the operation is unsuccessful, the current directory will remain unchanged.

| Status Code | Cause | Correction |
|---|---|---|
| **35**<br>Directory Error | An invalid directory path name was specified in the Key Number parameter. | Make sure that only a valid directory path name is specified. |

# Get Directory (18)

## Function

The Get Directory (18) operation returns the current directory for a specified logical disk drive.

| Parameter | Before Call | After Call |
|---|---|---|
| **Position Block** | No value is required. | No value is returned. |
| **Data Buffer** | No value is required. | No value is returned. |
| **Data Buffer Length** | No value is required. | No value is returned. |
| **Key Buffer** | No value is required. | The Key Buffer contains the current directory, terminated by a binary zero. |
| **Key Number** | The Key Number parameter contains the drive number of the drive for which the current directory is to be returned. Specify drive numbers as 1 for A:, 2 for B: and so on. A zero value indicates the current drive. | No value is returned. |

| Status Code | Cause | Correction |
|---|---|---|
| **35**<br>Directory Error | An invalid drive number was specified in the Key Buffer. | Make sure that only a valid drive number is specified. |

# Begin Transaction (19)

## Function

The Begin Transaction (19) operation defines the start of a transaction. All Btrieve operations following the Begin Transaction operation are included in the transaction until an End Transaction (20) operation is encountered. Within a transaction, all operations must occur or no operations within the transaction will occur.

| Parameter | Before Call | After Call |
|---|---|---|
| **Position Block** | No value is required. | No value is returned. |
| **Data Buffer** | No value is required. | No value is returned. |
| **Data Buffer Length** | No value is required. | No value is returned. |
| **Key Buffer** | No value is required. | No value is returned. |
| **Key Number** | No value is required. | No value is returned. |

## Notes

Transactions are used to ensure logical data integrity (i.e., that the files involved do not contain incomplete or conflicting data). A transaction is defined as the set of Btrieve operations performed between the Begin Transaction and End Transaction operations.

Workstation Btrieve uses a pre-image system to track database transactions. NetWare Btrieve uses NetWare's Transaction Tracking System (TTS) instead of pre-imaging for files flagged with the Transactional attribute (i.e., FLAG *.BTR +T). From the application's point of view, the behavior of a Btrieve transaction is the same, whether pre-imaging or TTS is being used.

When pre-imaging, a Begin Transaction (19) operation causes all pages that are modified to be stored in the pre-image file associated with each file within the transaction. The pre-image files continue to grow until the transaction is ended or aborted.

The three operations associated with transactions are Begin Transaction (19), End Transaction (20), and Abort Transaction (21). The Begin Transaction operation marks the start of a transaction. The End Transaction operation marks the end of a transaction and makes permanent (commits) all modifications within the transaction. The Abort Transaction operation causes a rollback to undo all operations that occurred within the transaction.

A Reset (28) operation *also* aborts a transaction.

A file cannot be closed within a transaction. All files that are accessed within a transaction are locked for the duration of the transaction. A file becomes locked on the first operation that accesses the file AFTER the Begin Transaction operation.

The number of files that can be involved within a transaction is set at the time Btrieve is loaded (this value defaults to zero). For NetWare Btrieve, the BSETUP program is used to set the number of files in a transaction. For workstation Btrieve, the /N: load parameter is used.

The Btrieve transaction file (named BTRIEVE.TRN for NetWare Btrieve and specified as a load parameter for workstation Btrieve) contains the names of the files involved in the transaction. BTRIEVE.TRN allows transactions to be spread over several file servers.

| Status Code | Cause | Correction |
|---|---|---|
| **36**<br>Transaction Error | Btrieve was not configured to support transactions. | Reload Btrieve and specify the maximum number of files to be included in any transaction. For NetWare Btrieve, the BSETUP setting, "Number of Files per Transaction" must be set properly. For workstation Btrieve, the /N: and /T: parameters must be specified. (For example, /N:6 /T:BTRIEVE.TRN allows six files to be involved in a transaction and sets BTRIEVE.TRN as the Btrieve transaction file.) |
| **37**<br>Transaction is Active | The Begin Transaction operation was attempted while a transaction was already in progress. | Do not attempt to nest transactions. |

## Available Biases

A No-Wait lock bias (+200 or +400) can be applied to the Begin Transaction operation (219 or 419). A Begin Transaction operation defaults to a Wait lock. If a file is locked (due to another transaction or an exclusive mode open), the first operation to access the file after the Begin Transaction will attempt to lock the file and fail. If the transaction was started with an opcode 219 or 419, a status 85 (File Locked) will be returned. If the transaction was started with an opcode 19, the first operation to access the file will lock up in a Wait lock situation which will only be cleared when the other process holding the file lock releases the file.

# End Transaction (20)

## Function

The End Transaction (20) operation defines the completion of a transaction. All Btrieve operations following the Begin Transaction operation are committed and made permanent and all file locks associated with the transaction are released.

| Parameter | Before Call | After Call |
|---|---|---|
| **Position Block** | No value is required. | No value is returned. |
| **Data Buffer** | No value is required. | No value is returned. |
| **Data Buffer Length** | No value is required. | No value is returned. |
| **Key Buffer** | No value is required. | No value is returned. |
| **Key Number** | No value is required. | No value is returned. |

## Notes

After an End Transaction operation, all file locks associated with the transaction are released.

The pre-image files associated with the transaction are discarded.

See "Begin Transaction (19)."

| Status Code | Cause | Correction |
|---|---|---|
| **38** Transaction Control File I/O Error | An error occurred when Btrieve tried to write to the transactional control file due to the file being deleted or lost. | All modifications to the Btrieve files within the transaction have been lost. The transaction process must be attempted again or abandoned. |

| Status Code | Cause | Correction |
|---|---|---|
| **39**<br>End/Abort Transaction Error | A transaction was not in effect. | Only use Abort Transaction operation within a transaction. |
| **74**<br>Transaction Abort | A transaction abort occurred before the End Transaction due to a Btrieve Abort Transaction (21) operation or a NetWare TTS error. | All modifications made to all Btrieve files within the transaction have been lost. The transaction process must be attempted again or abandoned. |

# Abort Transaction (21)

## Function

The Abort Transaction (21) operation terminates a transaction and results in a roll back and undoing of all operations made since the Begin Transaction (19) operation.

| Parameter | Before Call | After Call |
|---|---|---|
| **Position Block** | No value is required. | No value is returned. |
| **Data Buffer** | No value is required. | No value is returned. |
| **Data Buffer Length** | No value is required. | No value is returned. |
| **Key Buffer** | No value is required. | No value is returned. |
| **Key Number** | No value is required. | No value is returned. |

## Notes

After an End Transaction (20) operation, all file locks associated with the transaction are released.

A Reset (28) operation will also result in an abort transaction.

The pre-image files associated with the transaction are discarded.

See "Begin Transaction (19)."

| Status Code | Cause | Correction |
|---|---|---|
| **39**<br>End/Abort Transaction Error | A transaction was not in effect. | Only use Abort Transaction within a transaction. |

# Get Position (22)

## Function

The Get Position (22) operation returns the four-byte physical address of the current record.

| Parameter | Before Call | After Call |
|---|---|---|
| **Position Block** | The Position Block must have positioning established on the record with any retrieval operation other than a key-only Get operation. | The Get Position operation does not affect positioning. |
| **Data Buffer** | No value is required. | The Data Buffer contains the four-byte physical address (most significant word first) of the current record used in conjunction with the Get Direct (23) operation. |
| **Data Buffer Length** | No value is required. | The Data Buffer Length is always set to four. |
| **Key Buffer** | No value is required. | No value is returned. |
| **Key Number** | No value is required. | No value is returned. |

## Notes

Current positioning must be established before the Get Position operation.

To switch current key paths, issue a Get Position operation followed by a Get Direct (23) operation and specify the new current key path in the Key Number parameter.

The Get Position operation will not cause any file I/O as the record position is obtained from the Position Block.

The four-byte physical address of a record can also be obtained from offset 41 of the Position Block.

The Data Buffer parameter should be a pointer to a four-byte integer.

The Get Direct (23) operation can be issued directly following the Get Position operation without altering the Data Buffer. Remember to reset the Data Buffer Length parameter from four to the maximum record size anticipated on the Get Direct operation.

| Status Code | Cause | Correction |
|---|---|---|
| **3**<br>File Not Opened | The file was not properly opened or the Position Block was overwritten. | Make sure the file is opened and the Position Block is intact. |
| **8**<br>Invalid Position | Current positioning was not established. | Before performing the Get Position operation, perform a Get or Step operation to establish positioning. |

# Get Direct (23)

## Function

The Get Direct (23) operation retrieves the record by its four-byte record address. It places the record in the Data Buffer, establishes positioning on the next logical record, and places the current key value in the Key Buffer.

| Parameter | Before Call | After Call |
|---|---|---|
| **Position Block** | The Position Block must have been initialized by the Open operation. Current positioning is not required. | Positioning is established on the record whose address is specified in the Data Buffer. The Current, Next, and Previous pointers are updated based on the current key. |
| **Data Buffer** | The Data Buffer must contain a valid four-byte record address as is returned by the Get Position (22) operation. | The entire record image of the current record is placed in the Data Buffer. |
| **Data Buffer Length** | The Data Buffer Length must be set to the maximum anticipated size (in bytes) of the returned record. | The Data Buffer Length is set to the size of the returned record. |
| **Key Buffer** | The Key Buffer should be as large as the current key. | The current key value parameter of the record is placed in the Key Buffer. |
| **Key Number** | The Key Number (zero offset) of the current key path to be established. | The Key Number is not modified. |

## Notes

The Get Direct operation is the fastest method of retrieving a record.

The four-byte record address can be obtained from several sources:

- It can be obtained through the Get Position (22) operation.
- It can be obtained from the returned record address value from extended operations.

- It can be copied directly from the Position Block.
- It can be obtained from another source, such as a value from another file.

To switch current key paths, issue a Get Position (22) operation followed by a Get Direct operation and specify the new current key path in the Key Number parameter.

**Warning**
The current key value of the next record is always returned at the location pointed to by the Key Buffer pointer parameter. Make sure the Key Buffer pointer is pointing to a variable of large enough to accommodate the key value.

For variable-length records, Btrieve will return no more than the number of bytes specified in the Data Buffer Length parameter. If the record contains more bytes than specified, a status 22 (Data Buffer Length) is returned and the number of bytes specified is returned in the Data Buffer.

For variable-length records, the Data Buffer Length parameter specifies the overall length of the Data Buffer. This value is equal to the fixed record length plus the variable-data length.

| Status Code | Cause | Correction |
|---|---|---|
| **6**<br>Invalid Key Number | The Key Number parameter contained an invalid Key Number reference. | Make sure the Key Number parameter has a valid value. A valid Key Number range is zero to [n - 1] where n is the number of keys paths defined for the file. |
| **22**<br>Data Buffer Length | The value specified in the Data Buffer Length parameter is smaller than the size of the record. This is often the result of a Get Position operation setting the Data Buffer Length parameter to four. | Make sure that the value of the Data Buffer Length parameter is set large enough to accommodate the largest anticipated record. |
| **43**<br>Invalid Data Record Address | The Data Buffer contained an invalid four-byte record address. | Make sure a valid record address is specified by properly establishing positioning and issuing a Get Position (22) operation. |

# Positioning

**Non-Duplicate Key**
Positioning is established on the next highest value in current key path order.

**Duplicate Key**
Positioning is established on the next highest value or the next duplicate value in chronological order. For supplemental keys, the next duplicate is in physical record order.

## Available Bias Values

Apply record locking bias:

100 = single record Wait
200 = single record No-Wait
300 = multiple record Wait
400 = multiple record No-Wait

# Step Next (24)

## Function

The Step Next (24) operation retrieves the next record in physical address order. It places the record in the Data Buffer and establishes positioning on the next record.

| Parameter | Before Call | After Call |
|---|---|---|
| **Position Block** | The Position Block must have been initialized by the Open operation. It is not required to have positioning established before the Step Next operation. | Positioning is established on the next record address. |
| **Data Buffer** | The Data Buffer should be pointing to a buffer of the size specified in the Data Buffer Length parameter. | The entire record image of the next physical record is placed in the Data Buffer. |
| **Data Buffer Length** | The Data Buffer Length must be set to the maximum anticipated size (in bytes) of the returned record. | The Data Buffer Length is set to the size of the returned record. |
| **Key Buffer** | No value is required. | No value is returned. |
| **Key Number** | No value is required. | No value is returned. |

## Notes

Step Next is used to traverse a database in physical record order. Step Next does not actually require previous positioning, however it is recommended to begin traversal with the Step First (33) operation. Physical record traversal is much faster than index path traversal.

The Step Next operation establishes positioning on the next physical record. This is the next record address on the same data page or the following data page. The Step Next operation does not return a key value and index pages are not accessed. For this reason, the Step Next operation performs much faster than the Get Next (6) operation.

For variable-length records, Btrieve will return no more than the number of bytes specified in the Data Buffer Length parameter. If the record contains more bytes than specified, a status 22 (Data Buffer Length) is returned and the number of bytes specified is returned in the Data Buffer.

The Data Buffer Length parameter specifies the overall length of the Data Buffer. This value is equal to the fixed record length plus the variable-data length.

| Status Code | Cause | Correction |
|---|---|---|
| **3**<br>File Not Opened | The file was not opened properly | Perform the Open (0) operation, and use the same Position Block. |
| | The Position Block was overwritten. | Determine the cause and correct. An invalid pointer (e.g., Key Buffer pointer) can cause a Position Block to be overwritten. |
| **9**<br>End of File | The Step Next operation was issued while positioned on the last record address in the file. | Discontinue database traversal. |
| **22**<br>Data Buffer Length | The value specified in the Data Buffer Length parameter is smaller than the size of the current record. | Make sure that the value of the Data Buffer Length parameter is set to a value that is large enough to accommodate the largest anticipated record. |

## Positioning

Positioning is established on the physical next record. No index key path is established.

## Available Bias Values

Apply record locking bias:
- 100 = single record Wait
- 200 = single record No-Wait
- 300 = multiple record Wait
- 400 = multiple record No-Wait

## Extended Operations

Step Next Extended (38)

# Stop (25)

## Function

The Stop (25) operation removes the Btrieve TSR from workstation memory. With workstation Btrieve, the BTRIEVE.EXE program is removed. With client-server Btrieve, the BREQUEST.-EXE program is removed. If both BTRIEVE.EXE and BREQUEST.EXE are present, both are removed.

| Parameter | Before Call | After Call |
|---|---|---|
| **Position Block** | No value is required. | No value is returned. |
| **Data Buffer** | No value is required. | No value is returned. |
| **Data Buffer Length** | No value is required. | No value is returned. |
| **Key Buffer** | No value is required. | No value is returned. |
| **Key Number** | No value is required. | No value is returned. |

## Notes

The Stop operation deallocates all memory associated with the Btrieve TSR as long as Btrieve is the highest memory resident program hooked to Interrupt 7b.

The Stop operation closes all files and releases all resources associated with the workstation's connection.

An application cannot perform any other Btrieve operations until the Btrieve TSR is reloaded.

# Version (26)

## Function

The Version (26) operation returns the version and revision number of the workstation TSR or DLL.

| Parameter | Before Call | After Call |
|---|---|---|
| **Position Block** | No value is required. | No value is returned. |
| **Data Buffer** | No value is required. | A five-byte description is returned in the format outlined in the Notes section below. |
| **Data Buffer Length** | The Data Buffer Length must be set to five or greater. | The Data Buffer Length is set to five. |
| **Key Buffer** | No value is required. | No value is returned. |
| **Key Number** | No value is required. | No value is returned. |

## Notes

The Version operation only returns the version of the workstation component of Btrieve. Its use is limited in that it does not return the NetWare Btrieve version.

A five-byte description is returned in the Data Buffer in the following format:

- Two-byte integer containing version number
- Two-byte integer containing revision number
- One-byte type character:

  (N) NetWare Btrieve and Btrieve for DOS
  (P) Btrieve for OS/2
  (W) Btrieve for Windows

# Unlock (27)

## Function

The Unlock (27) operation releases locks placed on records.

| Parameter | Before Call | After Call |
|---|---|---|
| **Position Block** | For single-record locks, the Position Block must be initialized for the file that contains the locked record. | No value is returned. |
| **Data Buffer** | For a multiple record unlock, the Data Buffer must contain the four-byte address of the record to unlock and the Key Number parameter must be set to [-1]. | No value is returned. |
| **Data Buffer Length** | For a multiple record unlock (Key Number equals [-1]), the Data Buffer Length must be set to four, the length of the record address in the Data Buffer. | No value is returned. |
| **Key Buffer** | No value is required. | No value is returned. |
| **Key Number** | If the Key Number is set to zero or above, the Unlock operation unlocks a single-record lock based on current positioning. If the Key Number is set to [-1], the Unlock operation unlocks a multi-record lock based on the four-byte address in the Data Buffer. If the Key Number is set to [-2], the Unlock operation unlocks all multi-record locks independent of positioning and record address. | No value is returned. |

## Notes

There are three basic ways to use the Unlock operation based on the Key Number:

- To unlock a single record lock, set the Key Number to zero
- To unlock a specific multi-record lock, determine the address of the record to unlock with the Get Position (22) operation, pass the address of the record to be unlocked
- To Unlock all multi-record locks, and set the Key Number to [-2].

Issuing a single record unlock (Key Number equals zero) or a global multi-record unlock while there are no locked records will result in a status of zero.

| Status Code | Cause | Correction |
|---|---|---|
| **81**<br>Lock Error | An attempt was made to unlock a specific multi-record locked record (Key Number equals [-1]) and the record at the specified record address was not locked. | The Unlock operation with the Key Number equal to [-1] only works on locked records. Set Key Number to [-2] to unlock all records. |

## Positioning

The Unlock operation does not effect current positioning.

# Reset (28)

## Function

The Reset (28) operation releases all resources held by a workstation. It closes all opened files, aborts all pending transactions, and releases all locks.

| Parameter | Before Call | After Call |
|---|---|---|
| **Position Block** | No value is required. | No value is returned. |
| **Data Buffer** | No value is required. | No value is returned. |
| **Data Buffer Length** | No value is required. | No value is returned. |
| **Key Buffer** | If resetting another workstation, the Key Buffer must contain the connection ID of the other work-station (the Key Number must equal [-1]). Otherwise no value is required. | No value is returned. |
| **Key Number** | If the Key Number is set to zero or above, the Reset operation resets the current workstation. If the Key Number is set to [-1] or below, the Reset operation resets another workstation. | No value is returned. |

## Notes

Issuing a Reset operation at the beginning of an application insures that the workstation has no open files and no locks.

The Reset operation is the easy way to close all files to an application.

# Set Owner (29)

## Function

The Set Owner (29) operation assigns an owner name to a file, thus restricting access to applications not possessing the owner name.

| Parameter | Before Call | After Call |
|---|---|---|
| **Position Block** | The Position Block must be initialized to the open file receiving the owner name. | No value is returned. |
| **Data Buffer** | The Data Buffer contains the owner name (binary zero terminated) to be assigned to the file. The owner name can be up to eight characters. It must be a duplicate of the Key Buffer value. | No value is returned. |
| **Data Buffer Length** | No value is required. | No value is returned. |
| **Key Buffer** | The Key Buffer contains the owner name (binary zero terminated) to be assigned to the file. The owner name can be up to eight characters. It must be a duplicate of the Data Buffer parameter. | No value is returned. |
| **Key Number** | Determines owner security level:<br>**0** – Require an owner name for any access (read/write) and no data encryption is applied.<br>**1** – Permits read-only access without an owner name and no data encryption is applied.<br>**2** – Require an owner name for any access (read/write) and data encryption is applied.<br>**3** – Permits read-only access without an owner name and data encryption is applied. | No value is returned. |

## Notes

Applications opening a Btrieve file with an owner name must specify the owner name in the Data Buffer.

For Security Levels One and Three (permit read-only access without owner name), an application not specifying the owner name can open the file. In this case, the application can not issue the Insert (2), Update (3), Delete (4), Add Supplemental Index (31), or Drop Supplemental Index (32) operations. A status 46 (Access to File Denied) is the result of attempting a write operation on the file.

For encryption, Btrieve uses the owner name as the encryption key. Encryption can be a lengthy operation on larger files.

The file will become locked during this operation.

Once an owner name is set, it remains in effect until a Clear Owner (30) operation is issued.

| Status Code | Cause | Correction |
|---|---|---|
| **41**<br>Operation Not Allowed | A Set Owner operation was attempted within a transaction. | Do not attempt a Set Owner operation in a transaction. |
| **50**<br>Owner Already Set | The file already has an owner name set. | If a new owner name is desired, issue a Clear Owner (30) operation before the Set Owner operation. |
| **51**<br>Invalid Owner | The owner names in the Data Buffer and the Key Buffer do not match. | Make sure that the owner names in the Data Buffer and the Key Buffer match exactly. |

# Clear Owner (30)

## Function

The Clear Owner (30) operation removes the owner name of a file and disables security. If the file has been encrypted with the Set Owner (29) operation, the Clear Owner (30) operation decrypts the data file.

| Parameter | Before Call | After Call |
|---|---|---|
| **Position Block** | The Position Block must be initialized to the open file clearing the owner name. | No value is returned. |
| **Data Buffer** | No value is required. | No value is returned. |
| **Data Buffer Length** | No value is required. | No value is returned. |
| **Key Buffer** | No value is required. | No value is returned. |
| **Key Number** | No value is required. | No value is returned. |

## Notes

After the Clear Owner operation, an Btrieve no longer requires an owner name to access the file. If the file had been encrypted (with the Set Owner operation), Btrieve decrypts the file. This can be a time consuming operation with large data files.

| Status Code | Cause | Correction |
|---|---|---|
| **41**<br>Operation Not Allowed | A Clear Owner operation was attempted within a transaction. | Do not attempt a Clear Owner operation in a transaction. |

# Create Supplemental Index (31)

## Function

The Create Supplemental Index (31) operation create a temporary index that can be dropped when it is no longer needed. This index is stored as a part of the file.

| Parameter | Before Call | After Call |
|---|---|---|
| **Position Block** | The Position Block must be initialized for an open file. | No value is returned. |
| **Data Buffer** | The Data Buffer contains the definition of the supplemental index to be created consisting of one sixteen-byte key segment specification block for each key segment of the supplemental index key. An alternate collating sequence is defined following the key specification. See the notes on the Data Buffer format below. | No value is returned. |
| **Data Buffer Length** | No value is required. | No value is returned. |
| **Key Buffer** | No value is required. | No value is returned. |
| **Key Number** | No value is required. | No value is returned. |

## Notes

**Data Buffer Format**

The following tables describe the Data Buffer format for defining a supplemental index. There must be one Key Segment specification block for each key segment in the key. For segmented keys, contiguous key specification blocks define each segment of the key, with the segmented key flag specifying that the following block defines the next segment of the current key.

A Segmented key flag setting of zero marks the last segment for the current key.

**Key Segment Specification Block**
(one for each key segment defined)

| Description | Length | Function |
|---|---|---|
| **Key Position** | 2 | Location of key segment in record (1 relative) |
| **Key Length** | 2 | Length of key segment in bytes |
| **Key Flags** | 2 | Defines file characteristics (see next table) |
| **Reserved 1** | 4 | |
| **Extended Key Type** | 1 | Btrieve key type of segment |
| **Null Value** | 1 | Character considered to be the null value |
| **Reserved 2** | 4 | |

**Key Flags Definition**

| Flag | Decimal Value | Description |
|---|---|---|
| **Duplicates** | 1 | Allow duplicates |
| **Modifiable** | 2 | Allow key to be modified |
| **Binary** | 4 | 1=key is binary; 0=key is string |
| **Null** | 8 | The key is a null key |
| **Segmented** | 16 | The key is segmented with the following key segment |
| **Alternate Collating Sequence** | 32 | The key uses an alternate collating sequence |
| **Descending** | 64 | The index is in descending order |
| **Supplemental** | 128 | The key is defining a supplemental index |

**Key Flags Definition**

| Flag | Decimal Value | Description |
|---|---|---|
| **Extended Key Type** | 256 | The key is of an extended key type |
| **Manual** | 512 | The key is a manual key |

See the Create(14) operation for detailed description of the key flags parameter.

**Extended Key Types**

| Type | Value |
|---|---|
| **String** | 0 |
| **Integer** | 1 |
| **Float** | 2 |
| **Date** | 3 |
| **Time** | 4 |
| **Decimal** | 5 |
| **Money** | 6 |
| **Logical** | 7 |
| **Numeric** | 8 |
| **Bfloat** | 9 |
| **Lstring** | 10 |
| **Zstring** | 11 |
| **Unsigned Binary** | 12 |
| **Autoincrement** | 15 |

The file must first be opened and a transaction cannot be active.

The file will become locked while the index is begin created and creating a supplemental index can be a lengthy operation on large files.

The Key Number identifier for the new index becomes the next highest Key Number.

The new index operates exactly like a permanent index with the following exception: chronological order cannot be guaranteed with duplicate values. Duplicate key values will traverse in physical record address order.

Btrieve appends new index pages to the end of the file as needed.

Use the Drop Supplemental Index (32) operation to remove the index.

If the Create Supplemental Index operation fails due to a system error, the index will remain in the file but will yield a status 56 (Incomplete Index) on an attempt to access the index. The supplemental index should be dropped and recreated.

| Status Code | Cause | Correction |
|---|---|---|
| **2**<br>File I/O Error | A hardware or network malfunction occurred while the supplemental index was being created. | Correct the hardware or network malfunction, drop the supplemental index, and recreate. |
| **18**<br>Disk Full | There is no disk space available. | Free up disk space<br><br>Use the Extend (16) operation to use another disk or volume (not supported with NetWare v3.x ). |
| **22**<br>Data Buffer Length | The Data Buffer Length parameter is not long enough to accommodate the entire key specification. | Make sure the Data Buffer Length parameter is large enough to specify the size of the file specification including the alternate collating sequence (if present).<br><br>Make sure all file specification parameters are set correctly. |

| Status Code | Cause | Correction |
|---|---|---|
| **27**<br>Invalid Key Position | A key segment definition (position and length) exceeds the record length of the file being defined. | Ensure each key segment definition defines the key within the record. One way to determine which key specification block is causing the error is to create the file several times decrementing the Number of Indexes value each time until the error does not occur or only one key remains. |
| **29**<br>Invalid Key Length | The key length specified in one of the key specification blocks was less than zero or greater than 255 (the maximum key size). | Adjust the key length parameter in the key specification block causing the error. On way to determine which key specification block is causing the error, is to create the file several times decrementing the Number of Indexes value each time until the error does not occur or only one key remains. |
| **48**<br>Invalid Alternate Sequence | The first byte in the alternate collating sequence does not contain a hex AC. | Place a hex AC in the first byte of the definition.<br><br>Make sure that the alternate collating sequence directly follows the last key specification block. |
| **49**<br>Key Type Error | The key type specified in one of the key specification blocks contained an invalid key type.<br><br>An attempt was made to assign an alternate collating sequence to a non-string key type. | Make sure all key type parameters contain a proper key type.<br><br>Only assign an alternate collating sequence to a String, Lstring, or Zstring key type. |

# Drop Supplemental Index (32)

## Function

The Drop Supplemental Index (32) operation drops a temporary index that was created with the Create Supplemental Index (31) operation.

| Parameter | Before Call | After Call |
|---|---|---|
| **Position Block** | The Position Block must be initialized for the open file with the supplemental index. | No value is returned. |
| **Data Buffer** | No value is required. | No value is returned. |
| **Data Buffer Length** | No value is required. | No value is returned. |
| **Key Buffer** | No value is required. | No value is returned. |
| **Key Number** | This is the Key Number of the supplemental index to drop. | No value is returned. |

## Notes

Use Drop Supplemental Index (32) operation to remove an index added with the Create Supplemental Index (31) operation.

The file must first be opened and a transaction cannot be active.

The file will become locked while the index is begin dropped.

The index pages containing the supplemental index are returned to the free space list.

The file size will not become smaller after the Drop Supplemental Index operation.

The index identifiers for supplemental indexes above the index being dropped are decremented by one.

| Status Code | Cause | Correction |
|---|---|---|
| **2**<br>File I/O error | A hardware or network malfunction occurred while the supplemental index was being dropped. | Correct the hardware or network malfunction, repeat the Drop Supplemental Index operation. |
| **6**<br>Invalid Key Number | The Key Number parameter referenced an index that was not a supplemental index. | Specify a valid Key Number. |
| **41**<br>Operation Not Allowed | A Drop Supplemental Index was attempted within a transaction. | Do not attempt to drop a supplemental index within a transaction. |

# Step First (33)

## Function

The Step First (33) operation retrieves the first record in physical address order. It places the record in the Data Buffer and establishes positioning on the physical first record. The record is placed in the Data Buffer and positioning is established on the first physical record.

| Parameter | Before Call | After Call |
|---|---|---|
| **Position Block** | The Position Block must have been initialized by the Open operation. It is not required to have positioning established before the Step First operation. | Positioning is established on the first record for physical traversal. |
| **Data Buffer** | The Data Buffer should be the size specified in the Data Buffer Length parameter. | The entire record image of the first record is placed in the Data Buffer. |
| **Data Buffer Length** | The Data Buffer Length must be set to the maximum anticipated size (in bytes) of the returned record. | The Data Buffer Length is set to the size of the returned record. |
| **Key Buffer** | No value is required. | No value is returned. |
| **Key Number** | No value is required. | No value is returned. |

## Notes

The Step First operation is used to begin traversing a database in physical record order. Use the Step Next (24) operation to continue traversal. Physical record traversal is much faster than index path traversal.

The Step First operation positions on the first physical record. This is the first record address on the first data page in the file. The Step First operation does not return a key value and index pages are not accessed. For this reason, the Step First operation performs much faster than the Get First (12) operation.

For variable-length records, Btrieve will return no more than the number of bytes specified in the Data Buffer Length parameter. If the record contains more bytes than specified, a status 22 (Data Buffer Length) is returned and the number of bytes specified is returned in the Data Buffer

For variable-length records, the Data Buffer Length parameter specifies the overall length of the Data Buffer. This is equal to the fixed record length plus the variable data length.

| Status Code | Cause | Correction |
|---|---|---|
| **3**<br>File Not Opened | The file was not opened properly. | Perform the open operation, and use the same Position Block. |
| | The Position Block was over written. | Determine the cause and correct. An invalid pointer (e.g., Key Buffer pointer) can cause a Position Block to be overwritten. |
| **9**<br>End of File | The database has no records. | Use after records have been inserted. |
| **22**<br>Data Buffer Length | The value specified in the Data Buffer Length parameter is smaller than the size of the current record. | Make sure that the value of the Data Buffer Length parameter is set large enough to accommodate the largest anticipated record. |

## Positioning

Positioning is established on the physical first record. No index key path is established.

## Available Bias Values

Apply record locking bias:

100 = single record Wait
200 = single record No-Wait
300 = multiple record Wait
400 = multiple record No-Wait

# Step Last (34)

## Function

The Step Last (34) operation retrieves the last record in physical address order. It places the record in the Data Buffer and establishes positioning on the last record.

| Parameter | Before Call | After Call |
|---|---|---|
| **Position Block** | The Position Block must be initialized by the Open operation. It is not required to have positioning established before the Step Last operation. | Positioning is established on the last record for physical traversal. |
| **Data Buffer** | The Data Buffer pointer should be the size specified in the Data Buffer Length parameter. | The entire record image of the last record is placed in the Data Buffer. |
| **Data Buffer Length** | The Data Buffer Length must be set to the maximum anticipated size (in bytes) of the returned record. | The Data Buffer Length is set to the size of the returned record. |
| **Key Buffer** | No value is required. | No value is returned. |
| **Key Number** | No value is required. | No value is returned. |

## Notes

Step Last is used to begin a reverse traversal of a database in physical record order. Use the Step Previous (35) operation to continue traversal.

The Step Last operation positions on the last physical record. This is the last record address on the last data page in the file. The Step Last operation does not return a key value and index pages are not accessed. For this reason, the Step Last operation performs much faster than the Get Last (13) operation.

For variable-length records, Btrieve will return no more than the number of bytes specified in the Data Buffer Length parameter. If the record contains more bytes than specified, a status

22 (Data Buffer Length) is returned and the number of bytes specified is returned in the Data Buffer

For variable-length records, the Data Buffer Length parameter specifies the overall length of the Data Buffer. This is equal to the fixed record length plus the variable-data length.

| Status Code | Cause | Correction |
|---|---|---|
| **3**<br>File Not Opened | The file was not opened properly. | Perform the open operation, and use the same Position Block. |
| | The Position Block was over written. | Determine the cause and correct. An invalid pointer (e.g., Key Buffer pointer) can cause a Position Block to be overwritten. |
| **9**<br>End of File | The database has no records. | Use after records have been inserted. |
| **22**<br>Data Buffer Length | The value specified in the Data Buffer Length parameter is smaller than the size of the current record. | Make sure that the value of the Data Buffer Length parameter is set large enough to accommodate the largest anticipated record. |

## Positioning

Positioning is established on the physical last record. No index key path is established.

## Available Bias Values

Apply record locking bias:

100 = single record Wait
200 = single record No-Wait
300 = multiple record Wait
400 = multiple record No-Wait

# Step Previous (35)

## Function

The Step Previous (35) operation retrieves the previous record in physical address order. It places the record in the Data Buffer and establishes positioning on the physical previous record.

| Parameter | Before Call | After Call |
|---|---|---|
| **Position Block** | The Position Block must have been initialized by the Open operation. It is not required to have positioning established before the Step Previous operation. | Positioning is established on the previous record (in physical order). |
| **Data Buffer** | The Data Buffer should be the size specified in the Data Buffer Length parameter. | The entire record image of the physical next record is placed in the Data Buffer. |
| **Data Buffer Length** | The Data Buffer Length must be set to the maximum anticipated size (in bytes) of the returned record. | The Data Buffer Length is set to the size of the returned record. |
| **Key Buffer** | No value is required. | No value is returned. |
| **Key Number** | No value is required. | No value is returned. |

## Notes

The Step Previous operation is used to perform a reverse traversal of a database in physical record order. Begin traversal with the Step Last (34) operation.

The Step Previous operation positions on the previous physical record. This is the previous record address on the same data page or the preceding data page. The Step Previous operation does not return a key value and index pages are not accessed. For this reason, The Step Previous operation performs much faster than the Get Previous (6) operation.

For variable-length records, Btrieve will return no more than the number of bytes specified in the Data Buffer Length parameter. If the record contains more bytes than specified, a status

22 (Data Buffer Length) is returned and the number of bytes specified is returned in the Data Buffer.

For variable-length records, the Data Buffer Length parameter specifies the overall length of the Data Buffer. This is equal to the fixed record length plus the variable-data length.

| Status Code | Cause | Correction |
|---|---|---|
| **3**<br>File Not Opened | The file was not opened properly. | Perform the Open (0) operation and use the same Position Block. |
| | The Position Block was overwritten. | Determine the cause and correct. An invalid pointer (e.g., Key Buffer pointer) can cause a Position Block to be incorrectly overwritten. |
| **9**<br>End of File | The Step Previous operation was issued while positioned on the first record address in the file. | Discontinue database traversal. |
| **22**<br>Data Buffer Length | The value specified in the Data Buffer Length parameter is smaller than the size of the previous record. | Make sure that the value of the Data Buffer Length parameter is set large enough to accommodate the largest anticipated record. |

## Positioning

Positioning is established on the physical next record. No index key path is established.

## Available Bias Values

Apply record locking bias:

100 = single record Wait
200 = single record No-Wait
300 = multiple record Wait
400 = multiple record No-Wait

## Extended Operation

Step Previous Extended (39)

# Get Next Extended (36)

## Function

The Get Next Extended (36) operation retrieves the next several records or sub-records that pass an optional filter condition. These records are returned in current key path order, starting at the current record. The number of records, the filter condition, and the sub-record specification are defined in the Data Buffer. The records or sub-records are returned in the Data Buffer along with record lengths and physical record address for each record.

| Parameter | Before Call | After Call |
|---|---|---|
| **Position Block** | The Position Block must have position established on the same key path as specified in the Key Number parameter. | Positioning is established on the last logical record examined by Btrieve on the key path specified by the Key Number parameter. |
| **Data Buffer** | Before the call, the Data Buffer contains an extended retrieval description containing three basic blocks of information:<br>• The Header specifies the total length of the Data Buffer and a control constant.<br>• The Filter specifies the filter condition that a record must pass in order to be returned and the maximum number of rejected records before control is returned.<br>• The Extractor specifies the sub-record or fields to return and the maximum number of records to be returned.<br>See notes below for detailed format. | After the call the Data Buffer contains returned data including the number of records retrieved followed by an array of records with the following information:<br>• Record length (used for variable-length records)<br>• Physical record address of record<br>• Record image based on the Extractor specification<br>See notes below for detailed format. |
| **Data Buffer Length** | The Data Buffer Length must be set to the either the size of the extended retrieval description or the size of the returned data, whichever is larger. | The Data Buffer Length is set to the size of the returned data. |

| Parameter | Before Call | After Call |
|---|---|---|
| **Key Buffer** | The Key Buffer should be as large as the key specified by the Key Number parameter. | The key value of the last record retrieved is returned. |
| **Key Number** | The Key Number (zero offset) of the current key path. | The Key Number is not modified. |

## Notes

Get Next Extended is used instead of multiple Get Next operations (6) for traversing a database in key path order where maximum network performance is desired. For NetWare Btrieve, if a filter is specified, the filtering logic takes place at the file server and only desired records are transmitted back to the workstation. In addition, by specifying an extractor (the bytes within the record or fields to be returned) the entire record need not be transmitted.

## Notes on Extended Operations

**Extended Get Description**
(format of Data Buffer before the Extended Get operation)

**Header** (one per call)

| Parameter | Length |
|---|---|
| **Data Buffer Length** | 2 |
| **Control Constant** (EG or UC) | 2 |

**Filter** (one per call)

| Parameter | Length |
|---|---|
| **Reject Count** | 2 |
| **Number of Logical Expressions Terms** | 2 |

**Filter Terms** (one per Number of Logical Expression Term)

| Parameter | Length |
|---|---|
| **Btrieve Data Type** | 1 |
| **Field Length** | 2 |
| **Field Offset** (zero relative) | 2 |
| **Comparison Code** (next table) | 1 |
| **Logical Expression**<br>(0 = last term, 1 = AND, 2 = OR) | 1 |
| **Comparison Constant/Comparison Field Offset**<br>(where n is equal to Field Length) | n or 2 |

**Comparison Codes**

| Code | Description |
|---|---|
| 1 | Equal |
| 2 | Greater than |
| 3 | Less than |
| 4 | Not equal |
| 5 | Greater than or equal |
| 6 | Less than or equal |

**Bias** (add to comparison code)

| Bias | Description |
|---|---|
| 32 | Use alt. collating sequence for strings |
| 64 | Compare with field, not a constant |
| 128 | Disable case sensitivity |

**Extended Get Extractor**
(specifies format of Data Buffer after the Extended Get occurs)

**Header** (one per call)

| Parameter | Length |
|---|---|
| **Number of Records Returned** | 2 |
| **Number of Fields to Extract** | 2 |

**Extractor Fields** (one for each field to be extracted)

| Parameter | Length |
|---|---|
| **Field Length** | 2 |
| **Field Offset** | 2 |

If the entire record is to be returned, set the Number of Fields to one, the Field Length to the record length, and the Field Offset to zero.

**Format of Returned Data**
(format of the Data Buffer after the extended retrieval operation is performed)

**Format of Returned Data**

| Data Buffer Portion | Length | Description |
|---|---|---|
| **Fixed Portion** | 2 | Number of records returned |
| **Repeating Portion** (one for each record retrieved) | 2 | Length of record image |
| | 4 | Physical Record address |
| | n | Record image |

## Notes on Implementation

The Number of Records Returned parameter (in the extractor description) instructs Btrieve to return only a specified number of records. The programmer decides how many records to retrieve based on the amount of available memory in the program.

The reject count variable in the filter condition is used to instruct Btrieve to return control once this number of records has been reached. If zero is specified, Btrieve assigns max integer as the reject count.

With the Extended Gets and Steps, Btrieve begins processing at the current record, and examines records in key path order for Gets and physical address order for Steps. Records that pass the filter condition (if present) are placed in an internal Btrieve output buffer to be returned (note: a filter condition is optional). The output buffer is transmitted to the workstation and control is returned to the calling program when one of the following occurs:

- The maximum number of records to return (as specified in the extractor) has been satisfied and a status 0 (Operation OK) is returned.
- The reject count has been exceeded and a status 60 (Reject Count) is returned.
- The end of file has been reached and a status 9 (End of File) is returned.
- Btrieve has determined that there are no more records that will pass the filter condition and a Status 64 (Filter Limit Reached) is returned.

If the current record is not to be included, place 'EG' in the header control constant. If the current record is to be included, place 'UC' in the header control constant.

"UC" is not supported for workstation-level Btrieve for DOS version 5.1x.

For Extended Gets, Btrieve always begins searching at the current record and does not automatically pre-position for optimal performance. To gain optimal performance on searches, if the filter condition includes a field that is one of the file's keys, use that key path and establish positioning on that key value (with Get Equal for or similar) before performing the extended operation.

Filter expressions are evaluated left to right and boolean order of precedence is not used. Thus, certain complex expressions cannot be supported.

In certain cases, Btrieve will determine that no more records will pass the filter condition and complete processing to avoid unnecessary delay. A status 64 (Filter Limit Reached) can occur when the current key path key definition matches a filter field definition.

Positioning is always established on the last record that Btrieve examined. If the reject count has been exceeded, this is the last rejected record.

**Warning**
The current key value of the last record returned is always returned at the location pointed to by the Key Buffer pointer parameter. Make sure the Key Buffer pointer is pointing to a variable large enough to accommodate the key value.

The Key Number parameter must be the same Key Number as the previous operation that established positioning.

| Status Code | Cause | Correction |
|---|---|---|
| 3<br>File Not Opened | The file was not opened properly. | Perform the open operation, and use the same Position Block for the Get Next. |
| | The Position Block was over written. | Determine the cause and correct. An invalid pointer (e.g., Key Buffer pointer) can cause a Position Block to be incorrectly overwritten. |
| 6<br>Invalid Key Number | The Key Number parameter contained an invalid Key Number reference. | Make sure the Key Number parameter has a valid value. A valid Key Number range is zero to (n - 1) where n is the number of keys paths defined for the file. |
| 7<br>Different Key Number | The Key Number value was different from the key path used to establish positioning. | Make sure the Key Number parameter specifies the same key path previously used to establish positioning. To change key paths while traversing perform a Get Position (22) followed by a Get Direct (23) with the new key path set in the Key Number parameter. |
| 9<br>End of File | The end of file has been reached. | Discontinue database retrieval. |
| 22<br>Data Buffer Length | The value specified in the Data Buffer Length parameter is not large enough to contain the returned records. | Make sure that the value of the Data Buffer Length parameter is set large enough to accommodate the largest anticipated record. |

| Status Code | Cause | Correction |
|---|---|---|
| **60**<br>Reject Count Reached | The number of records specified in the Reject Count parameter in the filter description was reached. | If more records that match the filter condition are believed to be in the file, repeat the operation. Otherwise discontinue record retrieval. |
| **62**<br>Incorrect Description | The header or filter description was incorrect and Btrieve was not able to perform the extended operation. | Examine the content of the Data Buffer before the extended operation, and make sure the description is formatted correctly. Workstation Btrieve version 5.1x does not support the "UC" control constant. See "Notes on Extended Operations." |
| **64**<br>Filter Limit Reached | A rejected record (from the filter condition) caused Btrieve to determine that no more records will satisfy the filter condition. This occurs when the current key path definition matches a filter field definition. | Discontinue record retrieval. |
| **65**<br>Incorrect Field Offset | The Extractor contains an invalid Field Offset. | Only specify offsets that are within the record. |

# Positioning

Positioning is established on the last record examined by Btrieve if a status 0 (Operation OK) is returned. Positioning is established on the last record in the Data Buffer. If a status 60 (Reject Count Reached) or status 64 (Filter Limit Reached) is returned, positioning is established on the last rejected record. The same positioning rules apply for duplicate and non-duplicate keys indexes as with the Get Next (6) operation.

# Get Previous Extended (37)

## Function

The Get Previous Extended (37) operation retrieves the previous several records or sub-records in current key path order that pass a filter condition starting at the current record. The number of records, filter condition, and sub-record specification are defined in the Data Buffer. The records or sub-records are returned in the Data Buffer along with record lengths and physical record address for each record.

| Parameters | Before Call | After Call |
|---|---|---|
| **Position Block** | The Position Block must have position established on the same key path as specified in the Key Number parameter. | Positioning is established on the last logical record examined by Btrieve in the current key path specified by the Key Number parameter. |
| **Data Buffer** | Before the call, the Data Buffer contains an extended retrieval description containing three basic blocks of information:<br>• The Header, which specifies the total length of the Data Buffer and a control constant,<br>• The Filter, which specifies the filter condition that a record must pass in order to be returned and the maximum number of rejected records before control is returned, and<br>• The Extractor, which specifies the sub-record or fields to return and the maximum number of records to be returned.<br>For a detailed format of the Data Buffer, see "Notes on Extended Operations" for Get Next Extended (36) operation. | After the call the Data Buffer contains returned data including including the number of records retrieved followed by an array of records with the following information:<br>• Record length (used for variable-length records)<br>• Physical record address of record<br>• Record image based on the Extractor specification<br>For detailed format, see "Notes on Extended Operations" under Get Next Extended (36) operation. |

| Parameters | Before Call | After Call |
|---|---|---|
| **Data Buffer Length** | The Data Buffer Length must be set to the larger of the following:<br>• The size of the extended retrieval description<br>• The size of the returned data | The Data Buffer Length is set to the size of the returned data. |
| **Key Buffer** | The Key Buffer should be as large as the current key size of the key specified by the Key Number parameter. | The current key value of the last record retrieved is returned. |
| **Key Number** | The current Key Number (zero offset) of the current key path. | The Key Number is not modified. |

## Notes

The Get Previous Extended operation is used instead of multiple Get Previous (7) operations for traversing a database in key path order where maximum network performance is desired. For NetWare Btrieve, if a filter is specified, the filtering logic takes place at the file server and only desired records are transmitted back to the workstation. In addition, by specifying an extractor (the bytes within the record or fields to be returned) the entire record need not be transmitted.

For a detailed format of extended operations Data Buffer format, and implementation notes, See "Notes on Extended Operations" under the Get Next Extended (36) operation.

**Warning**
The current key value of the last record returned is always returned at the location pointed to by the Key Buffer pointer parameter. Make sure the Key Buffer pointer is pointing to a variable of large enough to accommodate the key value.

The Key Number parameter must be the same Key Number as the previous operation that established positioning.

| Status Code | Cause | Correction |
|---|---|---|
| **3**<br>File Not Opened | The file was not opened properly. | Perform the open operation, and use the same Position Block for the Get Next. |
| | The Position Block was over written. | Determine the cause and correct. An invalid pointer (e.g., Key Buffer pointer) can cause a Position Block to be incorrectly overwritten. |
| **6**<br>Invalid Key Number | The Key Number parameter contained an invalid Key Number reference. | Make sure the Key Number parameter has a valid value. A valid Key Number range is zero to (n - 1) where n is the number of keys paths defined for the file. |
| **7**<br>Different Key Number | The Key Number value was different from the key path used to establish positioning. | Make sure the Key Number parameter specifies the same key path previously used to establish positioning. To change key paths while traversing perform a Get Position (22) followed by a Get Direct (23) with the new key path set in the Key Number parameter. |
| **9**<br>End of File | The end of file has been reached. | Discontinue database retrieval. |
| **22**<br>Data Buffer Length | The value specified in the Data Buffer Length parameter is not large enough to contain the returned records. | Make sure that the value of the Data Buffer Length parameter is set large enough to accommodate the largest anticipated record. |
| **60**<br>Reject Count Reached | The number of records specified in the Reject Count parameter in the filter description was reached. | If more records that match the filter condition are believed to be in the file, repeat the operation otherwise discontinue record retrieval. |

| Status Code | Cause | Correction |
|---|---|---|
| **62**<br>Incorrect Description | The header or filter description was incorrect and Btrieve was not able to perform the extended operation. | Examine the content of the Data Buffer before the extended operation, and make sure the description is formatted correctly. Workstation Btrieve version 5.1x does not support the "UC" control constant. See "Notes on Extended Operations." |
| **64**<br>Filter Limit Reached | A rejected record (from the filter condition) caused Btrieve to determine that no more records will satisfy the filter condition. This occurs when the current key path definition matches a filter field definition. | Discontinue record retrieval. |
| **65**<br>Incorrect Field Offset | The Extractor contains an invalid Field Offset. | Only specify offsets that are within the record. |

## Positioning

Positioning is established on the last record examined by Btrieve if a status 0 (Operation OK) is returned. Positioning is established on the last record in the Data Buffer. If a status 60 (Reject Count Reached) or status 64 (Filter Limit Reached) is returned, positioning is established on the last rejected record. The same positioning rules apply for duplicate and non-duplicate keys indexes as with the Get Previous (7) operation.

# Step Next Extended (38)

## Function

The Step Next Extended (38) operation retrieves the next several records or sub-records in physical record address order that pass a filter condition starting at the current record. The number of records, filter condition, and sub-record specification are defined in the Data Buffer. The records or sub-records are returned in the Data Buffer along with record lengths and physical record address for each record.

| Parameters | Before Call | After Call |
|---|---|---|
| **Position Block** | The Position Block must have position established on a record. | Positioning is established on the last physical record examined by Btrieve. |
| **Data Buffer** | Before the call, the Data Buffer contains an extended retrieval description containing three basic blocks of information:<br>• The Header, which specifies the total length of the Data Buffer and a control constant,<br>• The Filter, which specifies the filter condition that a record must pass in order to be returned and the maximum number of rejected records before control is returned, and<br>• The Extractor, which specifies the sub-record or fields to return and the maximum number of records to be returned.<br>For a detailed format of the Data Buffer, see "Notes on Extended Operations" for the Get Next Extended (36) operation. | After the call the Data Buffer contains returned data including the number of records retrieved followed by an array of records with the following information:<br>• Record length (used for variable-length records)<br>• Physical record address of record<br>• Record image based on the Extractor specification<br>For detailed format, see "Notes on Extended Operations" for the Get Next Extended (36) operation. |

| Parameters | Before Call | After Call |
|---|---|---|
| **Data Buffer Length** | The Data Buffer Length must be set to the larger of the following:<br>• The size of the extended retrieval description<br>• The size of the returned data | The Data Buffer Length set to the size of the returned data. |
| **Key Buffer** | No value is required. | No value is returned. |
| **Key Number** | No value is required. | No value is returned. |

## Notes

The Step Next Extended operation is used instead of multiple Step Next (24) operations for traversing a database in physical address order where maximum network performance is desired. For NetWare Btrieve, if a filter is specified, the filtering logic takes place at the file server and only desired records are transmitted back to the workstation. In addition, by specifying an extractor (the bytes within the record or fields to be returned) the entire record need not be transmitted.

For a detailed format of extended operations Data Buffer format, and implementation notes, See "Notes on Extended Operations" under the Get Next Extended (36) operation.

| Status Code | Cause | Correction |
|---|---|---|
| **3**<br>File Not Opened | The file was not opened properly. | Perform the open operation, and use the same Position Block. |
| | The Position Block was overwritten. | Determine the cause and correct. An invalid pointer (e.g., Key Buffer pointer) can cause a Position Block to be overwritten. |
| **9**<br>End of File | The end of file has been reached. | Discontinue record retrieval. |
| **22**<br>Data Buffer Length | The value specified in the Data Buffer Length parameter is not large enough to contain the returned records. | Make sure that the value of the Data Buffer Length parameter is set large enough to accommodate the largest anticipated record. |

| Status Code | Cause | Correction |
|---|---|---|
| **60**<br>Reject Count Reached | The number of records specified in the reject count parameter in the filter description was reached. | If more records that match the filter condition are believed to be in the file, repeat the operation otherwise discontinue record retrieval. |
| **62**<br>Incorrect Description | The header or filter description was incorrect and Btrieve was not able to perform the extended operation. | Examine the content of the Data Buffer before the extended operation, and make sure the description is formatted correctly. See "Notes on Extended Operations" under the Get Next Extended (36) operation. |
| **64**<br>Filter Limit Reached | A rejected record (from the filter condition) caused Btrieve to determine that no more records will satisfy the filter condition. This can occur when the current key path key definition matches a filter field definition. | Discontinue record retrieval. |
| **65**<br>Incorrect Field Offset | The extractor contains an invalid field offset. | Only specify offsets that are within the record. |

## Positioning

Positioning is established on the last record examined by Btrieve if a status 0 (Operation OK) is returned. Positioning is established on the last record in the Data Buffer. If a status 60 (Reject Count Reached) or status 64 (Filter Limit Reached) is returned, positioning is established on the last rejected record. The same positioning rules apply as for the Step Next (24) operation.

# Step Previous Extended (39)

## Function

The Step Previous Extended (39) operation retrieves the previous several records or sub-records in physical record address order that pass a filter condition starting at the current record. The number of records, filter condition, and sub-record specification are defined in the Data Buffer. The records or sub-records are returned in the Data Buffer along with record lengths and physical record address for each record.

| Parameter | Before Call | After Call |
|---|---|---|
| **Position Block** | The Position Block must have position established on a record. | Positioning is established on the last physical record examined by Btrieve. |
| **Data Buffer** | Before the call, the Data Buffer contains an extended retrieval description containing three basic blocks of information:<br>• The Header, which specifies the total length of the Data Buffer and a control constant,<br>• The Filter, which specifies the filter condition that a record must pass in order to be returned and the maximum number of rejected records before control is returned, and<br>• The Extractor, which specifies the sub-record or fields to return and the maximum number of records to be returned.<br>For a detailed format of the Data Buffer, see "Notes on Extended Operations" for the Get Next Extended (36) operation. | After the call the Data Buffer contains returned data including the number of records retrieved followed by an array of records with the following information:<br>• Record length (used for variable-length records)<br>• Physical record address of record<br>• Record image based on the Extractor specification<br>For detailed format, see "Notes on Extended Operations" for the Get Next Extended (36) operation. |
| **Data Buffer Length** | The Data Buffer Length must be set to the larger of the following:<br>• The size of the extended retrieval description<br>• The size of the returned data | The Data Buffer Length must be set to the size of the returned data. |

| Parameter | Before Call | After Call |
|---|---|---|
| **Key Buffer** | No value is required. | No value is returned. |
| **Key Number** | No value is required. | No value is returned. |

## Notes

The Step Previous Extended operation is used instead of multiple Step Previous (35) operations for traversing a database in physical address order where maximum network performance is desired. For NetWare Btrieve, if a filter is specified, the filtering logic takes place at the file server and only desired records are transmitted back to the workstation. In addition, by specifying an extractor (the bytes within the record or fields to be returned) the entire record need not be transmitted.

For a detailed format of extended operations Data Buffer format, and implementation notes, see "Notes on Extended Operations" for the Get Next Extended (36) operation.

| Status Code | Cause | Correction |
|---|---|---|
| **3**<br>File Not Opened | The file was not opened properly. | Perform the open operation, and use the same Position Block for the Get Next operation. |
| | The Position Block was over written. | Determine the cause and correct. An invalid pointer (e.g., Key Buffer pointer) can cause a Position Block to be incorrectly overwritten. |
| **6**<br>Invalid Key Number | The Key Number parameter contained an invalid Key Number reference. | Make sure the Key Number parameter has a valid value. A valid Key Number range is zero to (n - 1) where n is the number of keys paths defined for the file. |

| Status Code | Cause | Correction |
|---|---|---|
| **7**<br>Different Key Number | The Key Number value was different from the key path used to establish positioning. | Make sure the Key Number parameter specifies the same key path previously used to establish positioning. To change key paths while traversing perform a Get Position (22) followed by a Get Direct (23) with the new key path set in the Key Number parameter. |
| **9**<br>End of File | The end of file has been reached. | Discontinue database retrieval. |
| **22**<br>Data Buffer Length | The value specified in the Data Buffer Length parameter is not large enough to contain the returned records. | Make sure that the value of the Data Buffer Length parameter is set large enough to accommodate the largest anticipated record. |
| **60**<br>Reject Count Reached | The number of records specified in the Reject Count parameter in the filter description was reached. | If more records that match the filter condition are believed to be in the file, repeat the operation otherwise discontinue record retrieval. |
| **62**<br>Incorrect Description | The header or filter description was incorrect and Btrieve was not able to perform the extended operation. | Examine the content of the Data Buffer before the extended operation, and make sure the description is formatted correctly. Workstation Btrieve version 5.1x does not support the "UC" control constant. See "Notes on Extended Operations." |

## Positioning

Positioning is established on the last record examined by Btrieve if a status 0 (Operation OK) is returned. Positioning is established on the last record in the Data Buffer. If a status 60 (Reject Count Reached) or status 64 (Filter Limit Reached) is returned, positioning is established on the last rejected record. The same positioning rules apply as with the Step Previous (35) operation.

# Insert Extended (40)

## Function

The Insert Extended (40) operation inserts the set of records in the Data Buffer into a file. It updates all indexes and establishes positioning on the last record inserted for the key path specified in the Key Number parameter.

| Parameter | Before Call | After Call |
|---|---|---|
| **Position Block** | The Position Block is not required to have positioning established before the Extended Insert operation. | Positioning is established on the last inserted record. The Position Block contains pointers to the last inserted record and logical next and previous record in current key path order as specified by the Key Number parameter. |
| **Data Buffer** | The Data Buffer must be pointing to a buffer containing an array of record images (with length bytes) to be inserted. The Data Buffer must adhere to the format detailed in the "Notes" section below. | The Total Number of Records is updated to reflect the number of records inserted. |
| **Data Buffer Length** | The Data Buffer Length must be the length of the Data Buffer which contains all records to be inserted. | No value is returned. |
| **Key Buffer** | The Key Buffer pointer should be pointing to a buffer as large as the key size of the key specified by the Key Number parameter. | The key value (of the key specified by the Key Number) of the last record inserted is returned in the Key Buffer. |
| **Key Number** | This is the current key path (zero offset) on which to maintain positioning. | The Key Number is not modified. |

## Notes

| Data Buffer | Number of Bytes | Description |
|---|---|---|
| **Fixed portion** | 2 | Number of records inserted |
| **Repeating portion** (one for each record) | 2 + n | Length of the record image (in bytes) followed by the record image |

The Insert Extended operation is the fastest method for inserting multiple records, especially over busy networks.

For NetWare Btrieve, make sure that the /R load parameter is set to a value as large or larger than the amount of data being inserted as specified by the Data Buffer Length parameter.

The "length of record image" value is used for variable-length records but must be included with fixed-length records as well.

If an error occurs, such as a status 5 (Duplicate Key), all records will remain inserted up to the record causing the error. The number of records inserted is specified in the first byte of the Data Buffer.

The Insert Extended operation will not return control to the workstation until all records have been inserted.

For duplicate keys on permanent indexes, duplicate key records will always be retrieved in the chronological order in which they were inserted.

**Warning**
The current key value of the inserted record is always returned at the location pointed to by the Key Buffer pointer parameter. Make sure the Key Buffer pointer is pointing to a variable of large enough to accommodate the key value.

| Status Code | Cause | Correction |
|---|---|---|
| **2** I/O Error | An error occurred during a disk write. This can be the result of hardware failure or the Btrieve file being improperly overwritten by a non-Btrieve program. | The file must be recreated. |

| Status Code | Cause | Correction |
|---|---|---|
| **3**<br>File Not Opened | The file was not opened properly. | Perform the open operation, and use the same Position Block. |
| | The Position Block was overwrit-ten. | Determine the cause and correct. An invalid pointer (e.g., Key Buffer pointer) can cause a Position Block to be overwritten. |
| **5**<br>Duplicate Key Error | The record contained an key value already existing in a non-duplicate key path. | Determine the number of records actually inserted from the first two bytes of the Data Buffer and insert records starting after the record causing the error. |
| **14**<br>Pre-Image Open Error | Btrieve attempted to create the pre-image file and was unable due to the disk being full. | Data integrity cannot be ensured. Issue a reset command and remove files to provide sufficient disk space. |
| | Btrieve attempted to create the pre-image file and was unable due to insufficient access rights to the directory where the pre-image file is located. | Data integrity cannot be ensured. Proper access rights must be assigned to the workstation (see "Grant" command, NetWare man-ual). |
| **15**<br>Pre-image I/O Error | Btrieve attempted to write to the pre-image file and the disk is full. | Provide more disk space. |
| | The pre-image file was damaged. | Discontinue insertion. Data integ-rity cannot be ensured. |
| **18**<br>Disk Full | The disk is full and Btrieve attempted to expand the file. | Provide more disk space. |
| **22**<br>Data Buffer Length | The value specified in the Data Buffer Length parameter is smaller than the fixed record length. | Determine the proper record length and specify that value in the Data Buffer Length parameter. |
| **46**<br>Access to File Denied | The file was opened in read-only mode. | Open the file in normal mode. |
| | The file requires an owner name to Insert. | Open the file with the correct owner name. |

## Positioning

**Non-duplicate key path**
Positioning is established on the last record inserted for the key path specified in the Key Number parameter.

**Duplicate key path**
The last inserted record becomes the last record in the chain of duplicates. For permanent indexes, this becomes the last record in chronological order of insert. For supplemental indexes, the record becomes the last record in physical address order.

# A Btrieve Extended Key Types

This appendix describes Btrieve key data types. You specify key types during a Create (14) operation in each one-byte key type parameter. These data types are compatible with NetWare SQL field types.

| Key Data Type | Decimal Value |
|---|---|
| String | 0 |
| Integer | 1 |
| Float | 2 |
| Date | 3 |
| Time | 4 |
| Decimal | 5 |
| Money | 6 |
| Logical | 7 |
| Numeric | 8 |
| Bfloat | 9 |
| Lstring | 10 |
| Zstring | 11 |
| Unsigned Binary | 12 |
| Autoincrement | 15 |

## String (0)

A String key is a non-delimited ASCII character array. Strings values are compared from left to right and can be up to 255 bytes long.

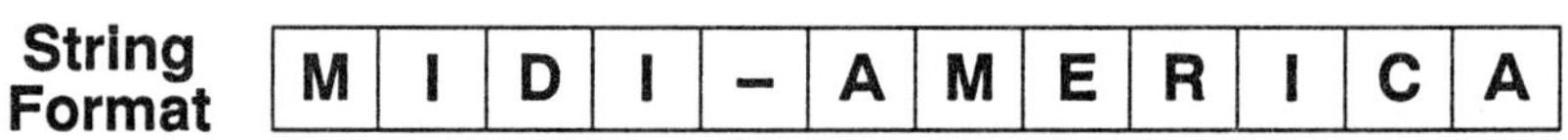


*Figure A.1: Example String type*

## Integer (1)

An Integer is a two- or four-byte signed whole number in an Intel binary integer format with the high-order and low-order bytes reversed.

## Float (2)

A Float type is an IEEE standard single and double precision real number. The internal format for a four-byte Float consists of a 23-bit mantissa, an eight-bit exponent biased by 127, and a sign bit.

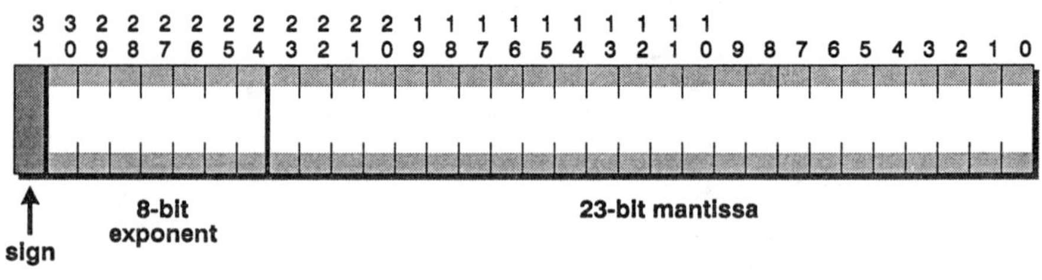


*Figure A.2.1: Example four-byte Float type*

An eight-byte Float consists of a 52-bit mantissa, an 11-bit exponent biased by 1023, and a sign bit.

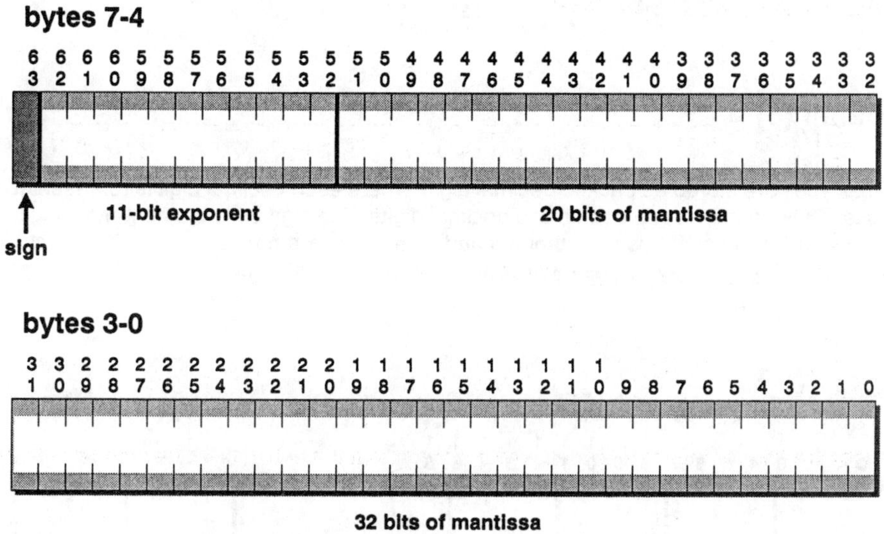


*Figure A.2.2: Example eight-byte Float type*

## Date (3)

Date types are stored in a 4-byte day, month, year format with a one-byte integer representing day, one-byte integer representing month, followed by a two-byte integer representing year.

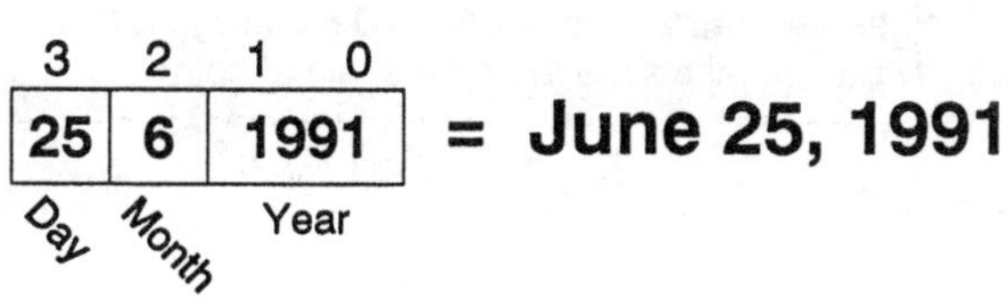


*Figure A.3: Example Date type*

## Time (4)

Time types are stored in a four-byte value where four integers represents hundredths of seconds, seconds, minutes, and hours.

## Decimal (5)

Decimal types are stored as packed decimal digits where each decimal digit is represented by four bits. Thus each byte represents two decimal digits. The sign bit is the right-most digit where F and C represent positive numbers and D represents a negative value. The decimal point is implied and all key values must contain the same number of decimals to collate properly.

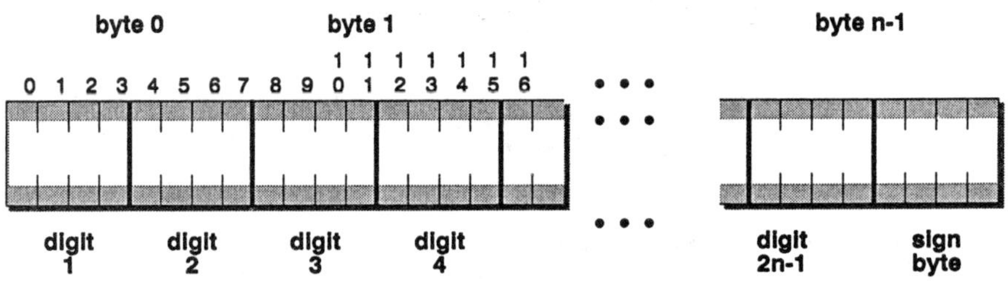


*Figure A.4: Example Decimal type*

## Money (6)

The Money type uses the same internal format as the Decimal type. It is assumed that Money types always have only two decimal places after the decimal point.

## Logical (7)

Logical types are stored as one or two-byte strings. The application determines what represents true and false.

## Numeric (8)

The Numeric type is stored as an ASCII string where each digit is represented by an ASCII character. The right-most byte of the number includes an embedded sign according to the following table:

***Figure A.5: Example Numeric type***

| Digit | Positive | Negative |
|---|---|---|
| 1 | 1 or A | J |
| 2 | 2 or B | K |
| 3 | 3 or C | L |
| 4 | 4 or D | M |
| 5 | 5 or E | N |
| 6 | 6 or F | O |
| 7 | 7 or G | P |
| 8 | 8 or H | Q |
| 9 | 9 or I | R |
| 0 | 0 or { | } |

## Bfloat (9)

The Bfloat type is used to support floating point values from older versions of BASIC (pre MS-BASIC 6.x). A Bfloat type can be a four- or eight-byte real number. A four-byte Bfloat type is stored with a 23-bit mantissa, an eight-bit exponent biased by 128, and a sign bit. An eight-byte Bfloat type is stored with a 55-bit mantissa, an eight-bit exponent biased by 128, and a sign bit.

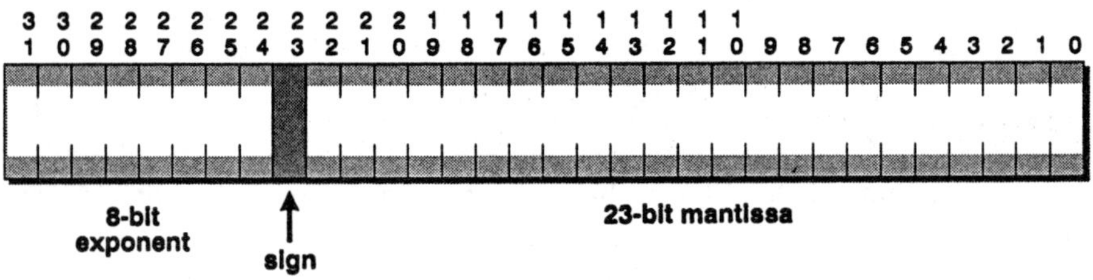


*Figure A.6: Example four-byte Bfloat type*

## Lstring (10)

The Lstring type supports Borland's Turbo Pascal string type where the length of the string is stored in the first byte of the character array. Only character values up to the length specified by the length byte are compared for collating. Characters beyond the string length are ignored.

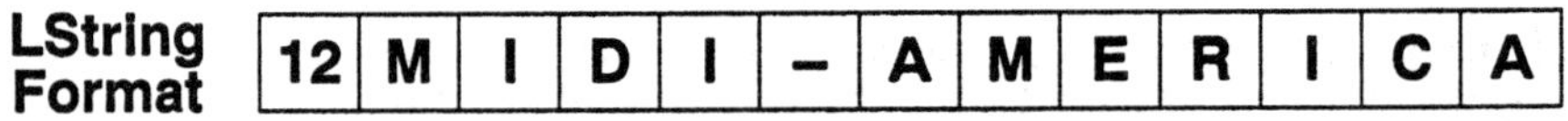


*Figure A.7: Example Lstring type*

## Zstring (11)

The Zstring type supports C Language's string type where the end of string is marked with a binary zero. Only character values up to the binary zero are compared for collating. Characters beyond the binary zero are ignored.

| | | | | | | | | | | | | | |
|---|---|---|---|---|---|---|---|---|---|---|---|---|---|
| **ZString Format** | M | I | D | I | – | A | M | E | R | I | C | A | Ø |

***Figure A.8: Example Zstring type***

## Unsigned Binary (12)

The Unsigned Binary type supports two- and four-byte unsigned integers compared a word at a time from right to left.

## Autoincrement (15)

The Autoincrement type is a two- or four- byte unsigned binary integer. An autoincrement key is used to automatically calculate the next highest integer value. Upon insert of an autoincrement key initialized to zero, the autoincrement value is calculated to be one plus the key buffer value after performing a Get Last (13) operation for the autoincrement key path. This value is reflected in the data buffer after the call. Autoincrement is not calculated on key values not equal to zero upon insert.

The following restrictions apply to the Autoincrement type:

- Duplicate key values are not supported.
- An autoincrement key cannot be part of a segmented key.
- An autoincrement key cannot overlap another key.

# B C Language Source Code Examples

This appendix contains source code listings of the example programs. These programs are available in machine readable form on the optional Tutorial Diskette available through MIDI America. The following programs are included:

| | |
|---|---|
| INCLUDES.C | — Define Btrieve Constants. |
| BCREATE.C | — Create Customer File. |
| BINSERT.C | — Insert records from input file. |
| BTRAVI.C | — Traverse in index order. |
| BTRAVP.C | — Traverse in physical record order. |
| BSEARCH.C | — Perform indexed search on customer number. |
| BUPDATE.C | — Perform updates on records as specified by input file. |
| BGROUP.C | — Display a group of records use the sales rep index. |
| BSINDEX.C | — Create supplemental index using alternate collating sequence. |
| BXINSERT.C | — Use extended inserts to insert variable length records. |
| BXGET.C | — Retrieve a set of customer records with no filter. |
| BXGETF.C | — Retrieve a set of customer records with a zip code range filter. |
| BUPM.C | — Multi-user version of BUPDATE.C |
| BUPT.C | — Use transactions on BUPM.C |

# INCLUDES.C

```
//
//  INCLUDES.C INCLUDE FILES FOR EXAMPLE PROGRAMS
//  AUTHOR:    FRANK A. LEO / THE ILLUSTRATED GUIDE TO BTRIEVE
//  DATE:      OCTOBER 17, 1991
//
//
#include "wat2btrv.c"
#include "b_const.c"
#include "ch_const.c"
#include <stdio.h>
#include <string.h>
#include <stdlib.h>
#include <time.h>
#include <process.h>
#include <dos.h>

// DEFINE THE BTRIEVE CALL WITH CASTING
#define Cp(expr)  ((char *)expr)
#define S(expr)  ((short )expr)
#define P(expr)  ((unsigned short *)expr)
#define BTRV(op,pos,buf,len,key,keyn) BTRV(S(op),Cp(pos), Cp(buf), P(len),
Cp(key), S(keyn))
```

# BCREATE.C

```
//
//  BCREATE.C  CREATE EXAMPLE WITH WATCOM C v8.0 AND BTRIEVE 5.10
//  AUTHOR:    FRANK A. LEO / THE ILLUSTRATED GUIDE TO BTRIEVE
//  DATE:      OCTOBER 17, 1991
//
//  Create the example customer file. See Customer_Record_Type for
//  file definition.
//
#include "includes.c"
#define MAX_NOTE_SIZE  2000
//
// BTRIEVE CREATE STRUCTURES
//
struct KeySpec
        { int   KeyPos;
          int   KeyLen;
          int   KeyFlags;
          long  KeyTot;
          char  KeyType;
          char  Reserved[5]; };

struct File_Description_Type
        { int   RecLen;
          int   PageSize;
          int   IndxCnt;
          long  RecTot;
          int   FileFlags;
          char  Reserved[2];
          int   Allocation;
          struct KeySpec KeyBuf[24]; };
//
// BTRIEVE DATA TYPE STRUCTURES
//
struct date_type
        {  char  day;
           char  month;
           int   year;  };
//
// APPLICATION STRUCTURE
//
struct  Customer_Record_Type{
        int     cust_number;          // key 0
        char    cust_name[30];        // key 1
        char    company[60];          // key 2.2 (10)
        char    addr_1[30];
        char    addr_2[30];
        char    city[30];
        char    state[2];
        char    zip[9];               // key 2.1
        char    country[3];
        char    phone[10];
        char    sales_rep[3];         // key 3.1
        struct  date_type next_date;  // key 3.2
        char    dollar_vol[10];
        int     record_flag;
        char    notes[MAX_NOTE_SIZE];  };
```

```
//
// BTRIEVE FUNCTION VARIABLES
//
int     Stat;
char    PosBlk[128];
struct  File_Description_Type FileBuf;
struct  Customer_Record_Type  CustRecBuf;
int     BufLen;
char    bFileName[] = {"CUSTOMER.DTR "};
int     Keyno;
//
main()
{
    Create_Customer ();
}
//
//
//  CREATE CUSTOMER.BTR FILE
//
void Create_Customer() {
  FileBuf.RecLen = sizeof(CustRecBuf) - MAX_NOTE_SIZE;
  FileBuf.PageSize = 1024;
  FileBuf.IndxCnt = 4;
  FileBuf.FileFlags = B_VARIABLE_LENGTH;

  // SETUP KEY SPECS

  //--------------------------------------------------------------------------

  FileBuf.KeyBuf[0].KeyPos = 1;          // KEY 0 BY CUSTOMER NUMBER
  FileBuf.KeyBuf[0].KeyLen = 2;
  FileBuf.KeyBuf[0].KeyFlags = B_EXTENDED_KEY_TYPE;
  FileBuf.KeyBuf[0].KeyType  = B_AUTOINC;

  //--------------------------------------------------------------------------

  FileBuf.KeyBuf[1].KeyPos = 3;          // KEY 1 BY CUSTOMER NAME *10
  FileBuf.KeyBuf[1].KeyLen = 10;
  FileBuf.KeyBuf[1].KeyFlags = B_EXTENDED_KEY_TYPE |
                               B_DUPLICATES |
                               B_MODIFIABLE ;
  FileBuf.KeyBuf[1].KeyType  = B_STRING;

  //--------------------------------------------------------------------------

  FileBuf.KeyBuf[2].KeyPos   = 185;       // KEY 2 BY >ZIPCODE BY COMPANY
  FileBuf.KeyBuf[2].KeyLen   = 9;
  FileBuf.KeyBuf[2].KeyFlags = B_EXTENDED_KEY_TYPE |
                               B_DUPLICATES |
                               B_MODIFIABLE |
                               B_SEGMENTED;
  FileBuf.KeyBuf[2].KeyType  = B_STRING;
  //
  FileBuf.KeyBuf[3].KeyPos   = 33;        // KEY 2 BY ZIPCODE BY >COMPANY
  FileBuf.KeyBuf[3].KeyLen   = 10;
  FileBuf.KeyBuf[3].KeyFlags = B_EXTENDED_KEY_TYPE |
                               B_DUPLICATES |
                               B_MODIFIABLE;
  FileBuf.KeyBuf[3].KeyType  = B_STRING;
```

```
    //--------------------------------------------------------------------------

    FileBuf.KeyBuf[4].KeyPos   = 207;       //KEY 3 BY >REP BY NEXT_DATE
    FileBuf.KeyBuf[4].KeyLen   = 3;
    FileBuf.KeyBuf[4].KeyFlags = B_EXTENDED_KEY_TYPE |
                                 B_DUPLICATES |
                                 B_MODIFIABLE;
    FileBuf.KeyBuf[4].KeyType  = B_STRING;
    //
    FileBuf.KeyBuf[5].KeyPos   = 210;       //KEY 3 BY REP BY >NEXT_DATE
    FileBuf.KeyBuf[5].KeyLen   = 4;
    FileBuf.KeyBuf[5].KeyFlags = B_EXTENDED_KEY_TYPE |
                                 B_DUPLICATES |
                                 B_MODIFIABLE |
                                 B_SEGMENTED;
    FileBuf.KeyBuf[5].KeyType  = B_DATE;

    //--------------------------------------------------------------------------

    BufLen = sizeof(FileBuf);
    Stat = BTRV(B_CREATE, PosBlk, &FileBuf, &BufLen, bFileName, 0);
    if(Stat != 0)
            printf("Error Creating Customer File.  Status = %d\n", Stat);
    else
            printf("Customer File created successfully\n");
    return;
}
```

# BINSERT.C

```
//
// BINSERT.C   INSERT EXAMPLE WITH WATCOM C v8.0 AND BTRIEVE 5.10
// AUTHOR:     FRANK A. LEO / THE ILLUSTRATED GUIDE TO BTRIEVE
// DATE:       OCTOBER 17, 1991
//
// Insert records from a comma delimited ASCII text input file into
// the example customer database file.
//
#include "includes.c"
#define MAX_NOTE_SIZE  2000
#define MAX_FIELD_SIZE 30
//
// FUNCTION PROTOTYPES
//
// Read a CUSTOMER record from an input SDF file
int fReadSDF_CustRec(struct Customer_Record_Type *CustRecBuf,
                     FILE *SDFfile );

// Read a field from an input SDF file
int fReadSDF_Field(char *fieldPtr,
                   int   Flength,
                   int   Ftype,
                   FILE *SDFfile   );

//
// BTRIEVE DATA TYPE STRUCTURES
//
struct date_type
       { char  day;
         char  month;
         int   year;  };
//
// APPLICATION STRUCTURES
//
// Btrieve file CUSTOMER.BTR record format
// Note: Key segments are denoted by "key k.s",
//       where k is the key number and s is the
//       segment. No s means a non segmented key.
//       If the segment length is smaller than the
//       field, the key segment length is denoted
//       with (l) where l is the segment length.
//
struct  Customer_Record_Type{
        int     cust_number;          // key 0
        char    cust_name[30];        // key 1 (10)
        char    company[60];          // key 2.2 (10)
        char    addr_1[30];
        char    addr_2[30];
        char    city[30];
        char    state[2];
        char    zip[9];               // key 2.1
        char    country[3];
        char    phone[10];
        char    sales_rep[3];         // key 3.1
        struct  date_type next_date;  // key 3.2
        char    dollar_vol[10];
```

```
        int     record_flag;
        char    notes[MAX_NOTE_SIZE];  };
//
// BTRIEVE FUNCTION VARIABLES
//
int     Stat;
char    CustPosBlk[128];
struct  Customer_Record_Type  CustRecBuf;
int     BufLen;
char    KeyBuf[255];
char    bFileName[13];
int     Keyno;
// INPUT FILE VARIABLES
FILE    *SDFfile;
char    inChar;
// TIMING VARIABLES
double RecPerSec, BeginTime, EndTime, d_time;
//
char temparr[MAX_FIELD_SIZE];
int  tempint;
long ctr;
main()
{
    Open_Customer ();
    SDFfile  = fopen("CUSTOMER.SDF","r");
    BeginTime = (double) clock();
    fReadSDF_CustRec(&CustRecBuf, SDFfile);          // Read the first record.
                                                     // Place in data buffer.
    ctr = 0;
    while ( ! feof(SDFfile) )  {                     // Loop until end of file.
       BufLen = sizeof(CustRecBuf) - MAX_NOTE_SIZE   // Calc. record length.
              + strlen(CustRecBuf.notes) + 1;
       printf("%crecord %ld, length = %d", CHR_CAR_RETURN, ++ctr, BufLen);
       Keyno=0;                                 // Maintain positioning on key 0.
       Stat    = BTRV(B_INSERT, CustPosBlk,     // Insert record into Btr. file
              &CustRecBuf, &BufLen, &KeyBuf, Keyno);
       if(Stat != 0)                            // Check for error conditions.
           printf("Error Inserting Customer Record. Status = %d\n", Stat);
       fReadSDF_CustRec(&CustRecBuf, SDFfile);       // Read the next record
                                                     // from the input file.
    }
    EndTime = (double) clock();
    d_time    = (EndTime - BeginTime) / CLK_TCK;
    Close_Customer ();
    fclose( SDFfile );
    RecPerSec = ctr / d_time;
    printf ("inserted %ld records in %6.2f seconds
             or %6.2f records per second\n",
             ctr, d_time, RecPerSec);
}
//
//
// fReadSDF_CustRec: read a record from the CUSTOMER database
// input SDF file. Place the record in the databuffer
//
int fReadSDF_CustRec(struct Customer_Record_Type *CustRecBuf,
                     FILE *SDFfile )
{
   CustRecBuf->cust_number = 0;
   fReadSDF_Field(&CustRecBuf->cust_name, 30, B_STRING, SDFfile);
```

```
        if feof( SDFfile ) return(0);
    fReadSDF_Field(&CustRecBuf->company, 60, B_STRING, SDFfile);
    fReadSDF_Field(&CustRecBuf->addr_1, 30, B_STRING, SDFfile);
    fReadSDF_Field(&CustRecBuf->addr_2, 30, B_STRING, SDFfile);
    fReadSDF_Field(&CustRecBuf->city, 30, B_STRING, SDFfile);
    fReadSDF_Field(&CustRecBuf->state, 2, B_STRING, SDFfile);
    fReadSDF_Field(&CustRecBuf->zip, 9, B_STRING, SDFfile);
    fReadSDF_Field(&CustRecBuf->country, 3, B_STRING, SDFfile);
    fReadSDF_Field(&CustRecBuf->phone, 10, B_STRING, SDFfile);
    fReadSDF_Field(&CustRecBuf->sales_rep, 3, B_STRING, SDFfile);
    fReadSDF_Field( (char *) &CustRecBuf->next_date, 4, B_DATE, SDFfile);
    fReadSDF_Field(&CustRecBuf->dollar_vol, 10, B_NUMERIC, SDFfile);
    fReadSDF_Field( (char *) &CustRecBuf->record_flag, 2, B_STRING, SDFfile);
    fReadSDF_Field(&CustRecBuf->notes, MAX_NOTE_SIZE, B_NOTE, SDFfile);
    return( sizeof( &CustRecBuf)-MAX_NOTE_SIZE + strlen(CustRecBuf->notes) );
}
//
// fReadSDF: read the next field in SDFfile and convert to the
// Btrieve data type specified by fType and fLength. Place the
// results in the fieldPtr location
//
//

int fReadSDF_Field(char    *fieldPtr,
                   int     fLength,
                   int     fType,
                   FILE    *SDFfile )
{
    int i,j;
    char temparr[MAX_FIELD_SIZE];
    int  tempint;
    switch ( fType ) {
       //
       case B_STRING: {
          do {
             inChar = fgetc(SDFfile);          //Read the double quotes
             if ( feof( SDFfile ) ) return(0);
           } while (inChar != CHR_DOUBLE_QT && inChar != CHR_CAR_RETURN);
          if (inChar == CHR_CAR_RETURN) {      // if a carrage return
             inChar = fgetc(SDFfile);          // read linefeed, return
             return(0);
          }
          i=0;
          inChar = fgetc(SDFfile);
          while (inChar != CHR_DOUBLE_QT) {    // read string value
             fieldPtr[i++] = inChar;
             inChar = fgetc(SDFfile);
           }
          for (j=i; j<fLength; j++)            //pad with blanks
              fieldPtr[j] = ' ';
          do { inChar = fgetc(SDFfile); }      // Read the comma
             while (inChar != CHR_COMMA );
       } break;
       //
       case B_NUMERIC: {
          for (j=0; j<fLength; j++)            //initialize with blanks
             fieldPtr[j] = ' ';
          i = 0;
          temparr[i] = fgetc(SDFfile);
          if (temparr[i] == CHR_COMMA) break;
```

```
        while (TRUE) {
           if (temparr[i] == CHR_COMMA ||
               temparr[i] == CHR_LINE_FEED) break; // read to comma
           if ( feof( SDFfile ) ) return(0);
           temparr[++i] = fgetc(SDFfile);
        }
         memcpy(&fieldPtr[fLength-i+1], &temparr[0], i+1);
         if (temparr[i] == CHR_LINE_FEED) inChar = fgetc(SDFfile);
                                                // read the line feed
      } break;
      //
      case B_DATE: {
           for (j=0; j<fLength; j++)           //initialize with zeros
              fieldPtr[j] = 0;
           for (i=0; i < 4; i++){
               temparr[i] = fgetc(SDFfile);         // read year
               if (temparr[i] == CHR_COMMA) break;
           }
           temparr[4] = 0;
           tempint = (int) atoi(temparr);
           memcpy(&fieldPtr[2], &tempint, 2);
           temparr[0] = fgetc(SDFfile);             // read month
           if (temparr[0] == CHR_COMMA) break;
           temparr[1]   = fgetc(SDFfile);           // read month
           temparr[2] = 0;
           fieldPtr[1] = (char) atoi(temparr);
           temparr[0] = fgetc(SDFfile);             // read month
           if (temparr[0] == CHR_COMMA) break;
           temparr[1]   = fgetc(SDFfile);           // read month
           temparr[2] = 0;
           fieldPtr[0] = (char) atoi(temparr);
           inChar = fgetc(SDFfile);                 // read comma
      } break;
      case B_NOTE: {
         do {inChar = fgetc(SDFfile); }             // Read the double quotes
           while (inChar != CHR_DOUBLE_QT );
         i = 0;
         inChar = fgetc(SDFfile);
         if (inChar == CHR_COMMA) break;
         while (inChar != CHR_DOUBLE_QT &&
              i <= fLength) {                       // read string value
           fieldPtr[i++] = inChar;
           inChar = fgetc(SDFfile);
          }
         fLength = i;
         fieldPtr[fLength] = 0;
      } break;

   };
   return (fLength);
}
```

# BTRAVI.C

```
//
//  BTRAVI.C    INDEX TRAVERSAL EXAMPLE WITH WATCOM C v8.0 AND BTRIEVE 5.10
//  AUTHOR:     FRANK A. LEO / THE ILLUSTRATED GUIDE TO BTRIEVE
//  DATE:       NOVEMBER 2, 1991
//
//  Traverse customer database in index order.
//
#include "includes.c"
#define MAX_NOTE_SIZE  2000
#define MAX_FIELD_SIZE 30
//
// FUNCTION PROTOTYPES
//
// Print the customer record.
Print_CustRec(struct Customer_Record_Type *CustRecBuf);

//
// BTRIEVE DATA TYPE STRUCTURES
//
struct date_type
        {  char  day;
           char  month;
           int   year;  };
//
// APPLICATION STRUCTURES
//
// Btrieve file CUSTOMER.BTR record format
// Note: Key segments are denoted by "key k.s",
//       where k is the key number and s is the
//       segment. No s means a non segmented key.
//       If the segment length is smaller than the
//       field, the key segment length is denoted
//       with (l) where l is the segment length.
//
struct  Customer_Record_Type{
        int     cust_number;           // key 0
        char    cust_name[30];         // key 1 (10)
        char    company[60];           // key 2.2 (10)
        char    addr_1[30];
        char    addr_2[30];
        char    city[30];
        char    state[2];
        char    zip[9];                // key 2.1
        char    country[3];
        char    phone[10];
        char    sales_rep[3];          // key 3.1
        struct  date_type next_date;   // key 3.2
        char    dollar_vol[10];
        int     record_flag;
        char    notes[MAX_NOTE_SIZE];  };
//
// BTRIEVE FUNCTION VARIABLES
//
int     Stat;
char    CustPosBlk[128];
struct  Customer_Record_Type  CustRecBuf;
```

```
int      BufLen;
char     KeyBuf[255];
char     bFileName[13];
int      Keyno;
//
//
//
main()
{
    Open_Customer ();
    Keyno =  1;                                    // Use the name key.
    BufLen = sizeof(CustRecBuf);
    Stat   = BTRV(B_GET_FIRST, CustPosBlk,
           &CustRecBuf, &BufLen, KeyBuf, Keyno);
    if(Stat != 0 )
       printf("Error Getting First Customer Record. Status = %d\n", Stat);
    while (Stat == 0)    {
                                                   // Loop until end of file.
       Print_CustRec(&CustRecBuf);
       BufLen = sizeof(CustRecBuf);                // Reset Buffer length to max.
       Stat   = BTRV(B_GET_NEXT, CustPosBlk,      // Get the next record.
                &CustRecBuf, &BufLen,
                KeyBuf, Keyno);
       if(Stat != 0 && Stat != B_END_OF_FILE)  // Check for error conditions.
          printf("Error Getting Next Customer Record. Status = %d\n", Stat);
    }
    Close_Customer ();
}
//
//
//  PRINT SELECTED FIELDS IN CUSTOMER RECORD
//
Print_CustRec(struct Customer_Record_Type *CustRecBuf)
{
   CustRecBuf->company[30]= 0;
   printf("%3d %s \n",CustRecBuf->cust_number, CustRecBuf->cust_name);
   printf("    %s \n",CustRecBuf->company);
   printf("    %s \n \n",CustRecBuf->notes);
}
```

# BTRAVP.C

```
//
// BTRAVP.C    PHYSICAL ORDER TRAVERSAL EXAMPLE
//             WITH WATCOM C v8.0 AND BTRIEVE 5.10
// AUTHOR:     FRANK A. LEO / THE ILLUSTRATED GUIDE TO BTRIEVE
// DATE:       NOVEMBER 2, 1991
//
// Traverse customer database in physical record order.
//
#include "includes.c"
#define MAX_NOTE_SIZE  2000
//
// FUNCTION PROTOTYPES
//
// Print the customer record.
Print_CustRec(struct Customer_Record_Type *CustRecBuf);

//
// BTRIEVE DATA TYPE STRUCTURES
//
struct date_type
        { char  day;
          char  month;
          int   year;  };
//
// APPLICATION STRUCTURES
//
// Btrieve file CUSTOMER.BTR record format
// Note: Key segments are denoted by "key k.s",
//       where k is the key number and s is the
//       segment. No s means a non segmented key.
//       If the segment length is smaller than the
//       field, the key segment length is denoted
//       with (l) where l is the segment length.
//
struct  Customer_Record_Type{
        int     cust_number;          // key 0
        char    cust_name[30];        // key 1 (10)
        char    company[60];          // key 2.2 (10)
        char    addr_1[30];
        char    addr_2[30];
        char    city[30];
        char    state[2];
        char    zip[9];               // key 2.1
        char    country[3];
        char    phone[10];
        char    sales_rep[3];         // key 3.1
        struct  date_type next_date;  // key 3.2
        char    dollar_vol[10];
        int     record_flag;
        char    notes[MAX_NOTE_SIZE];  };
//
// BTRIEVE FUNCTION VARIABLES
//
int     Stat;
char    CustPosBlk[128];
struct  Customer_Record_Type  CustRecBuf;
```

```
int     BufLen;
char    KeyBuf[255];
char    bFileName[13];
int     Keyno;
//
//
//
main()
{
    Open_Customer ();
    BufLen = sizeof(CustRecBuf);
    Stat   = BTRV(B_STEP_FIRST, CustPosBlk,
            &CustRecBuf, &BufLen, &KeyBuf, Keyno);
    if(Stat != 0 )
       printf("Error Getting First Customer Record. Status = %d\n", Stat);
    while (Stat == 0)    {                          // Loop until end of file.
       Print_CustRec(&CustRecBuf);
       BufLen = sizeof(CustRecBuf);                 // Reset Buffer length to max
       Stat   = BTRV(B_STEP_NEXT, CustPosBlk,       // Get the next record.
                &CustRecBuf, &BufLen,
                &KeyBuf, Keyno);
       if(Stat != 0 && Stat != B_END_OF_FILE)  // Check for error conditions.
          printf("Error Getting Previous Customer Record.
                 Status = %d\n", Stat);
    }
    Close_Customer ();
}
//
//
//  PRINT SELECTED FIELDS IN CUSTOMER RECORD
//
Print_CustRec(struct Customer_Record_Type *CustRecBuf)
{
   CustRecBuf->cust_name[30] = 0;
   CustRecBuf->company[60]= 0;
   CustRecBuf->dollar_vol[11]= 0;

   printf("%3d %s \n", CustRecBuf->cust_number,
          CustRecBuf->cust_name);
   printf("    %s  Dollar Vol: %s \n",CustRecBuf->company,
          CustRecBuf->dollar_vol);
   printf("    %s \n \n",CustRecBuf->notes);
}
```

# BSEARCH.C

```
//
//  BSEARCH.C  INDEXED SEARCH EXAMPLE
//             WITH WATCOM C v8.0 AND BTRIEVE 5.10
//  AUTHOR:    FRANK A. LEO
//  DATE:      NOVEMBER 2, 1991
//
//  Perform an indexed search on the customer database from an
//  input customer number.
//
#include "includes.c"
#define MAX_NOTE_SIZE  2000
#define MAX_FIELD_SIZE 30
//
// FUNCTION PROTOTYPES
//
// Print the customer record.
Print_CustRec(struct Customer_Record_Type *CustRecBuf);

//
// BTRIEVE DATA TYPE STRUCTURES
//
struct date_type
        { char  day;
          char  month;
          int   year;  };

//
// APPLICATION STRUCTURES
//
// Btrieve file CUSTOMER.BTR record format
// Note: Key segments are denoted by "key k.s",
//       where k is the key number and s is the
//       segment. No s means a non segmented key.
//       If the segment length is smaller than the
//       field, the key segment length is denoted
//       with (l) where l is the segment length.
//
struct  Customer_Record_Type{
        int     cust_number;          // key 0
        char    cust_name[30];        // key 1 (10)
        char    company[60];          // key 2.2 (10)
        char    addr_1[30];
        char    addr_2[30];
        char    city[30];
        char    state[2];
        char    zip[9];               // key 2.1
        char    country[3];
        char    phone[10];
        char    sales_rep[3];         // key 3.1
        struct  date_type next_date;  // key 3.2
        char    dollar_vol[10];
        int     record_flag;
        char    notes[MAX_NOTE_SIZE];  };
//
// BTRIEVE FUNCTION VARIABLES
//
```

```
int     Stat;
char    CustPosBlk[128];
struct  Customer_Record_Type  CustRecBuf;
int     BufLen;
char    KeyBuf[255];
char    bFileName[13];
int     Keyno;
int     Cust_No_Key;
//
//
//
main()
{
    Open_Customer ();
    Keyno =  0;                               // Use the Customer Number key.
    printf("customer number: ");
    scanf("%d", &Cust_No_Key);
    BufLen = sizeof(CustRecBuf);
    Stat   = BTRV(B_GET_EQUAL, CustPosBlk,
            &CustRecBuf, &BufLen, &Cust_No_Key, Keyno);
    if(Stat == 0 )
       Print_CustRec(&CustRecBuf);
    else
       printf("Record not found. Status = %d\n", Stat);
    Close_Customer ();
}
//
//
//  PRINT SELECTED FIELDS IN CUSTOMER RECORD
//
Print_CustRec(struct Customer_Record_Type *CustRecBuf)
{
   CustRecBuf->company[30]= 0;
   printf("%3d %s \n",CustRecBuf->cust_number,
          CustRecBuf->cust_name);
   printf("    %s \n",CustRecBuf->company);
   printf("    %s \n \n",CustRecBuf->notes);
}
```

# BUPDATE.C

```
//
//  BUPDATE.C  UPDATE EXAMPLE WITH WATCOM C v8.0 AND BTRIEVE 5.10
//  AUTHOR:    FRANK A. LEO
//  DATE:      OCTOBER 17, 1991
//
//  Make updates to records in the customer database file as
//  specified by an SDF input file contining a company number
//  followed by a new dollar amount value to be updated.
//
#include "includes.c"
#define MAX_NOTE_SIZE  2000
#define MAX_FIELD_SIZE 30
//
// FUNCTION PROTOTYPES
//
// Read a field from an input SDF file
int fReadSDF_Field(char *fieldPtr,
                   int   Flength,
                   int   Ftype,
                   FILE *SDFfile   );

//
// BTRIEVE DATA TYPE STRUCTURES
//
struct date_type
        { char  day;
          char  month;
          int   year;  };
//
// APPLICATION STRUCTURES
//
// Btrieve file CUSTOMER.BTR record format
// Note: Key segments are denoted by "key k.s",
//       where k is the key number and s is the
//       segment. No s means a non segmented key.
//       If the segment length is smaller than the
//       field, the key segment length is denoted
//       with (l) where l is the segment length.
//
struct  Customer_Record_Type{
        int     cust_number;          // key 0
        char    cust_name[30];        // key 1 (10)
        char    company[60];          // key 2.2 (10)
        char    addr_1[30];
        char    addr_2[30];
        char    city[30];
        char    state[2];
        char    zip[9];               // key 2.1
        char    country[3];
        char    phone[10];
        char    sales_rep[3];         // key 3.1
        struct  date_type next_date;  // key 3.2
        char    dollar_vol[10];
        int     record_flag;
        char    notes[MAX_NOTE_SIZE];  };
//
```

```
// BTRIEVE FUNCTION VARIABLES
//
int      Stat;
char     CustPosBlk[128];
struct   Customer_Record_Type  CustRecBuf;
int      BufLen;
char     KeyBuf[255];
char     bFileName[13];
int      Keyno;
int      Cust_No_Key;
// INPUT FILE VARIABLES
FILE     *SDFfile;
char     SDFCust_No[5];
char     temparr[MAX_FIELD_SIZE];
char     inChar;

//

main()
{
    Open_Customer ();
    SDFfile  = fopen("UPDATES.SDF","r");      // Open update SDF file
    fReadSDF_Field(&SDFCust_No, 5, B_NUMERIC, SDFfile);
    Keyno = 0;
    while ( ! feof(SDFfile) )  {              // Loop through update file
       Cust_No_Key = (int) atoi(SDFCust_No);  // Read customer number
       printf("Searching for customer: %d.",
                 Cust_No_Key);
       BufLen = sizeof(CustRecBuf);           // Set buffer length to max
       Stat = BTRV(B_GET_EQUAL,CustPosBlk,    // Search for record
             &CustRecBuf,&BufLen, &Cust_No_Key, Keyno);
       fReadSDF_Field(&CustRecBuf.dollar_vol, 10,  // Read new dollar amount
                       B_NUMERIC, SDFfile);
       if(Stat == 0 ) {                       // If record found,
          printf(".record found.");
          Stat = BTRV(B_UPDATE, CustPosBlk,   // then update record
                      &CustRecBuf, &BufLen,
                      &Cust_No_Key, Keyno);
             if(Stat == 0 )
                printf(".updated. %c", CHR_CAR_RETURN);
             else
                printf("\nerror updating, status = %d", Stat);

       }
       else {
          printf("\nrecord not found, status = %d,
                 rejecting update.\n", Stat);
       }
       fReadSDF_Field(&SDFCust_No, 5, B_NUMERIC, SDFfile);
    }
    Close_Customer ();
    fclose( SDFfile );
}
```

# BGROUP.C

```
//
// BGROUP.C    SUB-LEVEL GROUPING EXAMPLE
//             WITH WATCOM C v8.0 AND BTRIEVE 5.10
// AUTHOR:     FRANK A. LEO
// DATE:       NOVEMBER 4, 1991
//
// Display a group of records with a common sales rep code
// entered from the keyboard.
//
//
#include "includes.c"
#define MAX_NOTE_SIZE  2000
#define MAX_KEY_SIZE   255
#define MAX_FIELD_SIZE 30
//
// FUNCTION PROTOTYPES
//
// Print the customer record.
Print_CustRec(struct Customer_Record_Type *CustRecBuf);

//
// BTRIEVE DATA TYPE STRUCTURES
//
struct date_type {
           char  day;
           char  month;
           int   year;  };
//
// APPLICATION STRUCTURES
//
// Btrieve file CUSTOMER.BTR record format
// Note: Key segments are denoted by "key k.s",
//       where k is the key number and s is the
//       segment. No s means a non segmented key.
//       If the segment length is smaller than the
//       field, the key segment length is denoted
//       with (l) where l is the segment length.
//
struct  Customer_Record_Type{
        int     cust_number;          // key 0
        char    cust_name[30];        // key 1 (10)
        char    company[60];          // key 2.2 (10)
        char    addr_1[30];
        char    addr_2[30];
        char    city[30];
        char    state[2];
        char    zip[9];               // key 2.1
        char    country[3];
        char    phone[10];
        char    sales_rep[3];         // key 3.1
        struct  date_type next_date;  // key 3.2
        char    dollar_vol[10];
        int     record_flag;
        char    notes[MAX_NOTE_SIZE];  };
//
// KEY BUFFER STRUCTURES
```

```
//
struct ZipCodeKeyType {
        char      zip_code[9];
        char      company[10]; };

struct SalesRepKeyType {
        char              sales_rep[3];
        struct date_type  next_date;
        char              dollar_vol[10]; };

union {
        int                     CustNo_Key;
        char                    CustName_Key[10];
        struct ZipCodeKeyType   ZipCode_Key;
        struct SalesRepKeyType  SalesRep_Key;
        char                    General_Key[MAX_KEY_SIZE];
      } KeyBuf;

//
// BTRIEVE FUNCTION VARIABLES
//
int     Stat;
char    CustPosBlk[128];
struct  Customer_Record_Type  CustRecBuf;
int     BufLen;
char    bFileName[13];
int     Keyno;
char    SearchValue[4];
//
//
//
main()
{
    Open_Customer ();
    Keyno =  3;                             // Use Sales Rep Key
    printf("Enter Rep Code: ");             // Prompt for Rep Code
    gets(SearchValue);
    BufLen = sizeof(CustRecBuf);
    memcpy(&KeyBuf.SalesRep_Key.sales_rep,  // Copy search value
           &SearchValue, 3);                // into key buffer

    Stat   = BTRV(B_GET_GREATER_OR_EQ, CustPosBlk, // Perform Search
            &CustRecBuf, &BufLen, &KeyBuf, Keyno);
    if(Stat != 0 )
       printf("Record not found. Status = %d\n", Stat);
    while ((Stat == 0 ) &&                   // Loop while not EOF,
          !memcmp(&KeyBuf, SearchValue, 3)) {  // and key value matches
       Print_Rep_Report(&CustRecBuf);
       BufLen = sizeof(CustRecBuf);          // Reset Buffer length to max
       Stat   = BTRV(B_GET_NEXT, CustPosBlk,  // Get the next record
               &CustRecBuf, &BufLen,
               &KeyBuf, Keyno);
       if(Stat != 0 && Stat != B_END_OF_FILE)  // Trap for error conditions.
          printf("Error Retrieving Customer Recort. Status = %d\n", Stat);
    }
    Close_Customer ();
}
//
//
//  PRINT SELECTED FIELDS IN CUSTOMER RECORD
```

```
//
Print_Rep_Report(struct Customer_Record_Type *CustRecBuf)
{
   char DspStr[MAX_FIELD_SIZE];
   int dmonth, dday, dyear;
   // SETUP DISPLAY VARIABLES

   dmonth = (int) CustRecBuf->next_date.month;
   dday   = (int) CustRecBuf->next_date.day;
   dyear  = (int) CustRecBuf->next_date.year;

   memcpy(&DspStr, CustRecBuf->sales_rep, 3);
   DspStr[3]=0;
   printf("\n %s %2d\\%2d\\%4d ", DspStr, dmonth, dday, dyear);
   memcpy(&DspStr[0], &CustRecBuf->cust_name, 30);
   DspStr[30]=0;
   printf(" %s", DspStr);

}
```

# BSINDEX.C

```
//
//  BSINDEX.C   SUPPLEMENTAL INDEX USING
//              AN ALTERNATE COLLATING SEQUENCE
//              WITH WATCOM C v8.0 AND BTRIEVE 5.10
//  AUTHOR:     FRANK A. LEO
//  DATE:       NOVEMBER 2, 1991
//
//  Create a supplemental index using a segmented key and
//  alternate collating sequence.
//
#include "includes.c"
#define MAX_NOTE_SIZE  2000
#define MAX_FIELD_SIZE 30
//
// FUNCTION PROTOTYPES
//
// Print the customer record.
Print_CustRec(struct Customer_Record_Type *CustRecBuf);

//
// BTRIEVE DATA TYPE STRUCTURES
//
struct date_type
        {  char  day;
           char  month;
           int   year;  };
//
// APPLICATION STRUCTURES
//
// Btrieve file CUSTOMER.BTR record format
// Note: Key segments are denoted by "key k.s",
//       where k is the key number and s is the
//       segment. No s means a non segmented key.
//       If the segment length is smaller than the
//       field, the key segment length is denoted
//       with (l) where l is the segment length.
//       Supplemental index keys are denoted with supp key.
//
struct  Customer_Record_Type{
        int     cust_number;         // key 0
        char    cust_name[30];       // key 1 (10)    supp key 4.2 (10)
        char    company[60];         // key 2.2 (10)  supp key 4.1 (20)
        char    addr_1[30];
        char    addr_2[30];
        char    city[30];
        char    state[2];
        char    zip[9];              // key 2.1
        char    country[3];
        char    phone[10];
        char    sales_rep[3];        // key 3.1
        struct  date_type next_date; // key 3.2
        char    dollar_vol[10];
        int     record_flag;
        char    notes[MAX_NOTE_SIZE];  };
//
// BTRIEVE FUNCTION VARIABLES
```

```
//
int     Stat;
char    CustPosBlk[128];
struct  Customer_Record_Type  CustRecBuf;
int     BufLen;
char    KeyBuf[255];
char    bFileName[13];
int     Keyno;
//
//
//
main()
{
    Open_Customer ();
    Create_Supp_Index ();
    Keyno =  4;
    BufLen = sizeof(CustRecBuf);
    Stat   = BTRV(B_GET_FIRST, CustPosBlk,
            &CustRecBuf, &BufLen, KeyBuf, Keyno);
    if(Stat != 0 )
       printf("Error Getting First Customer Recort. Status = %d\n", Stat);
    while (Stat == 0)   {                      // Loop until end of file
       Print_CustRec(&CustRecBuf);
       BufLen = sizeof(CustRecBuf);            // Reset Buffer length to max
       Stat   = BTRV(B_GET_NEXT, CustPosBlk,   // Get the next record
                &CustRecBuf, &BufLen,
                KeyBuf, Keyno);
       if(Stat != 0 && Stat != B_END_OF_FILE)  // Check for error conditions
          printf("Error Inserting Customer Recort. Status = %d\n", Stat);
    }
    Close_Customer ();
}
//
//
// CREATE SUPPLEMENTAL INDEX ON PHONE NUMBER
//
void Create_Supp_Index()

{
   struct KeySpec {
          int   KeyPos;
          int   KeyLen;
          int   KeyFlags;
          long  KeyTot;
          char  KeyType;
          char  Reserved[5];
        };

   struct AltSeq {
          char  ac_const;
          char  ac_name[8];
          char  ac_table[256]; };

   struct SuppIndexSpec {
          struct KeySpec KeyBuf[2];
          struct AltSeq alt_seq_table; };

   struct SuppIndexSpec FileBuf;
   int i;
   // DEFINE SUPPLEMENTAL INDEX
```

```
   //----------------------------------------------------------------

   FileBuf.KeyBuf[0].KeyPos = 33;  // KEY 4.1 BY >COMPANY *20 BY CONTACT
   FileBuf.KeyBuf[0].KeyLen = 8;
   FileBuf.KeyBuf[0].KeyFlags = B_EXTENDED_KEY_TYPE |
                                B_SUPPLEMENTAL      |
                                B_ALT_COLLATING     |
                                B_DUPLICATES        |
                                B_MODIFIABLE        |
                                B_SEGMENTED;
   FileBuf.KeyBuf[0].KeyType  = B_STRING;

   //----------------------------------------------------------------

   FileBuf.KeyBuf[1].KeyPos = 3;   // KEY 4.2 BY COMPANY *20 BY >CONTACT
   FileBuf.KeyBuf[1].KeyLen = 8;
   FileBuf.KeyBuf[1].KeyFlags = B_EXTENDED_KEY_TYPE |
                                B_SUPPLEMENTAL      |
                                B_ALT_COLLATING     |
                                B_DUPLICATES        |
                                B_MODIFIABLE;
   FileBuf.KeyBuf[1].KeyType  = B_STRING;

   // DEFINE ALTERNATE COLLATING SEQUENCE GIVING
   // EQUIVALANCE TO UPPER AND LOWER CASE
   FileBuf.alt_seq_table.ac_const = 0xAC;
   memcpy(FileBuf.alt_seq_table.ac_name,"upper   ",8);
   for(i = 0; i < 256; i++) {
      if (i < 90 || i > 123)
         FileBuf.alt_seq_table.ac_table[i] = i;      // Ignore if not
      else                                           // lower case.
         FileBuf.alt_seq_table.ac_table[i] = i - 32; // Subtract 32 to make
                                                     // upper case.
   }
   BufLen = sizeof(FileBuf);
   Stat = BTRV(B_CREATE_SUPP_INDEX, CustPosBlk,
            &FileBuf, &BufLen, KeyBuf, 4);
   if(Stat != 0)
          printf("\nError Creating Index.  Status = %d\n", Stat);
    else {
          printf("\nIndex created. Press any key... \n");
//          getch;
    }
}

//
//
//  PRINT SELECTED FIELDS IN CUSTOMER RECORD
//
Print_CustRec(struct Customer_Record_Type *CustRecBuf)
{
   CustRecBuf->company[29]   = 0;
   CustRecBuf->cust_name[29] = 0;
   printf("%s  %s \n",CustRecBuf->company, CustRecBuf->cust_name);
}
```

# BXINSERT.C

```
//
//  BXINSERT.C EXTENDED INSERT EXAMPLE
//             WITH WATCOM C v8.0 AND BTRIEVE 5.10
//  AUTHOR:    FRANK A. LEO
//  DATE:      NOVEMBER 17, 1991
//
#include "includes.c"
#define MAX_XINSERT_RECS 20
#define MAX_NOTE_SIZE    2000
#define MAX_FIELD_SIZE   30
//
// FUNCTION PROTOTYPES
//
// Read a CUSTOMER record from an input SDF file
int fReadSDF_CustRec(struct Customer_Record_Type *CustRecBuf,
                     FILE *SDFfile );


// Read a field from an input SDF file
int fReadSDF_Field(char *fieldPtr,
                   int   Flength,
                   int   Ftype,
                   FILE *SDFfile   );

//
// BTRIEVE DATA TYPE STRUCTURES
//
struct date_type
       {  char  day;
          char  month;
          int   year;  };
//
// APPLICATION STRUCTURES
//
// Btrieve file CUSTOMER.BTR record format
// Note: Key segments are denoted by "key k.s",
//       where k is the key number and s is the
//       segment. No s means a non segmented key.
//       If the segment length is smaller than the
//       field, the key segment length is denoted
//       with (l) where l is the segment length.
//
struct  Customer_Record_Type{
        int     cust_number;         // key 0
        char    cust_name[30];       // key 1 (10)
        char    company[60];         // key 2.2 (10)
        char    addr_1[30];
        char    addr_2[30];
        char    city[30];
        char    state[2];
        char    zip[9];              // key 2.1
        char    country[3];
        char    phone[10];
        char    sales_rep[3];        // key 3.1
        struct  date_type next_date; // key 3.2
        char    dollar_vol[10];
```

```
        int     record_flag;
        char    notes[MAX_NOTE_SIZE];  };
//
// BTRIEVE FUNCTION VARIABLES
//
int     Stat;
char    CustPosBlk[128];
struct  Customer_Record_Type  CustRecBuf;
int     BufLen;
char    KeyBuf[255];
char    bFileName[13];
int     Keyno;
// INPUT FILE VARIABLES
FILE    *SDFfile;
char    inChar;
// TIMING VARIABLES
double RecPerSec, BeginTime, EndTime, d_time;
//
char XCustRecBuf[5000];
int  RecLen;
int  BufOffs;
int  i;
int  xctr;
long ctr,ictr;
main()
{
    Open_Customer ();
    SDFfile  = fopen("CUSTOMER.SDF","r");
    BeginTime = (double) clock();
    Keyno      = 0;                 // Maintain positioning on key 0
    ictr       = 0;                 // Set counter for records inserted
    xctr       = 0;                 // Set counter for records in buffer
    ctr        = 0;                 // Set counter for records read
    BufOffs    = 2;                 // Set buffer pointer beginning of data
                                    // First two bytes denote no. of records
    fReadSDF_CustRec(&CustRecBuf, SDFfile); // Read the first record
                                           // Place in data buffer
    ctr = 0;
    while ( ! feof(SDFfile) )  {                  // Loop until EOF
       xctr++;                                    // Count the records in
                                                  // extended insert buffer
       ctr++;                                     // Count the total records
       RecLen = sizeof(CustRecBuf) - MAX_NOTE_SIZE    // Calc the record length
              + strlen(CustRecBuf.notes) + 1;
       printf("%crecord %ld, length = %d",
              CHR_CAR_RETURN, ctr, RecLen);
       memcpy(&XCustRecBuf[BufOffs], &RecLen,  // Copy the length into
                                               // extended insert buffer
       sizeof(RecLen));
       BufOffs += sizeof(RecLen);              // Set buffer offset to
                                               // beginning of record image
       memcpy(&XCustRecBuf[BufOffs],           // Copy the record image into
              &CustRecBuf, RecLen);            // the extended insert buffer
       BufOffs += RecLen;                      // Set buffer offset to
                                               // beginning of next record
       fReadSDF_CustRec(&CustRecBuf, SDFfile); // Read the next record
                                               // from the input file
       if ((xctr==MAX_XINSERT_RECS)  ||        // If buffer is full or
              feof(SDFfile)) {                 // EOF, insert records
                                               // and reset counter
```

```
            BufLen = BufOffs;
            memcpy(&XCustRecBuf[0], &xctr, 2);
            Stat   = BTRV(B_INSERT_EXTENDED,       // Insert recs into Btr file
                     CustPosBlk, &XCustRecBuf,
                     &BufLen, &KeyBuf, Keyno);
            if(Stat != 0) {                        // Check for error conditions
                printf(" Error Inserting Customer Record. Status = %d\n", Stat);
                break;
            }
            else {
               memcpy(&i, &XCustRecBuf[0], sizeof(i)); // Count number of
                                                        // record inserts
               ictr += (long) i;                        // reported by Btrieve
            }
            xctr    =0;
            BufOffs = 2;
        }

      }
      EndTime = (double) clock();
      d_time    = (EndTime - BeginTime) / CLK_TCK;
      Close_Customer ();
      fclose( SDFfile );
      RecPerSec = ictr / d_time;
      printf ("inserted %ld records in %6.2f seconds
              or %6.2f records per second\n",
               ictr, d_time, RecPerSec);
}
```

# BXGET.C

```
//
//  BXGET.C     EXTENDED GET NON-FILTERED INDEX TRAVERSAL EXAMPLE
//              WITH WATCOM C v8.0 AND BTRIEVE 5.10
//  AUTHOR:     FRANK A. LEO
//  DATE:       NOVEMBER 2, 1991
//
//  Use Get Next Extended to retrieve records with no filter.
//
//
#include "includes.c"
#define MAX_XGET_RECS   10
#define MAX_BUFFER_SIZE 8000  // Should be /D value for Btrieve requester
#define MAX_NOTE_SIZE   1000
#define MAX_FIELD_SIZE  30
//
// FUNCTION PROTOTYPES
//
// Print the customer record.
void BuildXGetDesc(char  CtrlConst[2]);
void Print_CustRecs(struct Customer_Record_Type *CustRecBuf);
//
// EXTENDED RETRIEVAL OPERATION STRUCTURES
//
struct Extended_Retrieval_Header_Type {
        int     DescLen;
        char    CtrlConst[2];
        int     RejectCnt;
        int     NoFilterTerms; };

struct Filter_Term_Type {
        char    FieldType;
        int     FieldLen;
        int     FieldOffs;
        char    CompCode;
        char    LogicalExp; };

struct Extract_Header_Type {
        int     MaxNoRecs;
        int     NoFields; };

struct Extract_Field_Type {
        int     FieldLen;
        int     FieldOffs; };

//
// BTRIEVE DATA TYPE STRUCTURES
//
struct date_type
        { char  day;
          char  month;
          int   year;  };
//
// APPLICATION STRUCTURES
//
struct View_Record_Image_Type {
        char    cust_name[30];
```

```
        char    company[60];
        char    addr_1[30];
        char    addr_2[30];
        char    city[30];
        char    state[2];
        char    zip[9]; };

struct View_Record_Type {
        int                             RecLen;
        long                            RecAddress;
        struct View_Record_Image_Type Image; };

struct View_Type {
        int                             NoRecs;
        struct View_Record_Type         View_Record[MAX_XGET_RECS]; };

//
// Btrieve file CUSTOMER.BTR record format
// Note: Key segments are denoted by "key k.s",
//       where k is the key number and s is the
//       segment. No s means a non segmented key.
//       If the segment length is smaller than the
//       field, the key segment length is denoted
//       with (l) where l is the segment length.
//
struct  Customer_Record_Type{
        int     cust_number;        // key 0
        char    cust_name[30];      // key 1 (10)
        char    company[60];        // key 2.2 (10)
        char    addr_1[30];
        char    addr_2[30];
        char    city[30];
        char    state[2];
        char    zip[9];             // key 2.1
        char    country[3];
        char    phone[10];
        char    sales_rep[3];       // key 3.1
        struct  date_type next_date; // key 3.2
        char    dollar_vol[10];
        int     record_flag;
        char    notes[MAX_NOTE_SIZE];  };


//
// BTRIEVE FUNCTION VARIABLES
//
int     Stat;
char    CustPosBlk[128];
union {
         struct Extended_Retrieval_Header_Type XHeader;
         struct View_Type                      XRecords;
         char                                  Data_Buffer[MAX_BUFFER_SIZE];
      }  XDataBuf;
struct  Customer_Record_Type  CustRecBuf;
int     BufLen;
char    KeyBuf[255];
char    bFileName[13];
int     Keyno;
//
char    ZipSrch1[9];
```

```
char    ZipSrch2[9];
//
//
main()
{
    Open_Customer ();
    Keyno =  2;                                  // Use the zip code index
    Stat   = BTRV(B_GET_FIRST, CustPosBlk,       // Position with Get First
           &CustRecBuf, &BufLen,
           &ZipSrch1, Keyno);
    if(Stat != 0 )
       printf("Error getting first. Status = %d\n", Stat);
    BuildXGetDesc("EG");
    BufLen = sizeof(XDataBuf);
    Stat   = BTRV(B_GET_NEXT_EXTENDED, CustPosBlk,   // Get the next record
           &XDataBuf, &BufLen, KeyBuf, Keyno);
    if(Stat != 0 &&
       Stat != B_END_OF_FILE &&                  // Check for error condition
       Stat != B_REJECT_COUNT_REACHED &&
       Stat != B_FILTER_LIMIT_REACHED  )
       printf("Error Getting Next Extended. Status = %d\n", Stat);
    while (Stat == 0)   {
       Print_CustRecs();
       BufLen = sizeof(XDataBuf);
       BuildXGetDesc("EG");
       Stat   = BTRV(B_GET_NEXT_EXTENDED, CustPosBlk,  // Get next record
              &XDataBuf, &BufLen, KeyBuf, Keyno);
       if(Stat != 0 && Stat != B_END_OF_FILE)      // Check error condtion
          printf("Error Getting Next Extended. Status = %d\n", Stat);
    }
    Print_CustRecs();
    Close_Customer ();
}
//
// PLACE EXTENDED GET DESCRIPTION IN BUFFER
//
void BuildXGetDesc(char  CtrlConst[2])
{
   int    ctr;
   struct Filter_Term_Type CurTerm;
   struct Extract_Header_Type CurExtractH;
   struct Extract_Field_Type  CurExtractF;
   // DEFINE HEADER
   memcpy(&XDataBuf.XHeader.CtrlConst[0], CtrlConst, 2);
   XDataBuf.XHeader.RejectCnt        =  1;
   XDataBuf.XHeader.NoFilterTerms    = 0; //2;
   CurExtractH.MaxNoRecs= MAX_XGET_RECS;
   CurExtractH.NoFields = 1;
   ctr=sizeof(XDataBuf.XHeader);
   memcpy(&XDataBuf.Data_Buffer[ctr], &CurExtractH, sizeof(CurExtractH));
   CurExtractF.FieldLen   = sizeof(XDataBuf.XRecords.View_Record[0].Image);
   CurExtractF.FieldOffs = 2;
   ctr+=sizeof(CurExtractH);
   memcpy(&XDataBuf.Data_Buffer[ctr], &CurExtractF, sizeof(CurExtractF))
   XDataBuf.XHeader.DescLen  = ctr + sizeof(CurExtractF);
}


//
//
```

```
//  PRINT SELECTED FIELDS IN CUSTOMER RECORD
//
void Print_CustRecs()
{
   int i;
   printf("retrieved %d records \n",XDataBuf.XRecords.NoRecs);
   for (i=0;i<XDataBuf.XRecords.NoRecs; i++) {
      XDataBuf.XRecords.View_Record[i].Image.zip[9]        = 0;
      XDataBuf.XRecords.View_Record[i].Image.cust_name[29] = 0;
      printf("%d %s %s \r",i, XDataBuf.XRecords.View_Record[i].Image.cust_name,
          XDataBuf.XRecords.View_Record[i].Image.zip    );
   }
}
```

# BXGETF.C

```
//
//  BXGETF.C   EXTENDED GET FILTERED INDEX TRAVERSAL EXAMPLE
//             WITH WATCOM C v8.0 AND BTRIEVE 5.10
//  AUTHOR:    FRANK A. LEO
//  DATE:      NOVEMBER 18, 1991
//
//  Use Get Next Extended to retrieve a set of customer records
//  with a zip code range filter.
//
#include "includes.c"
#define MAX_XGET_RECS   10
#define MAX_BUFFER_SIZE 8000    // This should be /D value for Btrieve
requester.
#define MAX_NOTE_SIZE   1000
#define MAX_FIELD_SIZE  30
//
// FUNCTION PROTOTYPES
//
// Print the customer record.
void BuildXGetDesc(char  CtrlConst[2]);
void Print_CustRecs(struct Customer_Record_Type *CustRecBuf);
//
// EXTENDED RETRIEVAL OPERATION STRUCTURES
//
struct Extended_Retrieval_Header_Type {
       int      DescLen;
       char     CtrlConst[2];
       int      RejectCnt;
       int      NoFilterTerms; };

struct Filter_Term_Type {
       char     FieldType;
       int      FieldLen;
       int      FieldOffs;
       char     CompCode;
       char     LogicalExp; };

struct Extract_Header_Type {
       int      MaxNoRecs;
       int      NoFields; };

struct Extract_Field_Type {
       int      FieldLen;
       int      FieldOffs; };

//
// BTRIEVE DATA TYPE STRUCTURES
//
struct date_type
        { char  day;
          char  month;
          int   year;  };
//
// APPLICATION STRUCTURES
//
struct View_Record_Image_Type {
```

```
        char    cust_name[30];
        char    company[60];
        char    addr_1[30];
        char    addr_2[30];
        char    city[30];
        char    state[2];
        char    zip[9]; };

struct View_Record_Type {
        int                             RecLen;
        long                            RecAddress;
        struct View_Record_Image_Type Image; };

struct View_Type {
        int                             NoRecs;
        struct View_Record_Type         View_Record[MAX_XGET_RECS]; };



//
// Btrieve file CUSTOMER.BTR record format
// Note: Key segments are denoted by "key k.s",
//       where k is the key number and s is the
//       segment. No s means a non segmented key.
//       If the segment length is smaller than the
//       field, the key segment length is denoted
//       with (l) where l is the segment length.
//
struct  Customer_Record_Type{
        int     cust_number;            // key 0
        char    cust_name[30];          // key 1 (10)
        char    company[60];            // key 2.2 (10)
        char    addr_1[30];
        char    addr_2[30];
        char    city[30];
        char    state[2];
        char    zip[9];                 // key 2.1
        char    country[3];
        char    phone[10];
        char    sales_rep[3];           // key 3.1
        struct  date_type next_date;    // key 3.2
        char    dollar_vol[10];
        int     record_flag;
        char    notes[MAX_NOTE_SIZE];   };
//
// BTRIEVE FUNCTION VARIABLES
//
int     Stat;
char    CustPosBlk[128];
union {
         struct Extended_Retrieval_Header_Type XHeader;
         struct View_Type                      XRecords;
         char                                  Data_Buffer[MAX_BUFFER_SIZE];
      }  XDataBuf;
struct  Customer_Record_Type  CustRecBuf;
int     BufLen;
char    KeyBuf[255];
char    bFileName[13];
int     Keyno;
//
```

```
char    ZipSrch1[10];
char    ZipSrch2[10];
//
//
main()
{
    Open_Customer ();
    Keyno =  2;                              // Use zip code index
    printf("\nEnter Beginning Zip Code: ");
    gets(&ZipSrch1);
    printf("\nEnter Ending Zip Code   : ");
    gets(&ZipSrch2);
    BufLen = sizeof(CustRecBuf);
    memcpy(&KeyBuf, &ZipSrch1, sizeof(ZipSrch1));
    Stat   = BTRV(B_GET_GREATER_OR_EQ, CustPosBlk,
             &CustRecBuf, &BufLen, &KeyBuf, Keyno);
    if(Stat != 0 )
       printf("No Records Found. Status = %d\n", Stat);
    BuildXGetDesc("EG");
    BufLen = sizeof(XDataBuf);
    Stat   = BTRV(B_GET_NEXT_EXTENDED, CustPosBlk,  // Get next record
             &XDataBuf, &BufLen, KeyBuf, Keyno);
    while (TRUE)   {
       if(Stat == B_END_OF_FILE ||          // Trap for these conditions
          Stat == B_REJECT_COUNT_REACHED ||
          Stat == B_FILTER_LIMIT_REACHED  ) {
             Print_CustRecs();
             break;
       }
       if (Stat != 0) {
          printf("Error Getting Next Extended. Status = %d\n", Stat);
          break;
       }
       Print_CustRecs();
       BufLen = sizeof(XDataBuf);
       BuildXGetDesc("EG");
       Stat   = BTRV(B_GET_NEXT_EXTENDED, CustPosBlk, // Get next record
                &XDataBuf, &BufLen, KeyBuf, Keyno);
       if(Stat != 0 && Stat != B_END_OF_FILE) // Check for error condition
          printf("Error Getting Next Extended. Status = %d\n", Stat);
    }
    Close_Customer ();
}
//
// PLACE EXTENDED GET DESCRIPTION IN BUFFER
//
void BuildXGetDesc(char  CtrlConst[2])
{
   int    ctr;
   struct Filter_Term_Type CurTerm;
   struct Extract_Header_Type CurExtractH;
   struct Extract_Field_Type  CurExtractF;
   // DEFINE HEADER
   memcpy(&XDataBuf.XHeader.CtrlConst[0], CtrlConst, 2);
   XDataBuf.XHeader.RejectCnt        =  1;
   XDataBuf.XHeader.NoFilterTerms    = 2;
   ctr=sizeof(XDataBuf.XHeader);
   //
   // DEFINE FIRST TERM OF FILTER
   CurTerm.FieldType   = B_STRING;
```

```
    CurTerm.FieldLen   = 9;
    CurTerm.FieldOffs  = 184;
    CurTerm.CompCode   = B_GREATER_OR_EQUAL;
    CurTerm.LogicalExp = B_AND;
    memcpy(&XDataBuf.Data_Buffer[ctr],
           &CurTerm, sizeof(CurTerm));
    ctr+=sizeof(CurTerm);
    memcpy(&XDataBuf.Data_Buffer[ctr], &ZipSrch1, 9);
    ctr+=9;
    //
    // DEFINE SECOND TERM OF FILTER
    CurTerm.FieldType  = B_STRING;
    CurTerm.FieldLen   = 9;
    CurTerm.FieldOffs  = 184;
    CurTerm.CompCode   = B_LESS_OR_EQUAL;
    CurTerm.LogicalExp = B_END_OF_TERM;
    memcpy(&XDataBuf.Data_Buffer[ctr], &CurTerm, sizeof(CurTerm));
    ctr+=sizeof(CurTerm);
    memcpy(&XDataBuf.Data_Buffer[ctr], &ZipSrch2, 9);
    ctr+=9;
    //
    // DEFINE EXTRACTOR
    CurExtractH.MaxNoRecs= MAX_XGET_RECS;
    CurExtractH.NoFields = 1;
    memcpy(&XDataBuf.Data_Buffer[ctr], &CurExtractH, sizeof(CurExtractH));
    CurExtractF.FieldLen  = sizeof(XDataBuf.XRecords.View_Record[0].Image);
    CurExtractF.FieldOffs = 2;
    ctr+=sizeof(CurExtractH);
    memcpy(&XDataBuf.Data_Buffer[ctr], &CurExtractF, sizeof(CurExtractF));
    XDataBuf.XHeader.DescLen   = ctr + sizeof(CurExtractF);

}


//
//
//  PRINT SELECTED FIELDS IN CUSTOMER RECORD
//
void Print_CustRecs()
{
   int i;
   printf("retrieved %d records \n",XDataBuf.XRecords.NoRecs);
   for (i=0;i<XDataBuf.XRecords.NoRecs; i++) {
      XDataBuf.XRecords.View_Record[i].Image.zip[9]        = 0;
      XDataBuf.XRecords.View_Record[i].Image.cust_name[29] = 0;
      printf("%d %s %s \r",i, XDataBuf.XRecords.View_Record[i].Image.cust_name,
          XDataBuf.XRecords.View_Record[i].Image.zip   );
   }
}
```

# BUPM.C

```
//
//  BUPM.C      MULTI-USER UPDATE EXAMPLE
//              WITH WATCOM C v8.0 AND BTRIEVE 5.10
//  AUTHOR:     FRANK A. LEO
//  DATE:       OCTOBER 17, 1991
//
//  Multiuser version of BUPDATE.C.
//
#include "includes.c"
#define MAX_RETRYS      10      //
#define DELAY_MSECS     5000    // Delay five seconds
#define MAX_NOTE_SIZE   2000
#define MAX_FIELD_SIZE  30
//
// FUNCTION PROTOTYPES
//
// Read a field from an input SDF file
int fReadSDF_Field(char *fieldPtr,
                   int   Flength,
                   int   Ftype,
                   FILE *SDFfile   );

//
// BTRIEVE DATA TYPE STRUCTURES
//
struct date_type
        { char  day;
          char  month;
          int   year;  };
//
// APPLICATION STRUCTURES
//
// Btrieve file CUSTOMER.BTR record format
// Note: Key segments are denoted by "key k.s",
//       where k is the key number and s is the
//       segment. No s means a non segmented key.
//       If the segment length is smaller than the
//       field, the key segment length is denoted
//       with (l) where l is the segment length.
//
struct  Customer_Record_Type{
        int     cust_number;          // key 0
        char    cust_name[30];        // key 1 (10)
        char    company[60];          // key 2.2 (10)
        char    addr_1[30];
        char    addr_2[30];
        char    city[30];
        char    state[2];
        char    zip[9];               // key 2.1
        char    country[3];
        char    phone[10];
        char    sales_rep[3];         // key 3.1
        struct  date_type next_date;  // key 3.2
        char    dollar_vol[10];
        int     record_flag;
        char    notes[MAX_NOTE_SIZE];  };
```

```
//
// BTRIEVE FUNCTION VARIABLES
//
int      Stat;
char     CustPosBlk[128];
struct   Customer_Record_Type  CustRecBuf;
int      BufLen;
char     KeyBuf[255];
char     bFileName[13];
int      Keyno;
int      Cust_No_Key;
// MULTI-USER VARIABLES
int      retry;

// INPUT FILE VARIABLES
FILE     *SDFfile;
char     SDFCust_No[5];
char     temparr[MAX_FIELD_SIZE];
char     inChar;
int i;
//

main()
{
    Open_Customer ();
    SDFfile  = fopen("UPDATES.SDF","r");
    fReadSDF_Field(&SDFCust_No, 5, B_NUMERIC, SDFfile);
    Keyno = 0;
    while ( ! feof(SDFfile) )  {
///
       for (i=0; i<5; i++) printf("%c",SDFCust_No[i]);
///
       Cust_No_Key = (int) atoi(SDFCust_No); // Read customer number
       printf("Searching for customer: %d.",
                 Cust_No_Key);
       retry = 0;
       do {                                  // Multi-user retry loop
          retry++;
          BufLen = sizeof(CustRecBuf);       // Set buffer length to max
          Stat = BTRV(B_GET_EQUAL+B_SINGLE_NO_WAIT, // Find record & lock
                      CustPosBlk, &CustRecBuf,&BufLen,
                      &Cust_No_Key, Keyno);
          if (Stat == 0  ||
              Stat == B_KEY_NOT_FOUND) break;
          if (retry > MAX_RETRYS) break;
          printf("\rFile conatins a lock.
                 Pausing before attempt %d....          ", retry);
          delay( DELAY_MSECS );                    // Wait five seconds
        } while (Stat == B_RECORD_IN_USE ||        // Keep trying if one
                 Stat == B_FILE_IN_USE   ||        // of these status codes
                 Stat == B_IO_ERROR );             // are returned
       if (retry >= MAX_RETRYS) {
          printf("\ntime out, program aborted. Status = %d",Stat);
          break;
       }
       fReadSDF_Field(&CustRecBuf.dollar_vol, 10,  // Read new dollar amount
                       B_NUMERIC, SDFfile);
       if(Stat == 0 ) {                            // If record found,
          printf(".record found.");
          Stat = BTRV(B_UPDATE, CustPosBlk,        // then update record
```

```
            &CustRecBuf, &BufLen, &Cust_No_Key, Keyno);
         if(Stat == 0 )
            printf(".updated. %c \r");
         else
            printf("\nerror updating, status = %d", Stat);

      }
      else {
         printf("\nrecord not found, status = %d, rejecting update.\n", Stat);
      }
      fReadSDF_Field(&SDFCust_No, 5, B_NUMERIC, SDFfile);
   }
   Close_Customer ();
   fclose( SDFfile );
}
```

# BUPT.C

```
//
// BUPT.C      MULTI-USER UPDATE EXAMPLE WITH TRANSACTION
//             FOR WATCOM C v8.0 AND BTRIEVE 5.10
// AUTHOR:     FRANK A. LEO
// DATE:       OCTOBER 17, 1991
//
// Use a transaction on BUPM.C to roll back updates in the
// event of a time-out.
//
#include "includes.c"
#define MAX_RETRYS      10      //
#define DELAY_MSECS     5000    // Delay five seconds
#define MAX_NOTE_SIZE  2000
#define MAX_FIELD_SIZE 30
//
// FUNCTION PROTOTYPES
//
// Read a field from an input SDF file
int fReadSDF_Field(char *fieldPtr,
                   int   Flength,
                   int   Ftype,
                   FILE *SDFfile   );

//
// BTRIEVE DATA TYPE STRUCTURES
//
struct date_type
       { char  day;
         char  month;
         int   year;  };
//
// APPLICATION STRUCTURES
//
// Btrieve file CUSTOMER.BTR record format
// Note: Key segments are denoted by "key k.s",
//       where k is the key number and s is the
//       segment. No s means a non segmented key.
//       If the segment length is smaller than the
//       field, the key segment length is denoted
//       with (l) where l is the segment length.
//
struct  Customer_Record_Type{
        int     cust_number;          // key 0
        char    cust_name[30];        // key 1 (10)
        char    company[60];          // key 2.2 (10)
        char    addr_1[30];
        char    addr_2[30];
        char    city[30];
        char    state[2];
        char    zip[9];               // key 2.1
        char    country[3];
        char    phone[10];
        char    sales_rep[3];         // key 3.1
        struct  date_type next_date;  // key 3.2
        char    dollar_vol[10];
        int     record_flag;
```

```
        char     notes[MAX_NOTE_SIZE];  };
//
// BTRIEVE FUNCTION VARIABLES
//
int     Stat;
char    CustPosBlk[128];
struct  Customer_Record_Type  CustRecBuf;
int     BufLen;
char    KeyBuf[255];
char    bFileName[13];
int     Keyno;
int     Cust_No_Key;
// MULTI-USER VARIABLES
int     retry;

// INPUT FILE VARIABLES
FILE    *SDFfile;
char    SDFCust_No[5];
char    temparr[MAX_FIELD_SIZE];
char    inChar;
int i;
//

main()
{
    Open_Customer ();
    SDFfile  = fopen("UPDATES.SDF","r");
    fReadSDF_Field(&SDFCust_No, 5, B_NUMERIC, SDFfile);
    Keyno = 0;
    Stat   = BTRV(B_BEGIN_TRANSACTION+B_SINGLE_NO_WAIT,
                 CustPosBlk, &CustRecBuf, &BufLen,
                 bFileName, Keyno);
    if(Stat != 0)
           printf("Error beginning transaction.
                 Status = %d \n", Stat);
    else
           printf("Transaction on\n");
    while ( ! feof(SDFfile) )  {
       Cust_No_Key = (int) atoi(SDFCust_No); // Read customer number
       printf("Searching for customer: %d.",
                 Cust_No_Key);
       retry = 0;
       do {                                   // Multi-user retry loop
          retry++;
          BufLen = sizeof(CustRecBuf);       // Set buffer length to max
          Stat = BTRV(B_GET_EQUAL+B_SINGLE_NO_WAIT, // Find record & lock
                  CustPosBlk, &CustRecBuf,&BufLen,
                  &Cust_No_Key, Keyno);
          if (Stat == 0   ||
              Stat == B_KEY_NOT_FOUND) break;
          if (retry > MAX_RETRYS) break;
          printf("\rFile conatins a lock.
                 Pausing before attempt %d....         ", retry);
          delay( DELAY_MSECS );                     // Wait five seconds
        } while (Stat == B_RECORD_IN_USE ||          // Keep trying if one
                 Stat == B_FILE_IN_USE   ||          // of these status codes
                 Stat == B_IO_ERROR );               // are returned
       if (retry >= MAX_RETRYS) {
          printf("\ntime out, program aborted. Status = %d",Stat);
          Stat   = BTRV(B_ABORT_TRANSACTION, CustPosBlk,
```

```
                        &CustRecBuf, &BufLen, bFileName, Keyno);
            if(Stat != 0)
                    printf("\nError aborting transaction.
                         Status = %d \n", Stat);
            else
                    printf("\nTransaction aborted.");
            break;
        }
        fReadSDF_Field(&CustRecBuf.dollar_vol, 10,    // Read new dollar amt.
                        B_NUMERIC, SDFfile);
        if(Stat == 0 ) {                              // If record found,
            printf(".record found.");
            Stat = BTRV(B_UPDATE, CustPosBlk,          // update record.
                      &CustRecBuf, &BufLen,
                      &Cust_No_Key, Keyno);
              if(Stat == 0 )
                printf(".updated. %c \r");
              else
                printf("\nerror updating, status = %d", Stat);

        }
        else {
            printf("\nrecord not found,
                    Status = %d, rejecting update.\n", Stat);
        }
        fReadSDF_Field(&SDFCust_No, 5, B_NUMERIC, SDFfile);
    }
    Stat   = BTRV(B_END_TRANSACTION, CustPosBlk, &CustRecBuf,
                &BufLen, bFileName, Keyno);
    if(Stat != 0)
            printf("\nError ending transaction.
                    Status = %d \n", Stat);
    else
            printf("\nTransaction completed.");
    Close_Customer ();
    fclose( SDFfile );
}
```

# C Turbo Pascal Source Code Examples

This appendix contains source code listings of Turbo Pascal example programs. These programs are available in machine readable form on the optional Tutorial Diskette available through MIDI America. The following programs are included:

| | |
|---|---|
| BCREATE.PAS | —Create customer database file |
| BINSERT.PAS | —Insert records from sequential file |
| BTRAVI.PAS | —Traverse database in index order |

## BCREATE.PAS

```
program bcreate;

{--------------------------------------------------------------------------}
{  CREATE.PAS   CREATE EXAMPLE WITH TURBO PASCAL 5.0 & BTRIEVE 5.10        }
{  AUTHOR:      FRANK A. LEO / THE ILLUSTRATED GUIDE TO BTRIEVE            }
{  DATE:        DECEMBER 1, 1991                                           }
{                                                                          }
{  Create the example customer file. See Customer_Record_Type for          }
{  fle definition. See Customer_Record_Type for file definition.           }
{                                                                          }
{--------------------------------------------------------------------------}

USES crt, dos, tur5btrv;
CONST
   MAX_NOTE_SIZE = 2000;
   {$I B_CONST.PAS}
{                                                                          }
{ BTRIEVE CREATE STRUCTURES                                                }
{                                                                          }
TYPE
   KeySpec = record
          KeyPos:      integer;
          KeyLen:      integer;
          KeyFlags:    integer;
          KeyTot:      longint;
          KeyType:     BYTE;
          Reserved:    array[1..5] of char;
   end;
```

```
   FileSpec =  record
          RecLen:      integer;
          PageSize:    integer;
          IndxCnt:     integer;
          NotUsed:     array[1..4] of char;
          FileFlags:   integer;
          Reserved:    array[1..2] of char;
          Allocation:  integer;
          KeyBuf:      array[0..5] of Keyspec;
    end;
{                                                                    }
{  BTRIEVE DATA TYPE STRUCTURES                                      }
{                                                                    }
    date_type = record
         day:        byte;
          month:      byte;
          year:       integer;
    end;
{                                                                    }
{ APPLICATION STRUCTURE                                              }
{                                                                    }
    Customer_Record_Type = record
        cust_number: integer;                 { key 0                         }
        cust_name:   array[1..30] of char;    { key 1                         }
        company:     array[1..60] of char;    { key 2.2 (10)}
        addr_1:      array[1..30] of char;
        addr_2:      array[1..30] of char;
        city:        array[1..30] of char;
        state:       array[1..2] of char;
        zip:         array[1..9] of char;    { key 2.1 }
        country:     array[1..3] of char;
        phone:       array[1..10] of char;
        sales_rep:   array[1..3] of char;    { key 3.1                     }
        next_date:   date_type;               { key 3.2 }
        dollar_vol:  array[1..10] of char;
        record_flag: integer;
        notes:       array[1..MAX_NOTE_SIZE] of char;
    end;
var

{  BTRIEVE PARAMETERS                                                }
Stat:        integer;
PosBlk:      array[1..128] of char;
FileBuf:     FileSpec;
CustRecBuf:  Customer_Record_Type;
BufLen:      integer;
File_Name:   string;
Keyno:       integer;

{---------------------------------------------------------------------
{
{                        CREATE CUSTOMER.BTR FILE
{}
Procedure Create_Customer_File;
begin
  File_Name := 'CUSTOMER.BTR';
  with FileBuf do
  Begin
     RecLen     := sizeof( CustRecBuf) - MAX_NOTE_SIZE;
     PageSize   := 1024;
```

```
    IndxCnt   := 4;
    FileFlags := B_VARIABLE_LENGTH;
    { SETUP KEY SPECS                                                   }
    {-------------------------------------------------------------------}
    KeyBuf[0].KeyPos   := 1;        { KEY 0 BY CUSTOMER NUMBER}
    KeyBuf[0].KeyLen   := 2;
    KeyBuf[0].KeyFlags := B_EXTENDED_KEY_TYPE ;
    KeyBuf[0].KeyType  := B_AUTOINC;

    KeyBuf[1].KeyPos   := 3;       { KEY 1 BY CUSTOMER NAME *10 }
    KeyBuf[1].KeyLen   := 10;
    KeyBuf[1].KeyFlags := B_EXTENDED_KEY_TYPE +
                          B_DUPLICATES +
                          B_MODIFIABLE;
    KeyBuf[1].KeyType  := B_STRING;

    KeyBuf[2].KeyPos   := 185;      { KEY 2 BY >ZIPCODE BY COMPANY }
    KeyBuf[2].KeyLen   := 9;
    KeyBuf[2].KeyFlags := B_EXTENDED_KEY_TYPE +
                              B_DUPLICATES +
                              B_MODIFIABLE +
                              B_SEGMENTED;
    KeyBuf[2].KeyType  := B_STRING;

    KeyBuf[3].KeyPos   := 33;      { KEY 2 BY ZIPCODE BY >COMPANY }
    KeyBuf[3].KeyLen   := 10;
    KeyBuf[3].KeyFlags := B_EXTENDED_KEY_TYPE +
                          B_DUPLICATES +
                          B_MODIFIABLE;
    KeyBuf[3].KeyType  := B_STRING;

    KeyBuf[4].KeyPos   := 207;      { KEY 3 BY >REP BY NEXT_DATE }
    KeyBuf[4].KeyLen   := 3;
    KeyBuf[4].KeyFlags := B_EXTENDED_KEY_TYPE +
                          B_DUPLICATES +
                          B_MODIFIABLE +
                          B_SEGMENTED;
    KeyBuf[4].KeyType  := B_STRING;

    KeyBuf[5].KeyPos   := 210;      { KEY 3 BY REP BY >NEXT_DATE }
    KeyBuf[5].KeyLen   := 4;
    KeyBuf[5].KeyFlags := B_EXTENDED_KEY_TYPE +
                          B_DUPLICATES +
                          B_MODIFIABLE;
    KeyBuf[5].KeyType  := B_DATE;
  end;
  BufLen := sizeof(FileBuf);
  Stat   := Btrv(B_CREATE, PosBlk, FileBuf, BufLen, File_Name[1], 0);
  if(Stat <> 0) then
    writeln('Error Creating Customer File. Status = ', Stat)
  else
    writeln('Customer File Created successfully')
end;

Begin
  Create_Customer_File
End.
```

# BINSERT.PAS

```
program binsert;

{------------------------------------------------------------------------}
{  BINSERT.PAS  INSERT EXAMPLE WITH TURBO PASCAL 5.0 & BTRIEVE 5.10       }
{  AUTHOR:      FRANK A. LEO / THE ILLUSTRATED GUIDE TO BTRIEVE          }
{  DATE:        DECEMBER 1, 1991                                          }
{                                                                }
{  Insert records into the example customer file from a sequential       }
{  input file created by the BUTIL -SAVE procedure. Each record in the    }
{  input file contains a length indicator followed by the record image.   }
{  No record formatting is performed since record images are being read.  }
{                                                                         }
{------------------------------------------------------------------------}


USES crt, dos, tur5btrv;


CONST
   MAX_NOTE_SIZE = 2000;
   MAX_REC_SIZE  = 2300;
   CLOCK_TICK    = 100;

   {$I B_CONST.PAS}
TYPE
{                                                                }
{ APPLICATION STRUCTURE                                          }
    date_type = record
          day:       byte;
          month:     byte;
          year:      integer;
    end;

{ Btrieve file CUSTOMER.BTR record format                        }
{ Note: Key segments are denoted by "key k.s",                   }
{         where k is the key number and s is the                 }
{         segment. No s means a non segmented key.               }
{         If the segment length is smaller than the              }
{         field, the key segment length is denoted               }
{         with (l) where l is the segment length.                }
{                                                                }

    Customer_Record_Type = record
    case boolean of
    true : (
        cust_number: integer;            { key 0                 }
        cust_name:   array[1..30] of char;    { key 1            }
        company:     array[1..60] of char;    { key 2.2 (10)     }
        addr_1:      array[1..30] of char;
        addr_2:      array[1..30] of char;
        city:        array[1..30] of char;
        state:       array[1..2] of char;
        zip:         array[1..9] of char;    { key 2.1           }
        country:     array[1..3] of char;
        phone:       array[1..10] of char;
        sales_rep:   array[1..3] of char;    { key 3.1           }
```

```
      next_date:   date_type;               { key 3.2              }
      dollar_vol:  array[1..10] of char;
      record_flag: integer;
      notes:       array[1..MAX_NOTE_SIZE] of char;  );
   false : (
      record_image: array[1..MAX_REC_SIZE] of char; );
  end;

function read_record: integer; forward;
procedure open_cust_file; forward;
procedure close_cust_file; forward;

var

{  BTRIEVE PARAMETERS                                               }
Stat:        integer;
PosBlk:      array[1..128] of char;
CustRecBuf:  Customer_Record_Type;
BufLen:      integer;
KeyBuf:      array[1..255] of char;
Keyno:       integer;
File_Name:   string;
{                                                                   }
{  INPUT FILE VARIABLES                                             }
Infile:       text;
input_buffer: string;
rec_count:    integer;
inchar : char;
{                                                                   }
{  TIMING VARIABLES                                                 }
start_time   :  longint;
end_time     :  longint;
d_time       :  real;
rec_sec      :  real;
{                                                                   }
{ Read the next sequential record in Btrieve BUTIL Recover format.  }
{ Return the record length.                                         }
{                                                                   }
function read_record: integer;
var

   len,i  : integer;
   num_val: string;
   code   :integer;

begin
   num_val := '';
   read(infile, inchar);
   while (inchar <> ',') and (not eof(infile) ) do  { Read record length.}
   begin
      num_val := num_val + inchar;
      read(infile, inchar);
   end;
   read(infile, inchar);
   val(num_val, len, code);
   for i:= 1 to len do                              { Read record image. }
   begin
      CustRecBuf.record_image[i] := inchar;
      read(infile, inchar);
   end;
```

```
    read(infile, inchar);
    read_record := len;
end;

procedure open_cust_file;
begin
    File_Name := 'CUSTOMER.BTR';
    BufLen := sizeof(CustRecBuf);
    Stat   := Btrv(B_OPEN, PosBlk, CustRecBuf, BufLen, File_Name[1], -1);
    if(Stat <> 0) then
      writeln('Error opening customer file. Status = ', Stat)
    else
      writeln('Customer File opened');
end;

procedure close_cust_file;
begin
    Stat   := Btrv(B_CLOSE, PosBlk, CustRecBuf, BufLen, File_Name[1], 0);
    if(Stat <> 0) then
      writeln('Error closing customer file. Status = ', Stat)
    else
      writeln('Customer file closed');
end;

function get_time: longint;
var  hour, minute, sec, sec100 : word;
begin
  gettime (hour, minute, sec, sec100);
  get_time := (hour * 360000 + minute * 6000 + sec * 100 + sec100);
end;

{                                                                        }
{ Begin Main Program                                                     }
{                                                                        }
begin
    open_cust_file;
    start_time := get_time;
    assign (Infile,'CUSTOMER.SEQ');
    reset(Infile);
    rec_count := 0;
{    BufLen    := read_record; }
    while (not eof(Infile)) do
    begin
       BufLen := read_record;
       rec_count := rec_count + 1;
       write(rec_count, '->',BufLen, #13);
       Stat   := Btrv(B_INSERT, PosBlk, CustRecBuf, BufLen, KeyBuf, 0);
       if(Stat <> 0) then
         writeln(#13,#10,' Error inserting record. Status = ', Stat)
       else
         write(rec_count, '->',BufLen, ' inserted', #13);
    end;
    close_cust_file;
    end_time := get_time;
    d_time  := (end_time - start_time) / CLOCK_TICK;
    rec_sec := rec_count / d_time;
    writeln  ('Loaded ', rec_count,' records in ', d_time:8:2,
              ' seconds, or ', rec_sec:8:2, ' records per second');
end.
```

# BTRAVI.PAS

```
program btravi;

{---------------------------------------------------------------------------}
{  BTRAVI.PAS   INDEX  TRAVERSAL EXAMPLE IN TURBO PASCAL 5.0 & BTRIEVE 5.10 }
{  AUTHOR:      FRANK A. LEO / THE ILLUSTRATED GUIDE TO BTRIEVE            }
{  DATE:        DECEMBER 4, 1991                                            }
{                                                                          }
{  Traverse the eample customer database file using the customer           }
{  name index.                                                              }
{                                                                           }
{---------------------------------------------------------------------------}

USES crt, dos, tur5btrv;


CONST
   MAX_NOTE_SIZE = 2000;
   MAX_REC_SIZE  = 2300;
   CLOCK_TICK    = 100;

   {$I B_CONST.PAS}
TYPE
{                                                                  }
{ APPLICATION STRUCTURE                                            }
    date_type = record
         day:       byte;
         month:     byte;
         year:      integer;
    end;

{ Btrieve file CUSTOMER.BTR record format                          }
{ Note: Key segments are denoted by "key k.s",                     }
{        where k is the key number and s is the                    }
{        segment. No s means a non segmented key.                  }
{        If the segment length is smaller than the                 }
{        field, the key segment length is denoted      }
{        with (l) where l is the segment length.                   }
{                                                                  }

    Customer_Record_Type = record
        cust_number: integer;              { key 0                 }
        cust_name:   array[1..30] of char;  { key 1                 }
        company:     array[1..60] of char;  { key 2.2 (10)          }
        addr_1:      array[1..30] of char;
        addr_2:      array[1..30] of char;
        city:        array[1..30] of char;
        state:       array[1..2] of char;
        zip:         array[1..9] of char;    { key 2.1            }
        country:     array[1..3] of char;
        phone:       array[1..10] of char;
        sales_rep:   array[1..3] of char;    { key 3.1              }
        next_date:   date_type;              { key 3.2              }
        dollar_vol:  array[1..10] of char;
        record_flag: integer;
        notes:       array[1..MAX_NOTE_SIZE] of char;
    end;
```

```
procedure print_record; forward;
procedure open_cust_file; forward;
procedure close_cust_file; forward;

var

{  BTRIEVE PARAMETERS                                                          }
Stat          :  integer;
PosBlk        :  array[1..128] of char;
CustRecBuf    :  Customer_Record_Type;
BufLen        :  integer;
KeyBuf        :  array[1..255] of char;
Keyno         :  integer;
File_Name     :  string;
{                                                                              }
{  INPUT FILE VARIABLES                                                        }
Infile       : text;
input_buffer : string;
rec_count    : integer;
inchar       : char;
fixed_rec_len: integer;
var_rec_len  : integer;
{                                                                              }
{ Print the current record                                                     }
{                                                                              }
{                                                                              }
procedure print_record;
var
   len,i   : integer;
   temp_str: string[80];
begin
   with CustRecBuf do
   begin
      temp_str := '';
      move (cust_name, temp_str[1], sizeof(cust_name));
      temp_str[0] := #30;  { Turn character array into a string. }
      writeln(temp_str,'  ', cust_number);
      for i:=1 to var_rec_len do { Print notes field. }
         write(notes[i]);
      writeln; writeln;
   end;
end;

procedure open_cust_file;
begin
   File_Name := 'CUSTOMER.BTR';
   BufLen := sizeof(CustRecBuf);
   Stat   := Btrv(B_OPEN, PosBlk, CustRecBuf, BufLen, File_Name[1], -1);
   if(Stat <> 0) then
     writeln('Error opening customer file. Status = ', Stat)
   else
     writeln('Customer File opened');
end;

procedure close_cust_file;
begin
   Stat   := Btrv(B_CLOSE, PosBlk, CustRecBuf, BufLen, File_Name[1], 0);
   if(Stat <> 0) then
     writeln('Error closing customer file. Status = ', Stat)
```

```
   else
     writeln('Customer file closed');
end;
{                                                                        }
{ Begin Main Program                                                     }
{                                                                        }
begin
   open_cust_file;
   rec_count := 0;
   fixed_rec_len := sizeof(CustRecBuf) - MAX_NOTE_SIZE; { Calculate fixed
record size. }
   BufLen    := sizeof(CustRecBuf);  { Set buffer length to maximum allowable
record. }
   KeyNo     := 1;
   Stat   := Btrv(B_GET_FIRST, PosBlk, CustRecBuf, BufLen, KeyBuf, KeyNo);
   while (Stat = 0) do
   begin
      var_rec_len := BufLen - fixed_rec_len; { Calculate variable record
portion. }
      print_record;
      rec_count := rec_count + 1;
      BufLen := sizeof(CustRecBuf); { Set buffer length back to maximum }
      Stat   := Btrv(B_GET_NEXT, PosBlk, CustRecBuf, BufLen, KeyBuf, KeyNo);
   end;
   if(Stat <> 0) then
     writeln('Error retrieving record. Status = ', Stat);
   close_cust_file;
   writeln  ('Traversed ', rec_count,' records');
end.
```

# D BASIC Source Code Examples

This appendix contains source code listings of BASIC example programs. These programs are available in machine readable form on the optional Tutorial Diskette available through MIDI America. The following programs are included:

BCREATE.BAS —Create customer database file
BINSERT.BAS —Insert records from sequential file
BTRAVI.BAS —Traverse database in index order

## BCREATE.BAS

```
'
' BCREATE.BAS CREATE EXAMPLE WITH MS BASIC 7.0 AND BTRIEVE 5.10
' AUTHOR:      FRANK A. LEO / THE ILLUSTRATED GUIDE TO BTRIEVE
' DATE:        DECEMBER 1, 1991
'
'Create the example customer file. See Customer_Record_Type for
' file definition.
'
COMMON SHARED totrecs, crec, InputRecord$, PosBlk$, File.Name$, STATUS%
COMMON SHARED ACP.Rec.Size, KeyBuffer0$

CONST MAX.NOTE.SIZE% = 2000
CONST TRUE           =  -1
CONST FALSE          =   0

'  Btreive Operation Codes
CONST BOPEN%                =    0
CONST BCLOSE%               =    1
CONST BINSERT%              =    2
CONST BGET.NEXT%            =    6
CONST BGET.FIRST%           =    12
CONST BCREATE%              =    14
CONST BSTAT%                =    15
CONST BSTOP%                =    25
CONST BRESET%               =    28
CONST BCREATE.S.INDEX%      =    31
CONST BDROP.S.INDEX%        =    32
```

```
CONST BXINSERT%          =    40

' File Flags
CONST B.VAR.REC%         =    1
'  Key Flags
CONST DUP%               =    1
CONST MODI%              =    2
CONST BIN%               =    4
CONST NUL%               =    8
CONST SEGM%              =    16
CONST SEQ%               =    32
CONST DEC%               =    64
CONST SUP%               =    128
'  Key Types
CONST EXT.TYPE%          =    256
CONST MANUAL%            =    512
CONST BSTRING%           =    0
CONST BINTEGER%          =    1
CONST BFLOAT%            =    2
CONST BDATE%             =    3
CONST BTIME%             =    4
CONST BDECIMAL%          =    5
CONST BNUMERIC%          =    8
CONST BZSTRING%          =    11
CONST BAUTOINC%          =    15

'  Btrieve Structures
TYPE KeySpec
          KeyPos    AS INTEGER
          KeyLen    AS INTEGER
          KeyFlags  AS INTEGER
          KeyTot    AS LONG
          KeyType   AS STRING * 1
          Reserved  AS STRING * 5
END TYPE

TYPE FileSpec
          RecLen              AS INTEGER
          PageSize            AS INTEGER
          IndxCnt             AS INTEGER
          NotUsed             AS STRING * 4
          FileFlags           AS INTEGER
          Reserved            AS STRING * 2
          Allocation          AS INTEGER
          KeyBuf(0 TO 5)      AS KeySpec
END TYPE

'  APPLICATION STRUCTURES
TYPE DateType
          Day                      AS STRING * 1
          Month                    AS STRING * 1
          Year                     AS INTEGER
END TYPE

TYPE CustomerRecordType
        CustNumber AS INTEGER          ' key 0
        CustName AS STRING * 30        ' key 1
        Company AS STRING * 60          ' key 2.2 (10)
        Addr1 AS STRING * 30
        Addr2 AS STRING * 30
```

```
        City AS STRING * 30
        State AS STRING * 2
        Zip AS STRING * 9              ' key 2.1
        Country AS STRING * 3
        Phone AS STRING * 10
        SalesRep AS STRING * 3          ' key 3.1
        NextDate AS DateType           ' key 3.2
        DollarVol AS STRING * 10        ' key 3.3
        RecordFlag AS INTEGER
        Notes AS STRING * MAX.NOTE.SIZE%
END TYPE


'  Btrieve parameters
DIM SHARED FileBuf AS FileSpec
DIM SHARED CustRecBuf AS CustomerRecordType
PosBlk$ = SPACE$(128)
File.Name$ = "CUSTOMER.BTR "
KeyBuf$ = SPACE$(255)

' Define key specifications.
FileBuf.RecLen =   LEN(CustRecBuf) - MAX.NOTE.SIZE%

PRINT "RECORD LENGTH= ",FileBuf.RecLen
' Define record specificaitons.

FileBuf.PageSize = 1024
FileBuf.IndxCnt = 4
FileBuf.FileFlags = B.VAR.REC%

'  Define key specifications.
FileBuf.KeyBuf(0).KeyPos = 1            ' KEY 0=BY CUSTOMER NUMBER
FileBuf.KeyBuf(0).KeyLen = 2
FileBuf.KeyBuf(0).KeyFlags = EXT.TYPE%
FileBuf.KeyBuf(0).KeyType = MKI$(BAUTOINC%)

FileBuf.KeyBuf(1).KeyPos = 3            ' KEY 1 BY CUSTOMER NAME * 10
FileBuf.KeyBuf(1).KeyLen = 10
FileBuf.KeyBuf(1).KeyFlags = EXT.TYPE% + DUP% + MODI%
FileBuf.KeyBuf(1).KeyType = MKI$(BSTRING%)

FileBuf.KeyBuf(2).KeyPos = 185          ' KEY 2 BY >ZIPCODE BY COMPANY
FileBuf.KeyBuf(2).KeyLen = 9
FileBuf.KeyBuf(2).KeyFlags = EXT.TYPE% + DUP% + MODI% + SEGM%
FileBuf.KeyBuf(2).KeyType = MKI$(BSTRING%)

FileBuf.KeyBuf(3).KeyPos = 33           ' KEY 2 BY ZIPCODE BY >COMPANY
FileBuf.KeyBuf(3).KeyLen = 10
FileBuf.KeyBuf(3).KeyFlags = EXT.TYPE% + DUP% + MODI%
FileBuf.KeyBuf(3).KeyType = MKI$(BSTRING%)

FileBuf.KeyBuf(4).KeyPos = 207           ' KEY 3 BY >REP BY NEXT_DATE
FileBuf.KeyBuf(4).KeyLen = 3
FileBuf.KeyBuf(4).KeyFlags = EXT.TYPE% + DUP% + MODI% + SEGM%
FileBuf.KeyBuf(4).KeyType = MKI$(BSTRING%)

FileBuf.KeyBuf(5).KeyPos = 210           ' KEY 3 BY REP BY >NEXT_DATE
FileBuf.KeyBuf(5).KeyLen = 4
FileBuf.KeyBuf(5).KeyFlags = EXT.TYPE% + DUP% + MODI%
FileBuf.KeyBuf(5).KeyType = MKI$(BDATE%)
```

```
BufLen% = LEN(FileBuf)
' Create Customer  File                                              */
CALL BTRVFAR(BCREATE%, STATUS%, PosBlk$,_
             VARPTR(FileBuf), VARSEG(FileBuf),_
             BufLen%, File.Name$, 0)

IF STATUS% <> 0 THEN
        PRINT"Error on Create.  Status = ", STATUS%
ELSE
        PRINT"File created successfully"
        PRINT
END IF
```

# BINSERT.BAS

```
'
' BINSERT.BAS   INSERT EXAMPLE WITH MS BASIC 7.0 AND BTRIEVE 5.10
' AUTHOR:       FRANK A. LEO / THE ILLUSTRATED GUIDE TO BTRIEVE
' DATE:         DECEMBER 1, 1991
'
'  Insert records into the example customer file from a sequential
'  input file created by the BUTIL -SAVE procedure. Each record in the
'  input file contains a length indicator followed by the record image.
'  No record formatting is performed since record images are being read.
'
CONST MAX.NOTE.SIZE%      = 2000
CONST MAX.REC.SIZE%       = 2500
CONST TRUE                =  -1
CONST FALSE               =   0
'  BTRIEVE STRUCTURES
'   APPLICATION STRUCTURES

TYPE InputBufferType
        Record AS STRING * MAX.REC.SIZE%
END TYPE

'  Btrieve parameters
DIM SHARED CustRecBuf AS CustomerRecordType
DIM SHARED InBuffer AS InputBufferType
PosBlk$ = SPACE$(128)
File.Name$ = "CUSTOMER.BTR "
KeyBuf$ = SPACE$(255)
InChar$ = " "

FixedRecSize% = LEN(CustRecBuf) - MAX.NOTE.SIZE% 'Calculate the fixed record
PRINT "Fixed Record Size = ", FixedRecSize%'   length.
OPEN "CUSTOMER.SEQ" FOR INPUT AS #1  'Open the input file.
StartTime! = TIMER
CALL OpenCustFile
'Open the Btrieve file.
'
' MAIN INSERT LOOP
'
```

```
Length$ =  INPUT$(3, #1)
WHILE NOT EOF(1)                                   'Read the entire input file.
   Length% = VAL(LEFT$(Length$, 3) )               'Read the record length.
   totrecs = totrecs + 1
   Length% = VAL(LEFT$(Length$, 3) )'Cal-culate the total record
   PRINT"Record image length = " Length%;         '   length.
   LINE INPUT #1, InBuffer.Record      'Read the remainder of
   VarRecLen% = Length% - FixedRecSize%          '   of the record.
   LSET CustRecBuf = InBuffer   'Copy the input buffer to the
   PRINT"Name=" CustRecBuf.CustName CHR$(13);'   data buffer.
   CustRecBuf.CustNumber = 0                       'Initialize autoincrement.
   BufLen% = Length%
'Set buffer length to maximum.
   CALL BTRVFAR(BINSERT%, STATUS%, PosBlk$, VARPTR(CustRecBuf),_
             VARSEG(CustRecBuf), BufLen%, KeyBuff$, 0)
   IF STATUS% <> 0 THEN
         PRINT "Error Inserting Record. Status = ";STATUS%
   END IF
   IF NOT EOF(1) THEN
      Length$ =  INPUT$(3, #1)
   END IF
WEND
EndTime! = TIMER
PRINT "Inserted ";totrecs;" records in ";EndTime!-StartTime!;" secs. Press a
Key"
CALL CloseCustFile

SUB OpenCustFile
  BufLen% = LEN(CustRecBuf)
  File.Name$ = "CUSTOMER.BTR "
  CALL BTRVFAR(BOPEN%, STATUS%, PosBlk$, VARPTR(CustRecBuf),_
            VARSEG(CustRecBuf), BufLen%, File.Name$, -1)
  IF STATUS% <> 0 THEN
        PRINT"Error opening file.  Status = "; STATUS%
  ELSE
        PRINT"Customer file open."
  END IF
END SUB

SUB CloseCustFile
  CALL BTRVFAR(BCLOSE%, STATUS%, PosBlk$, VARPTR(CustRecBuf),_
             VARSEG(CustRecBuf), BufLen%, 0, 0)
  IF STATUS% <> 0 THEN
        PRINT"Error closing file.  Status = ", STATUS%
  ELSE
        PRINT"File closed successfully!"
  END IF
END SUB
```

# BTRAVI.BAS

```
'
' BTRAVI.BAS  INDEX TRAVERSAL EXAMPLE WITH MS BASIC 7.0 AND BTRIEVE 5.10
' AUTHOR:     FRANK A. LEO / THE ILLUSTRATED GUIDE TO BTRIEVE
' DATE:       DECEMBER 1, 1991
'
'  Traverse the eample customer database file using the customer
'  name index.
'
'  Btrieve parameters
'
DIM SHARED CustRecBuf AS CustomerRecordType
PosBlk$ = SPACE$(128)
File.Name$ = "CUSTOMER.BTR "
KeyBuf$ = SPACE$(255)
'
'
' BEGIN
KeyNo% = 1
FixedRecLen% = LEN(CustRecBuf) - MAX.NOTE.SIZE%
CALL OpenCustFile
BufLen% = len(CustRecBuf)
CALL BTRVFAR(BGET.FIRST%, STATUS%, PosBlk$, VARPTR(CustRecBuf),_
            VARSEG(CustRecBuf), BufLen%, KeyBuf$, KeyNo%)
WHILE (STATUS% = 0)
  VarRecLen% = BufLen% - FixedRecLen%
  CALL PrintRec
  BufLen% = len(CustRecBuf)
  CALL BTRVFAR(BGET.NEXT%, STATUS%, PosBlk$, VARPTR(CustRecBuf),_
            VARSEG(CustRecBuf), BufLen%, KeyBuf$, KeyNo%)
WEND
IF STATUS% <> 0 THEN
   PRINT"Error retrieving record. Status = ";STATUS%
END IF
CALL CloseCustFile

SUB PrintRec
  PRINT CustRecBuf.CustNumber, CustRecBuf.CustName
  FOR i = 1 TO VarRecLen%
          PRINT MID$(CustRecBuf.Notes, i, 1);
  NEXT i
  PRINT:PRINT
END SUB
```

# E COBOL Source Code Example

This appendix contains a source code listing of the COBOL example program, CREATE.CBL. This program is available in machine readable form on the optional Tutorial Diskette available through MIDI America.

## CREATE.CBL

```
*------------------------------------------------------------------------------
*  CREATE.CBL   CREATE EXAMPLE WITH REALIA COBOL 3.x & BTRIEVE 5.10
*  AUTHOR:      FRANK A. LEO / THE ILLUSTRATED GUIDE TO BTRIEVE
*  DATE:        DECEMBER 8, 1991
*
*  Create the example customer file. See Customer_Record_Type for
*  file definition.
*
*------------------------------------------------------------------------------
*$CALL,COMP-5
 IDENTIFICATION DIVISION.
*
 PROGRAM-ID. BCREATE.
*
*CREATE A BTRIEVE FILE
*
*
 ENVIRONMENT DIVISION.
 CONFIGURATION SECTION.
 SOURCE-COMPUTER. IBM-PC.
 OBJECT-COMPUTER. IBM-PC.
*
*
 DATA DIVISION.
*
 WORKING-STORAGE SECTION.
*
* BTRIEVE OP CODES
*
 01 B-CREATE                          PIC 9(4) COMP-5 VALUE 14.
*
* FILE FLAGS
```

```
*
 01 NO-FILE-FLAG                    PIC 9(4) COMP-5 VALUE 0.
 01 VARIABLE-LENGTH                 PIC 9(4) COMP-5 VALUE 1.
 01 BLANK-TRUNCATION                PIC 9(4) COMP-5 VALUE 2.
 01 PRE-ALLOCATION                  PIC 9(4) COMP-5 VALUE 4.
 01 DATA-COMPRESSION                PIC 9(4) COMP-5 VALUE 8.
 01 KEY-ONLY                        PIC 9(4) COMP-5 VALUE 16.
 01 B10-FREE-SPACE                  PIC 9(4) COMP-5 VALUE 64.
 01 B20-FREE-SPACE                  PIC 9(4) COMP-5 VALUE 128.
 01 B30-FREE-SPACE                  PIC 9(4) COMP-5 VALUE 192.
*
* KEY FLAGS
*
 01 NO-KEY-FLAGS                    PIC 9(4) COMP-5 VALUE 0.
 01 DUPS                            PIC 9(4) COMP-5 VALUE 1.
 01 MODIFIABLE                      PIC 9(4) COMP-5 VALUE 2.
 01 BIN                             PIC 9(4) COMP-5 VALUE 4.
 01 NULL                            PIC 9(4) COMP-5 VALUE 8.
 01 SEGMENTED                       PIC 9(4) COMP-5 VALUE 16.
 01 DESC                            PIC 9(4) COMP-5 VALUE 64.
 01 SUPPLEMENTAL                    PIC 9(4) COMP-5 VALUE 128.
 01 EXTTYPE                         PIC 9(4) COMP-5 VALUE 256.
 01 MAN                             PIC 9(4) COMP-5 VALUE 512.
*
* KEY TYPES
*
 01 B-STRING                        PIC 9(4) COMP-5 VALUE 0.
 01 B-INTEGER                       PIC 9(4) COMP-5 VALUE 1.
 01 B-DATE                          PIC 9(4) COMP-5 VALUE 3.
 01 B-NUMERIC                       PIC 9(4) COMP-5 VALUE 8.
 01 B-AUTOINCREMENT                 PIC 9(4) COMP-5 VALUE 15.
*
 01 B-STATUS                        PIC 9(4) COMP-5 VALUE 0.
 01 KEY-NUMBER                      PIC 9(4) COMP-5 VALUE 0.
 01 BUF-LEN                         PIC 9(4) COMP-5 VALUE 0.
 01 FILE-NAME                       PIC X(13) VALUE SPACES.
 01 POSITION-BLOCK                  PIC X(128) VALUE SPACES.
 01 DATA-BUFFER.
    02 RECORD-LENGTH                PIC 9(4) COMP-5 VALUE 0.
    02 PAGE-SIZE                    PIC 9(4) COMP-5 VALUE 0.
    02 INDEX-COUNT                  PIC 9(4) COMP-5 VALUE 0.
    02 NOT-USED-1                   PIC X(4).
    02 FILE-FLAG                    PIC 9(4) COMP-5 VALUE 0.
    02 NOT-USED-1A                  PIC XX.
    02 PRE-ALLOC                    PIC 9(4) COMP-5 VALUE 0.
    02 KEY-SPECS OCCURS 6 TIMES.
       05 KEY-POSITION              PIC 9(4) COMP-5.
       05 KEY-LENGTH                PIC 9(4) COMP-5.
       05 KEY-FLAG                  PIC 9(4) COMP-5.
       05 NOT-USED-2                PIC X(4).
       05 KEY-TYPE                  PIC 9(4) COMP-5.
       05 FILLER                    PIC X(4).
 01 DSP-STATUS                      PIC 9(5) COMP-5.
*
*
*
 PROCEDURE DIVISION.
 BEGIN.
*
*    DEFINE THE FILE
```

```
     MOVE 225  TO RECORD-LENGTH.
     MOVE 1024 TO PAGE-SIZE.
     MOVE 4    TO INDEX-COUNT.
     MOVE VARIABLE-LENGTH TO FILE-FLAG.
*
*        KEY 0 BY CUSTOMER NUMBER
     MOVE 1 TO KEY-POSITION(1).
     MOVE 2 TO KEY-LENGTH(1).
     MOVE EXTTYPE TO KEY-FLAG(1).
     MOVE B-AUTOINCREMENT TO KEY-TYPE(1).
*
*       KEY 1 BY CUSTOMER NAME * 10
     MOVE 3  TO KEY-POSITION(2).
     MOVE 10 TO KEY-LENGTH(2).
     ADD EXTTYPE  DUPS MODIFIABLE
         GIVING KEY-FLAG(2).
     MOVE B-STRING TO KEY-TYPE(2).
*
*        KEY 2 BY >ZIPCODE BY COMPANY
     MOVE 185 TO KEY-POSITION(3).
     MOVE 9 TO KEY-LENGTH(3).
     ADD EXTTYPE DUPS MODIFIABLE
         SEGMENTED
         GIVING KEY-FLAG(3).
     MOVE B-STRING TO KEY-TYPE(3).
*
*        KEY 2 BY ZIPCODE BY >COMPANY
     MOVE 33 TO KEY-POSITION(4).
     MOVE 10  TO KEY-LENGTH(4).
     ADD EXTTYPE DUPS MODIFIABLE GIVING KEY-FLAG(4).
     MOVE B-INTEGER TO KEY-TYPE(4).
     MOVE 80   TO BUF-LEN.
*
*        KEY 3 BY >REP BY NEXT_DATE
     MOVE 207 TO KEY-POSITION(5).
     MOVE 3  TO KEY-LENGTH(5).
     ADD EXTTYPE DUPS MODIFIABLE
         SEGMENTED GIVING KEY-FLAG(5).
     MOVE B-STRING TO KEY-TYPE(5).
*
*
*        KEY 3 BY REP >BY NEXT_DATE
     MOVE 210 TO KEY-POSITION(6).
     MOVE 4  TO KEY-LENGTH(6).
     ADD EXTTYPE DUPS MODIFIABLE
         GIVING KEY-FLAG(6).
     MOVE B-DATE TO KEY-TYPE(6).

*
     MOVE 112 TO BUF-LEN.
     MOVE 'CUSTOMER.BTR ' TO FILE-NAME.
     CALL 'BTRV' USING B-CREATE, POSITION-BLOCK, DATA-BUFFER,
                     BUF-LEN, FILE-NAME, KEY-NUMBER.
     MOVE RETURN-CODE TO B-STATUS
     IF B-STATUS NOT = 0
       DISPLAY 'Error creating file. Status= ' B-STATUS
     ELSE
       DISPLAY 'File ' FILE-NAME ' created successfully'
     END-IF.
     STOP RUN.
```

# F Btrieve Status Codes

## 0
### Operation OK

The operation performed successfully.

## 2
### I/O Error

An error occurred during a disk read or write due to a damaged file, hardware error, or system error. A status 2 error can be the result of a poor network connection or improper network configuration. Repeated status 2s on the same file indicate that the file is probably severely damaged and should be recreated or restored from a current backup.

## 3
### File Not Opened

The operation cannot execute because the file is not open. A file must be opened before any other operation can be performed on it. A status 3 also occurs when the Position Block was improperly overwritten.

## 4
### Key Value Not found

The value in the Key Buffer was not found in the index specified by the Key Number on a search operation (Get Equal, Get Greater, Get Greater or Equal, Get Less Than, Get Less Than or Equal).

## 5
## *Duplicate Key Value*

An attempt was made to insert a record with a key field containing a duplicate key value to an index that does not allow duplicate values. Autoincrement keys must be initialized to zero or the autoincrement logic will not be applied and Btrieve will attempt to insert the Data Buffer key value into the index.

## 6
## *Invalid Key Number*

The value stored in the key number parameter was not valid for the file being accessed. The key number must be in the range of 0 to (n-1), where n is the number of key index paths including supplemental indexes.

## 7
## *Different Key Number*

An indexed traversal operation (Get Next or Get Previous) attempted to retrieve a record using a key path other than the key path on which positioning was established. To switch key paths, use the Get Position operation follow by a Get Direct operation specifying the new key path.

## 8
## *Invalid Positioning*

An attempt was made to update or delete a record when positioning was not properly established. A status 8 can also occur if the Position Block was improperly overwritten.

## 9
## *End Of File*

An attempt was made to read past the end or beginning of file:

- A Get Next was attempted and positioning was established on the logical last record, or
- A Get Previous was attempted while positioning was established on the logical first

record, or

- A Step Next was attempted while positioning was established on the physical last record, or
- A Step Previous was attempted while positioning was established on the physical first record.

## 10
## Modifiable Key Value Error

An Update operation was attempted that would change a non-modifiable key.

## 11
## Invalid File Name

An illegal file name was specified that the operating system would not accept. File names must be terminated with a binary zero or blank space.

## 12
## File Not Found

The file name specified does not exist. File names must be terminated with a binary zero or blank space.

## 13
## Extended File Error

Btrieve was not able to find the extension file for an extended file. The name of an extension file is stored in the File Control Record. If the extension file is moved or renamed an Extended File Error will result. To open a file with an extension file, both the primary and the extension file must be accessible.

## 14
## Pre-Image Open Error

The pre-image file could not be created or opened. There are three primary causes:

- The disk was full
- The pre-image file was erased, renamed, or damaged
- The user did not have proper access rights to the pre-image file

Opening the file in read-only mode is performed without opening the pre-image file. Use the BUTIL -RECOVER procedure or replace the file with its most recent backup.

## 15
## Pre-Image I/O Error

An I/O error occurred during the pre-imaging function. This is caused by a full disk or a damaged pre-image file. Use the BUTIL -RECOVER procedure or replace the file with its most recent backup.

## 16
## Expansion Error

An error occurred while writing the directory structure to disk prior to the creation of the expanded file partition. Either Btrieve was not able to close the file, or a new page was added to the file and Btrieve was not able to close and reopen the file to update the directory structure. Check for a disk hardware failure.

## 17
## Close Error

An error occurred while writing the directory table to disk before closing the file. Check for a hardware failure.

## 18
### Disk Full

The disk was full and the file could not be expanded as the result of an Insert operation.

## 19
### Unrecoverable Error

Automatic data recovery was not able to be performed. Use the BUTIL -RECOVER procedure or replace the file with its most recent backup.

## 20
### Record Manager Inactive

The Btrieve TSR (BTRIEVE.EXE or BREQUEST.EXE) was not loaded into memory.

## 21
### Key Buffer Too Short

The Key Buffer parameter was not long enough to accommodate the key value for the index path requested. This operation is only returned by a few interfaces.

## 22
### Data Buffer Length

The data buffer parameter was not long enough to accommodate the fixed record length of the file. Verify that the length of the data buffer is at least as long as the file's defined record length.

Before a retrieval operation, the Data Buffer Length parameter must be set to a size as large or larger than the retrieved record. For variable-length records, a status 22 indicates that the retrieved record was larger than the Data Buffer, and only a portion of the record was returned as much as the Data Buffer Length parameter specified.

For inserts, only the entire record will be inserted.

For the Create, Stat, and Add Supplemental Index operations the Data Buffer was not large enough to hold the file and key specifications. For the Create operation a status 22 may have resulted from the "Number of Indexes" parameter in the file specification indicating more key segments than are present or that the last key segment has the Segmented Flag set.

## 23
### Position Block Length

The position block parameter was not 128 bytes in length. This operation is only returned by a few interfaces.

## 24
### Page Size Error

The page size was invalid. A page size must be a multiple of 512 bytes and no larger than 4096. For the Create operation, a Page Size Error is often the result of an improper Data Buffer.

## 25
### Create I/O Error

The file specified could not be created due to a full disk or directory. This value is returned when an attempt is made to create over an existing file when the file is opened or the Key Number is set to (-1).

## 26
### Number of Keys

The number of keys specified was invalid. For files with a page size of 512, the maximum number of keys is eight. For larger page sizes, the maximum number of keys is 24.

## 27
## *Invalid Key Position*

The key segment position specified exceeded the defined record length for the file. Either the key position or the key position plus the key length was greater than the record length. For variable-length records, all keys must reside in the fixed record portion. For key-only files, the key must begin in the first byte of the record.

## 28
## *Invalid Record Length*

The record length specified (plus overhead for duplicates and variable-length records) must be less than or equal to the page size minus twelve, and greater than or equal to four bytes.

## 29
## *Invalid Key Length*

The key length specified must be greater than zero and cannot exceed 255. Btrieve requires that each key page in the file is large enough to hold at least eight keys.

## 30
## *Not a Btrieve File*

The file specified was not a valid Btrieve file. Either the file was not created by Btrieve, or it was created by an earlier version of Btrieve.

## 31
## *File Already Extended*

The file specified has already been extended. A file can only be extended once.

## 32
## *Extend I/O Error*

The file could not be extended due to the directory or file being full, or insufficient access rights to the file.

## 34
## *Invalid Extension Name*

The file name specified for the extended partition was invalid.

## 35
## *Directory Error*

An invalid drive or directory was specified on the Get Directory or Set Directory operations.

## 36
## *Transaction Error*

For workstation Btrieve, a Begin Transaction operation could not be performed because no transaction control filename was specified when Btrieve was loaded.

For NetWare Btrieve, the maximum number of concurrent transactions specified in BSETUP has been exceeded.

## 37
## *Transaction is Active*

A Begin Transaction was issued while another transaction was active in the application.

## 38
## Transaction Control File I/O Error

An error occurred when Btrieve attempted to write to the transaction control file due to the disk being full, insufficient access rights, or the transaction control file being deleted.

## 39
## End/Abort Transaction Error

An End or Abort Transaction operation was issued without a corresponding Begin Transaction operation.

## 40
## Transaction Max files

An attempt was made to update more files within a transaction than was specified as the maximum files in a transaction setting when Btrieve was loaded.

## 41
## Operation Not Allowed

An attempt was made to perform an operation that was not allowed at that particular time. This condition can occur from one of the following:

- A Step, Update, of Delete operation on a key only file
- A Get operation on a data-only file
- A Close, Set or Clear Owner, or Create or Drop Supplemental Index during a transaction

## 42
## Incomplete Accelerated Access

An attempt was made to open a file that was previously accessed in accelerated mode and never successfully closed. File integrity cannot be ensured. Use BUTIL -RECOVER or restore the latest backup.

## 43
## Invalid Record Address

An invalid address was specified for a Get Direct operation. The address used for a Get Direct operation should be obtained from a Get Position operation.

## 44
## Null Key Path

An attempt was made to use the Get Direct operation to establish an index path for a key whose value is null in the corresponding record. Btrieve cannot establish positioning based on a null key value.

## 45
## Inconsistent Key Flags

The key flags specification for a Create operation was inconsistent. If a key has multiple segments, the duplicate, modifiable, and null flags must be the same for each segment in the key.

## 46
## Access to file Denied

An attempt was made to perform an Update, Delete, or Insert operation on a file that was opened in Read-Only mode. Another cause is an attempt was made to update a file where the owner name was not specified.

## 47
## Maximum Open Files

The number of files opened in accelerated mode exceeded the number of buffers available in Btrieve's cache. When a file is opened in accelerated mode, Btrieve reserves on cache buffer for the file. Btrieve always reserves five empty buffers for index manipulation. Reload Btrieve with a smaller maximum page size parameter to allocate more buffers.

## 48
### Invalid Alternate Sequence Definition

The first byte of an alternate collating sequence definition did not contain an AC hex.

## 49
### Key Type Error

An attempt was made to create a file or supplemental index with an invalid extended key type, or tried to assign an alternate collating sequence to a non-string key type. A status 49 can also be caused by setting the alternate collating sequence bit and not supplying an alternate collating definition.

## 50
### Owner Already Set

An attempt was made to perform a Set Owner operation on a file that already has an owner name assigned. Use the Clear Owner operation to remove the previous owner before specifying a new owner.

## 51
### Invalid Owner

A Set Owner operation was attempted when the owner name in the Data Buffer did not match the owner name in the Key Buffer, or an attempt was made to open a file requiring an owner name without specifying the proper name.

## 52
### Error Writing Cache

An I/O error occurred while writing data to the cache. This occurs when Btrieve attempts to write data to a logical disk drive from a file that was previously opened in accelerated mode.

## 53
## *Invalid Interface*

An attempt was made to access a file containing variable-length records with a language interface from Btrieve v3.15 or earlier. To access files with variable-length records a interface version greater than 4.0 is required.

## 54
## *Variable Page Error*

During a Step Direct operation, Btrieve could not read all or part of the variable-length portion of a record. This error usually indicates file damage to one or more pages in the file.

## 55
## *Autoincrement Error*

An attempt was made to specify a segmented or duplicate flag for an autoincrement key type. An autoincrement key cannot be part of another key and cannot allow duplicates.

## 56
## *Incomplete Index*

A Create Supplemental Index or Drop Supplemental Index operation was interrupted and a partial index remains in the file. Perform a Drop Supplemental Index operation on the incomplete index.

## 57
## *Expanded Memory Error*

Workstation Btrieve received an error from the Expanded Memory Manager (This error does not apply to NetWare Btrieve). This error usually means that Btrieve was unable to save or restore the memory mapping register context, indicating an incompatibility with another application that uses expanded memory.

## 58
### Compression Buffer Too Short

An attempt was made to read or write a record that is longer than the value specified for the size of the compression buffer. Reload Btrieve with a larger "Maximum Compressed Record Size" option (/U for Workstation Btrieve) that is at least equal to the length of the largest record your application will access.

## 59
### File Already Exists

An attempt was made to create over an existing file while the key number parameter was (-1) indicating not to create over an existing file.

## 60
### Reject Count Reached

On an extended operation, Btrieve rejected the number of records specified by the "Reject Count" parameter in the filter description. The number of records retrieved before a status 60 is returned in the number of records parameter of the returned data buffer.

## 61
### Work Space Too Small

An extended operation exceeded Btrieve's internal buffer. The "Memory Size" load option (/M for Workstation Btrieve) must be increased.

## 62
### Incorrect Description

An extended operation passed Btrieve an invalid header or filter description.

## 63
### *Invalid Extended Insert Buffer*

An Insert Extended Operation passed an invalid data buffer format. This was caused by the buffer length being less than five bytes or the number of records being zero.

## 64
### *Filter Limit Reached*

During an extended get operation, Btrieve rejected a record and determined that no other records in the file would satisfy the filter condition. This happens only when the field definition of the first term in the filter condition matches the key definition of the current key path.

## 65
### *Incorrect Field Offset*

On an extended operation, the field offset of the extractor description fell outside the bounds of the record.

## 74
### *Automatic Transaction Abort*

An End Transaction operation was issued after the transaction was aborted either by the Abort Transaction operation or by NetWare's TTS (Transaction Tracking System). No file modification operations made after the Begin Transaction operation will take effect.

## 78
### *Deadlock Detected*

An attempt was made to initiate a transaction that would have resulted in a dead lock condition. A deadlock would occur if the first application was waiting for a lock to be cleared by the second application that was waiting for a lock to be cleared by the first application.

# 80
## Conflict Error

A file modification operation attempted to modify a record (or page for Workstation Btrieve) that was modified by another application since the time the record was retrieved. The record must be retrieved again before it can be modified. A status 80 can be prevented with record locking. If a record is locked, no other application can modify the record until the lock is cleared.

# 81
## Lock Error

A lock operation failed due to one of the following conditions:

- The Btrieve lock table was full. Increase the "Multiple Locks" load option (/L for workstation Btrieve).
- The Unlock operation passed an invalid record address.

# 82
## Lost Position

A traversal operation passed a position block with invalid positioning. Reestablish positioning on the current record with a Get Direct operation.

# 83
## Read Outside Transaction

An attempt was made to delete or update a record within a transaction that was retrieved outside of the transaction.

## 84
### Record Locked

An attempt was made to use a no-wait lock to update or lock a record that was currently locked, or to lock a file that has locked records. Continue to retry the operation until the record becomes unlocked. A wait lock bias will automatically retry until the record is freed.

## 85
### File Locked

An attempt was made to use a no-wait lock to update or lock a record in a file that is currently locked by another application. Continue to retry the operation until the file becomes unlocked. A wait lock bias will automatically retry until the file is freed.

## 86
### File Table Full

An attempt was made to open a file while Btrieve's internal file table was full. Reload Btrieve with a larger "Maximum Number of Open Files" option (/F parameter for workstation Btrieve), enough to handle all concurrently open files in the application.

## 87
### Handle Table Full

NetWare Btrieve or Btrieve for Windows attempted to open a file while Btrieve's internal file handle table was full. Reload Btrieve with a larger "Maximum Number of File Handles" option to handle all open files including data and pre-image files.

## 88
### Incompatible Mode Error

An attempt was made to open a file while another application had the same file open in an incompatible mode. If an application has a file opened in accelerated mode all other applications must open the file in accelerated mode.

# 90
## Redirection Device Table Full

An attempt was made to map to more network drives than can be handled by the NetWare Btrieve requester program (BREQUEST.EXE for DOS workstation Btrieve). Reload the requester program with a larger /R (for redirection table of mapped drives) or /S (for server table) options.

# 91
## Server Error

The NetWare Btrieve requester program was unable to establish a session with a Btrieve server. Make sure that NetWare Btrieve is loaded on the server where data files will be accessed and a proper mapping can be established.

# 92
## Transaction Table Full

An attempt was made to initiate a transaction on NetWare Btrieve while the transaction table was full. Reload NetWare Btrieve with a larger "Number of Concurrent Transactions" option.

# 93
## Incompatible Lock Type

An attempt was made to place a lock type that is incompatible lock type with other current locks. Single-record locks (+100, 200 bias) cannot be placed while multiple-record locks (+300, 400) are in place and visa versa.

# 94
## Permission Error

An attempt was made to open a file in Read-Write mode (Key Number = 0) or create a file in a directory where "Write" access rights are not granted.

## 95
## *Session No Longer Valid*

The Session between a Btrieve workstation (running the requester) and NetWare Btrieve was lost possibly due to NetWare Btrieve being unloaded or loss of drive mapping.

## 96
## *Communications Environment Error*

While loading NetWare Btrieve, the SPX connection table was full. Reload SPX specifying a higher value for the connection table. Refer to NetWare system documentation.

## 97
## *Data Message too Small*

An attempt was made to read or write a record whose length exceeded the "Maximum Record Length" load option (/D for the DOS requester). The "Maximum Record Length" option specifies the maximum size that a data buffer can be including multiple records for extended operations, and variable-length data. The "Maximum Record Length" parameter at the file server must be as large or larger than the requester's /D option.

## 98
## *Internal Transaction Error*

A NetWare TTS error was detected while executing a previous operation on a NetWare TTS file. An Abort Transaction operation must be performed.

# G Operation Code Quick Reference Tables

## Biases (by Bias Value)

| Bias Value | Bias Description | Category |
|---|---|---|
| **+50** | Key-Only Operation Bias | Miscellaneous |
| **+100** | Single-Record Wait Lock Bias | Lock Operation |
| **+200** | Single-Record NoWait Lock Bias | Lock Operation |
| **+300** | Multiple-Record Wait Lock Bias | Lock Operation |
| **+400** | Multiple-Record NoWait Lock Bias | Lock Operation |

## Biases (by Description)

| Bias Description | Bias Value | Category |
|---|---|---|
| **Key-Only Operation Bias** | 50 | Miscellaneous |
| **Single-Record Wait Lock Bias** | 100 | Lock Operation |
| **Single-Record NoWait Lock Bias** | 200 | Lock Operation |
| **Multiple-Record Wait Lock Bias** | 300 | Lock Operation |
| **Multiple-Record NoWait Lock Bias** | 400 | Lock Operation |

| Operation Code | Operation | Category |
|---|---|---|
| 1 | Close | Initialize |
| 2 | Insert | File Modification |
| 3 | Update | File Modification |
| 4 | Delete | File Modification |
| 5 | Get Equal | Retrieval/Search |
| 6 | Get Next | Retrieval/Traversal |
| 7 | Get Previous | Retrieval/Traversal |
| 8 | Get Greater Than | Retrieval/Search |
| 9 | Get Greater Than or Equal | Retrieval/Search |
| 10 | Get Less Than | Retrieval/Search |
| 11 | Get Less Than or Equal | Retrieval/Search |
| 12 | Get First | Retrieval/Traversal |
| 13 | Get Last | Retrieval/Traversal |
| 14 | Create | Create |
| 15 | Stat | Status |
| 16 | Extend | Miscellaneous |
| 17 | Set Directory | Miscellaneous |
| 18 | Get Directory | Miscellaneous |
| 19 | Begin Transaction | Transaction |
| 20 | End Transaction | Transaction |
| 21 | Abort Transaction | Transaction |
| 22 | Get Position | Direct Access |
| 23 | Get Direct | Direct Access |
| 24 | Step Next | Retrieval/Traversal |
| 25 | Stop | Initialize |
| 26 | Version | Status |
| 27 | Unlock | Lock Operation |
| 28 | Reset | Initialize |
| 29 | Set Owner | Initialize |
| 30 | Clear Owner | Initialize |
| 31 | Create Supplemental Index | Create |
| 32 | Drop Supplemental Index | Create |
| 33 | Step First | Retrieval/Traversal |
| 34 | Step Last | Retrieval/Traversal |
| 35 | Step Previous | Retrieval/Traversal |
| 36 | Get Next Extended | Retrieval/Traversal |
| 37 | Get Previous Extended | Retrieval/Traversal |
| 38 | Step Next Extended | Retrieval/Traversal |
| 39 | Step Previous Extended | Retrieval/Traversal |
| 40 | Insert Extended | File Modification |

| Operation | Operation Code | Category |
|---|---|---|
| Abort Transaction | 21 | Transaction |
| Begin Transaction | 19 | Transaction |
| Clear Owner | 30 | Initialize |
| Close | 1 | Initialize |
| Create | 14 | Create |
| Create Supplemental Index | 31 | Create |
| Delete | 4 | File Modification |
| Drop Supplemental Index | 32 | Create |
| End Transaction | 20 | Transaction |
| Extend | 16 | Miscellaneous |
| Get Direct | 23 | Direct Access |
| Get Directory | 18 | Miscellaneous |
| Get Equal | 5 | Retrieval/Search |
| Get First | 12 | Retrieval/Traversal |
| Get Greater Than | 8 | Retrieval/Search |
| Get Greater Than or Equal | 9 | Retrieval/Search |
| Get Last | 13 | Retrieval/Traversal |
| Get Less Than | 10 | Retrieval/Search |
| Get Less Than or Equal | 11 | Retrieval/Search |
| Get Next | 6 | Retrieval/Traversal |
| Get Next Extended | 36 | Retrieval/Traversal |
| Get Position | 22 | Direct Access |
| Get Previous | 7 | Retrieval/Traversal |
| Get Previous Extended | 37 | Retrieval/Traversal |
| Insert | 2 | File Modification |
| Insert Extended | 40 | File Modification |
| Reset | 28 | Initialize |
| Set Directory | 17 | Miscellaneous |
| Set Owner | 29 | Initialize |
| Stat | 15 | Status |
| Step First | 33 | Retrieval/Traversal |
| Step Last | 34 | Retrieval/Traversal |
| Step Next | 24 | Retrieval/Traversal |
| Step Next Extended | 38 | Retrieval/Traversal |
| Step Previous | 35 | Retrieval/Traversal |
| Step Previous Extended | 39 | Retrieval/Traversal |
| Stop | 25 | Initialize |
| Unlock | 27 | Lock Operation |
| Update | 3 | File Modification |
| Version | 26 | Status |

# Reader Survey

Tell us what you liked or did not like about
***The Illustrated Guide to Btrieve.***

What other books would you like to see offered?

What additional Btrieve utilities would you like to see offered?

***MIDI AMERICA***

**(404) 634-3334**

**Mail this form to: 2103 N. Decatur Rd., Suite 160**
**Decatur, GA 30033**

Cut along line

# Index


## Numerics

3GL (third generation language) 12
4GL (fourth generation language) 12

## A

Abort Transaction (21) 113, 199
accelerated mode 135
alternate collating sequence 95, 176, 188
Alternate Collating Sequence flag 182
alternate collating sequence key flag 69
alternate-collating sequence definition 53
architecture 53
ASCII files, reading 81
autoincrement 140
Autoincrement key type 257

## B

B.EXE 32
BASIC 27, 46
BCONSOLE monitoring utility 16, 31, 34
BDEBUG 32
Begin Transaction (19) 113, 195
Bfloat key type 255
Binary flag 181
binary key flag 69
blank truncation 59
Blank Truncation flag 178
Borland 27
BREQUEST.EXE 39, 63, 208
BROUTER 116, 126
BSETUP installation utility 16, 196
BSETUP.EXE 126
BSPXCOM.NLM 124
BSTART.NCF 124, 125
BSTOP.NCF 125
B-tree index 64
B-tree indexes 65
B-tree indexing 11, 12
B-tree node 60
Btrieve debuggers 32
Btrieve Developer's Kits 17
Btrieve Developers Kit 16
Btrieve file 53
Btrieve function call 43
Btrieve function executors 32
Btrieve interface 29
Btrieve NLM 15
Btrieve operations 40
Btrieve Requester 15
Btrieve requester 117
Btrieve utilities 31
Btrieve VAP 15
BTRIEVE.EXE 208
BTRIEVE.TRN 196
Btrieve/N 17
BTRTOOLS 37
BTRTOOLS.EXE 122
BTRVINIT function 49
BTRVSTOP function 49
Bullets 22, 51, 53
busy-wait 110
BUTIL 32, 33
BUTIL -CREATE 73
BUTL 37
BX.EXE 32, 37, 80

## C

C compiler for DOS 26
C compiler for NLMs 26
C Language 26, 46

C Language compilers 26
cache buffers 62
cache memory 54
cache swapping 87
calling Btrieve 39
case sensitivity 95
chronological order for duplicate keys 70
CLARION 29
Clear Owner (30) 215
client-based processing 16
client-server mode 15, 117
Clipper 29
Clone (with BUTIL) 33
Close (1) 138
closing 80
closing files 80
COBOL 28, 47
COBOL compilers 28
collating sequence 82
comma-separated SDF file 81
comparison codes for extended retrieval 231
compilers 25
CompuServe 22, 31
concurrency 109
Conflict Error 109
Create (14) 176
create coding example 77
create example program 261
Create Supplemental Index (31) 216
creating Btrieve files 37
creating files 73
current key 86
current record address 85

## D

Data Buffer 41, 44
Data Buffer for Create 176
Data Buffer Length 41
data compression 60
Data Compression flag 178
data dictionary 18, 19, 20, 35, 36
data encryption 213
data format 13, 77
data-only files 60
Date key type 253
dBase 81
Decimal key type 254
definition of Btrieve file 73
Delete (4) 146
Descending flag 182
descending key flag 69
design philosophy 53
DLL 48
DLL (dynamic link library) 39
doubly-linked list for duplicate keys 70
Drop Supplemental Index (32) 221
dropping a supplemental index 97
duplicate key indexes 69
duplicate key values 140
duplicate keys on permanent indexes 69
duplicate keys with Get Less Than 164
Duplicates flag 180
duplicates key flag 69

## E

End Transaction (20) 113, 197
establishing positioning 84, 91
exclusive mode 135
Extend (16) 191
extended get retrieval example program 282, 285
extended inserts 100
Extended Key Type flag 182
extended key types 183
extended operations 97
extended operations, control constant 103
extended operations, Data Buffer format 99
extended operations, extractor description 100
extended operations, filter description 100
extended operations, filter limit 102
extended operations, performance issues 98
extended operations, query description 100
extended operations, reject count 102
extended retrieval operations 102
extended type key flag 69
extractor for extended retrieval 229

## F

FCR (file control record) 53
FCR page 54
fields 18, 74
file access techniques 73
file architecture 53
File Control Record (FCR) 55
File in Use 114
file pages 53
file specification block 176, 188
File utilities 32
file utility 37
filter condition 233
filter expressions for extended retrieval 233
filter for extended retrieval 229
filtered extended get example program 289
fixed-length data pages 56
Float key type 252
flow of control 39
FORTRAN 28
fReadSDF_CustRec procedure 82
fReadSDF_CustRec subroutine 265
Free 179
Free space 55
Free Space flags 179
free space list 59
free space threshold 59, 77
function executor 112
function executors 37

## G

Get Direct (23) 202
Get Direct operation 58
Get Directory (18) 194
Get Equal (5) 89, 149
Get First (12) 170
Get Greater (8) 89, 158
Get Greater Than or Equal (9) 89, 161
Get Last (13) 173
Get Less Equal (11) 89
Get Less Than (10) 89, 164
Get Less Than or Equal (11) 167
Get Next (6) 152
Get Next Extended (36) 229
Get operations 84
Get Position (22) 200
Get Position operation 58
Get Previous (7) 155
Get Previous Extended (37) 236
GUPTA 29

## H

header for extended retrieval 229

## I

INCLUDES.C 77
INCLUDES.C example program 260
index order 84
index pages 60
index positioning 84
index traversal 85, 86
index traversal example program 268
indexed positioning 91
Insert (2) 140
Insert Extended (40) 246
insert extended example program 282
insert records example program 264
inserting records 81
installing NetWare v2.x Btrieve 126
installing NetWare v3.x Btrieve 124
Integer key type 252
integrity features 13
interface 45
interface modules 17
interface program 29
interfacing with Btrieve for DOS 45
interfacing with Btrieve for OS/2 50
interfacing with Btrieve for Windows 48
internal structure of Btrieve file 53
interrupt 7B 45
INTRFACE.DOC 45
Invalid Positioning 87

## K


Key Buffer 41, 44, 86
key buffer formatting 94
key flags 67, 93
key identifier 86
Key Number 41, 44, 86
key segment 77
key segment specification block 176, 180, 188, 216
key segment specifications 93
key segments 66, 67
key types 30, 67, 251
Key-Only flag 179
key-pointer 65


## L


licensing fee 18
load options for Btrieve 119
loading Btrieve for DOS 120
Loading Btrieve for OS/2 123
loading Btrieve for Windows 3.0 122
loading Btrieve in Windows DOS Box 128
loading Btrieve Requester for DOS 127
loading Btrieve requester for OS/2 128
loading Btrieve requester for Windows 127
loading NetWare Btrieve 124
lock bias 111
logical field 14
Logical key type 255
logical next record 86
logical next record address 85
logical previous record 86
logical previous record address 85
Lstring key type 30, 256


## M


Manual flag 182
manual key flag 69
maximum number of indexes 66
maximum number of records in file 58
memory scheme 62
mixed mode 118
Modifiable flag 180
modifiable key flag 69
Money key type 254
multiple record processing 97
multitasking 13
multi-user example program 293
multiuser programming 109


## N


NetWare 26
NetWare 2.x 15
NetWare 3.x 15
NetWare Btrieve 15
NetWare Lite 15
NetWare SQL 19, 20, 35, 36, 77
NetWare v3.x 34
network performance 98
network traffic considerations 111
NLMs, writing Btrieve 115
normal mode 135
Novell Education 23, 53
Novell support 13
Novell's Network C for NLM 115
no-wait lock 110
Null flag 181
null key flags 69
Numeric key type 255


## O


OpCode 41
Open (0) 134
Open (0) operation 80
opening files 80
operating modes, Btrieve 117
Operation Code 41, 44
operation codes 131
optimal page size 61
optimal page size, calculation of 76
OS/2, CONFIG.SYS 123
owner name for Open 134

## P

packing files 55
page size 54
page swapping 62
partial match search 161
Pascal 27, 48
Pascal compilers 27
passive concurrency 109
patches 21
performance as function of page size 75
performance considerations for page size 61
physical address 87
physical address order 84, 223, 227
physical record 56
physical record address 58
physical record length, calculation of 75
physical record traversal 87
physical traversal 87
physical traversal example program 268, 270
Position Block 41, 44, 80, 84, 85
positioning 84, 86
Preallocation flag 178
pre-imaging 63
pre-positioning 84
Professional Developers' Program 22
Programmer's Connection, the 36
Programmer's Shop, the 36

## Q

queries with extended operations 99

## R

read-only mode 135
record addressing 58
record fragmentation of variable records 77
record grouping 93
record grouping example program 276
record image 56, 57
record locking 110, 111
record manager 13, 25
Recover (with BUTIL) 33
recovering data 33
re-indexing 55
reject count 233
relational database manager 13
Reset (28) 212
root node 65
Root page of index 56
RQSHELLINIT function 49

## S

SDF format 81
search operations 89
search with index example program 272
search, global filtered 103
search, optimal 103
searching for records 89
segment 66
Segmented flag 181
segmented key type 69
segmented keys 177
server-based architecture 13
Set Directory (17) 193
Set Owner (29) 213
SHARE.EXE 80, 112
simulating multi-user environment 80
SoftCraft 11, 12, 17
software vendors (for Btrieve utilities) 36
source fix 21
SQL 35
SQL Access to Btrieve files 13
SQL field types 251
Stat (15) 188
Status Code 41, 44
Step First (33) 223
Step Last (34) 225
Step Next (24) 205
Step Next Extended (38) 240
Step operations 84
Step Previous (35) 227
Step Previous Extended (39) 243
Stop (25) 208
string data types 77
String key type 252
string key type 30
Structured Query Language 19

sub-field key 77
sub-level sorting 66, 93
sub-records 97
Supplemental flag 182
supplemental index 77
supplemental index example program 279
supplemental indexes 70, 95
supplemental key flag 69

## T

TASKID 129
TBMI 129
thread support 51
Time key type 254
tools for Btrieve 25
TPU (Turbo Pascal Unit) 45
Trace file 123
transaction example program 296
transaction processing 113
transaction rollback 113
transaction, initiating 114
traversal order 70
traversing 84
TSR 39
TSR (terminate and stay resident) 17
Turbo Pascal 27
Turbo Pascal interface 45
Tutorial Diskette 34, 37

## U

union option for key buffers 94
Unsigned Binary key type 257
Update (3) 143
update example program 293
update record example program 274
updating records 91
utilities 31

## V

variable portion of record 57
variable record pointer 59
variable-length data pages 56, 59
Variable-Length Record flag 178
variable-length records 140
verify mode 135
Version (26) 209
views 35
Visual BASIC 29

## W

wait lock 110
WATCOM C 44, 45
WBTRCALL DLL 48
WBTRCALL.DLL 122
Windows 37
Windows, SYSTEM.INI 122
Windows, WIN.IN 127
Windows, WIN.INI 123
workstation Btrieve 16, 117

## X

XQL 19
Xtrieve PLUS 18, 31, 35, 73, 81

## Z

Zstring key type 30, 257

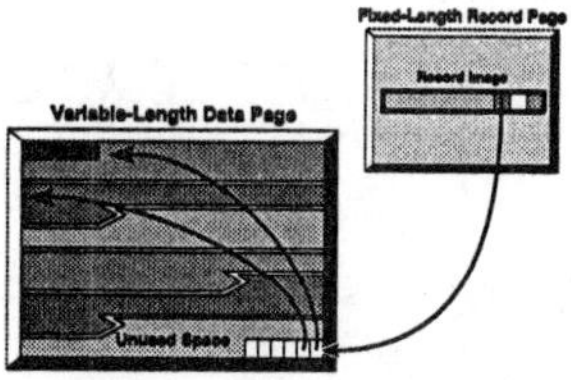


# YES!

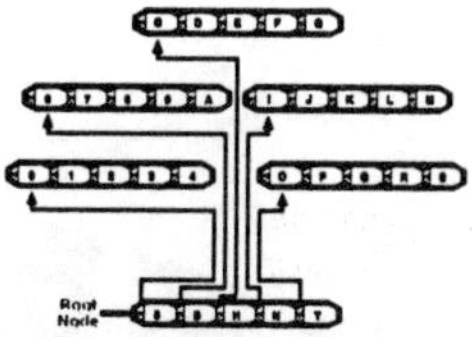


Please send me _______ copies of ***The Illustrated Guide to Btrieve*** at $29.95 per copy. • Include $4.00 per book for postage and handling.

Please send me _______ copies of the ***Tutorial Disk*** at $19.95 per copy. • If ordered without book, include $2.00 per disk for postage and handling.

**See the last section in Chapter Two for a description of "BX" - a Btrieve Function Executor and "BUTL" - a Btrieve File Utility Program, both included on the disk.**

NAME________________________________________

COMPANY_____________________________________

ADDRESS_____________________________________

CITY__________________________ST________ZIP____________

PHONE (O) __________________ PHONE (H) __________________

CARD NUMBER (CIRCLE ONE): VISA MASTER CARD DISCOVER AMERICAN EXPRESS

☐☐☐☐☐☐☐☐☐☐☐☐☐☐☐☐ ☐☐☐☐

CARD EXPIRATION

SIGNATURE ______________________________

***MIDI AMERICA***

**(404) 634-3334**

**Mail this form to: 2103 N. Decatur Rd., Suite 160**
**Decatur, GA 30033**

# Just Because You Own a Business Machin

## New! The Musical PC: How To Create an